MIKE STARR OF OSHAWA

Mike Starr of Oshawa
A Political Biography

Myron Momryk

MERCURY SERIES
HISTORY PAPER 57

CANADIAN MUSEUM OF HISTORY
AND UNIVERSITY OF OTTAWA PRESS

© 2017 Canadian Museum of History

All rights reserved. No part of this book may be reproduced or transmitted in any form or by any means electronic or mechanical, including photocopying, recording, or any retrieval system, without the written permission of the publisher.

**Co-published by
the Canadian Museum of History
and the University of Ottawa Press**

The University of Ottawa Press gratefully acknowledges the support extended to its publishing list by the Government of Canada, the Canada Council for the Arts, the Federation for the Humanities and Social Sciences through the Awards to Scholarly Publications Program and the University of Ottawa.

Copy editing: Rob Ferguson
Proofreading: Robbie McCaw
Typesetting: Édiscript enr.
Cover design: Édiscript enr.

Library and Archives Canada Cataloguing in Publication

Momryk, Myron, 1946-, author
Mike Starr of Oshawa: a political biography / Myron Momryk.

(Mercury series)
(History paper; 57)
Includes bibliographical references.
Issued in print and electronic formats.
ISBN 978-0-7766-2591-1 (softcover)
ISBN 978-0-7766-2592-8 (PDF)
ISBN 978-0-7766-2593-5 (EPUB)

1. Starr, Mike, 1910-2000. 2. Politicians—Ontario—Oshawa—Biography. 3. Biographies. I. Canadian Museum of History, issuing body II. Title. III. Series: Mercury series IV. Series: History paper (Canadian Museum of Civilization); 57

FC3099.O84Z49 2018   971.3'56092   C2017-908056-3
                                      C2017-908057-1

The Mercury Series

Strikingly Canadian and highly specialized, the *Mercury Series* presents research from the Canadian Museum of History and benefits from the publishing expertise of the University of Ottawa Press. Created in 1972, the *Mercury Series* is the Canadian Museum of History's primary vehicle for the publication of academic research, and includes numerous landmark contributions in the disciplines of Canadian history, archaeology, culture and ethnology. Books in the series are published in either English or French, and all include a second-language summary.

La Collection Mercure

Remarquablement canadienne et hautement spécialisée, la *Collection Mercure* réunit des ouvrages portant sur des recherches effectuées au Musée canadien de l'histoire, et elle s'appuie sur le savoir-faire des Presses de l'Université d'Ottawa. Mise sur pied en 1972, la *Collection Mercure* est le principal véhicule qu'utilise le Musée canadien de l'histoire pour publier ses recherches scientifiques. Elle comprend plusieurs contributions remarquables à l'histoire, à l'archéologie, à la culture et à l'ethnologie canadiennes. Les ouvrages de la série sont publiés en français ou en anglais, et ils comportent un résumé dans l'autre langue officielle

How To Order

All trade orders must be directed to the University of Ottawa Press:

    Web: www.press.uottawa.ca
    Email: puo-uop@uottawa.ca
    Phone: 613-562-5246

All other orders may be directed to either the University of Ottawa Press (as above) or to the Canadian Museum of History:

    Web: http://www.historymuseum.ca/shop/#publications
    Email: publications@historymuseum.ca
    Phone: 1-800-5550-5621 (toll-free)
    or 819-776-8387 (National Capital Region)
    Mail: Mail Order Services
    Canadian Museum of History
    100 Laurier Street
    Gatineau, QC K1A 0M8

Pour commander

Les libraires et autres détaillants doivent adresser leurs commandes aux Presses de l'Université d'Ottawa :

    Web : www.presses.uottawa.ca
    Courriel : puo-uop@uottawa.ca
    Téléphone : 613-562-5246

Les particuliers doivent adresser leurs commandes soit aux Presses de l'Université d'Ottawa (voir plus haut), soit au Musée canadien de l'histoire :

    Web : http://www.museedelhistoire.ca/magasiner/#publications
    Courriel : publications@museedelhistoire.ca
    Téléphone : 1-800-5550-5621 (numéro sans frais) – 819-776-8387 (région de la capitale nationale)
    Poste : Service des commandes postales
    Musée canadien de l'histoire
    100, rue Laurier
    Gatineau (Québec) K1A 0M8

Abstract

As a political pioneer, Michael Starr (1910–2000) accomplished many firsts and opened the political doors to other members of the various ethnocultural groups. The son of Ukrainian immigrants, he became involved in municipal affairs during the Depression and was elected alderman in Oshawa, Ontario in 1944. He was later elected Mayor of Oshawa, Member of Parliament and, in 1957, he was appointed to the federal cabinet in the government of the Honourable John Diefenbaker. This study focuses on Starr's federal election campaigns in Oshawa and across Canada. As Minister of Labour, he was faced with many national problems: seasonal unemployment, regional disparities, union negotiations, emerging militant Quebecois nationalism. Starr devoted most of his efforts both inside and outside the House of Commons to fighting unemployment across Canada despite constant criticism from the opposition parties. A notable achievement was his promotion of the Winter Works Program that encouraged year-round employment and fundamentally changed Canadian seasonal working traditions. He was a popular speaker among the ethnocultural groups from Eastern Europe and regularly criticized the human rights record of the Soviet Union. After the defeat of the Progressive Conservative government in the 1963 elections, Starr became an active member of the Opposition in Parliament. He remained loyal to Diefenbaker and for his loyalty, Diefenbaker appointed Starr as House Leader. Starr ran for the leadership of the Progressive Conservative Party in September, 1967. But with the entry of Diefenbaker in the leadership contest at the last minute, Starr lost his expected support and the campaign. In the 1968 federal election, Starr was defeated by fifteen votes by Edward Broadbent, who later became the national leader of the New Democratic Party. Starr was appointed Citizenship Court judge, serving in that post until 1972. Starr continued his career of public service and, from 1973 until 1980, Starr was Chairman of the Workmen's Compensation Board of Ontario. As he had developed a reputation for public service and fairness, he was appointed Co-Chairman of a federal task force in 1983 reviewing conflict of interest and post-employment guidelines for Members of Parliament. Starr continued to live in Oshawa and remained active through public service in the local community.

Résumé

Les réussites de Michael Starr (1910-2000), un pionnier en politique, ont ouvert les portes politiques pour d'autres membres de différents groupes ethnoculturels. Fils d'immigrants ukrainiens, il s'est impliqué dans le milieu municipal durant la Grande Dépression avant de se faire élire conseiller municipal à Oshawa, en Ontario, en 1944. Il a été élu maire d'Oshawa et membre de Parlement avant d'être nommé au cabinet fédéral du gouvernement de l'honorable John Diefenbaker en 1957. Cet ouvrage porte sur les campagnes électorales de Mike Starr à Oshawa et à travers le Canada. En tant que ministre du Travail, il a fait face à plusieurs problématiques nationales, dont le chômage saisonnier, les disparités régionales, les négociations syndicales et l'émergence d'un nationalisme militant québécois. Starr a consacré la plupart de ses efforts, à l'intérieur comme à l'extérieur de la Chambre des communes, à lutter contre le chômage partout au Canada, et ce, malgré les critiques constantes des partis de l'opposition. Sa promotion du programme de travaux d'hiver s'est avérée un succès notable, encourageant le travail à longueur d'année, et changeant de façon fondamentale les traditions saisonnières canadiennes du travail. Il était un orateur populaire parmi les groupes ethnoculturels de l'Europe de l'Est et critiquait régulièrement l'Union soviétique en matière des droits de la personne. Après la défaite du gouvernement progressiste-conservateur aux élections de 1963, Starr est alors devenu membre actif de l'opposition. Il est resté fidèle à Diefenbaker et, grâce à cette loyauté, ce dernier le nomme leader à la Chambre. Mike Starr a pris part à la course à la direction du Parti progressiste-conservateur en septembre 1967, mais a perdu son soutien attendu après l'entrée à la course de Diefenbaker à la dernière minute. Durant l'élection fédérale de 1968, il a perdu par quinze voix contre Edward Broadbent, qui est parvenu par la suite au poste de leader du Nouveau Parti démocratique. Mike Starr s'est vu nommé juge à la Cour de la citoyenneté, servant à ce titre jusqu'en 1972. Il a poursuivi une carrière à la fonction publique et, entre 1973 et 1980, a été président de la Commission des accidents du travail de l'Ontario. En raison de sa réputation en matière de service public et d'impartialité, en 1983 il a été nommé coprésident du groupe de travail chargé d'examiner les conflits d'intérêts et les lignes directrices sur l'après-mandat pour les membres du Parlement. Il a continué de vivre à Oshawa et de jouer un rôle actif dans la communauté locale à travers son service public.

Table of Contents

Abstract v

Résumé vi

Acknowledgements ix

Foreword xi

Introduction 1

Chapter 1
The Early Years 3

Chapter 2
Oshawa Municipal Politics 1944–1952 25

Chapter 3
Election Campaign for Ontario Riding, 1952 37

Chapter 4
Member of Parliament, 1952–1957 45

Chapter 5
Appointment as Minister of Labour, 1957 59

Chapter 6
The 1958 Federal Election 71

Chapter 7
Minister of Labour, 1958 77

Chapter 8
Minister of Labour, 1959 87

Chapter 9
Minister of Labour, 1960 101

Chapter 10
Minister of Labour, 1961 109

Chapter 11
Minister of Labour, 1962 123

Chapter 12
Politics in Ontario Riding, 1962 127

Chapter 13
Minister of Labour in a Minority Government, 1962-1963 135

Chapter 14
The 1963 Federal Election 145

Chapter 15
Member of Parliament and House Leader, 1963–1965 153

Chapter 16
The 1965 Federal Election in Ontario 167

Chapter 17
The Leadership Race, 1967 177

Chapter 18
The 1968 Federal Election 191

Chapter 19
Public Service, 1968–1973 205

Chapter 20
Public Service, 1973-1988 215

Chapter 21
Final Years and Mike Starr's Legacy 231

Bibliography 237

Acknowledgements

I would like to thank Dr. John Willis, editor of the Mercury Series, the Canadian Museum of History, for his encouragement and guidance, and the two anonymous readers for their comments and advice. Also, I am grateful to Elizabeth Schwaiger, University of Ottawa Press, for preparing the manuscript for publication. I would like to thank Prof. Bohdan Harasymiw, University of Calgary, who read a very early draft of the manuscript for his comments. In addition, I thank Danielle Peters and Janet Stanley for typing early versions of the manuscript. Thanks as well to Lee Wyndham of the Canadian Museum of History, and to Pascal Laplante of CMH Publishing.

A special thanks to Mike and Catherine Nicol and to Walter Kish from Oshawa for their co-operation in making available copies of illustrations relating to Mike Starr's life and career. Melissa Cole, Oshawa Museum, kindly provided photos of the Michael Starr Building in Oshawa. Mr. Grant Harper provided copies of posters from his private collection relating to Mike Starr's campaign for the leadership of the Progressive Conservative Party.

– Myron Momryk, Ottawa 2017

Foreword

Mike Starr was a notable Canadian politician: his 1957 appointment as Minister of Labour in the John Diefenbaker government created a sensation among the Ukrainian Canadian community, especially among post-Second World War immigrants challenged by social, political and economic adjustments. His appointment proved the son of Ukrainian immigrants could rise through the Canadian political system and reach the position of a cabinet minister, and provided a great morale boost. What were the steps in this political "ladder" to Ottawa? How did the Ukrainian community contribute to Starr's political career? This biography, a record of the political life and career of Mike Starr, answers some of these questions.

Introduction

I first heard Mike Starr's name from my father, who had read about Starr's appointment as the federal Minister of Labour in the newspaper. I was only in elementary school at the time but the news made an impact. To my father, a relatively recent arrival to Canada, having a person of Ukrainian descent appointed to the Cabinet was a remarkable event. Over time, I developed an interest in Starr's career: not only did I make him the subject of one of my Canadian history research papers while at university, I continued researching his career and compiling information. That interest only grew when I began working at Library and Archives Canada in the early 1980s; one of my areas of responsibility was community leaders and organizations, tracing their origins to Central and Eastern Europe. Whenever possible I examined archival and published sources mentioning Starr. A major obstacle was the lack of archival material produced by Mike Starr himself. Not only did Starr not systematically preserve archival material relating to his political career, he was not aware of the services available to him by Library and Archives Canada: when the Diefenbaker government was defeated in 1963 he destroyed his papers. Fortunately his wife, Anne, did compile news clippings, photographs and documents in scrapbooks, the two volumes of which were later borrowed by Library and Archives Canada and microfilmed. References to Starr in the memoirs of fellow cabinet ministers and Members of Parliament were few and uninformative. This biography, therefore, had to be researched and written using mostly secondary and other published sources.

In the course of my research in the 1980s, I contacted Starr several times at his home in Oshawa and arranged a number of interviews. On one occasion I even interviewed him on a GO bus travelling between Oshawa and Toronto and our last interview was in 1987 when he was visiting Ottawa after his appointment to the Refugee Status Advisory Committee. He was reluctant to be interviewed; however, towards the end of his life, Starr enjoyed reminiscing about his political successes. The interview filmed in 1998 and released as *Memoirs of the Honourable Michael Starr* provides a good summary of his career but this is the first biography of Mike Starr and his political career. Starr read an early version of it commenting only about the accuracy of various election results.

In the writing of Ukrainian Canadian history, there is a lack of publications on the post-Second World War period, especially on the Ukrainian community in eastern Canada. I hope this record of Mike Starr's political career is a contribution to Canadian ethnocultural and political history.

I have chosen to focus his story on the various election campaigns Starr contested in Oshawa: his political career, as are the careers of all politicians, was determined largely by the successes and failures of these campaigns. Some historical context is provided to better explain the campaigns at the municipal, provincial and federal levels. Important factors during these years were the evolution of ethnocultural groups in Oshawa, the role of labour unions in local politics and, at the national level, the impact of the Cold War on Starr's career. No attempt is made to analyze Starr in psychological terms, nor to assess his personal reasons for launching his political career.

Chapter 1
The Early Years

"Starr New Labor Minister"

This headline, which appeared in bold letters on the front page of the *Daily Times Gazette* on June 21, 1957, announced the remarkable achievement of one of Oshawa's own citizens on the national political scene. Along with Michael Starr's photograph, a summary of his life and career outlined his modest origins and the progress of his political career from alderman to Mayor of Oshawa to Member of Parliament. Almost every reference to Starr and his new appointment to the federal cabinet included some version of the statement that he was the "country's first federal minister of Ukrainian extraction."[1]

Starr's appointment as Minister of Labour[2] by Prime Minister John Diefenbaker, publicized in newspapers across Canada, created a sensation in the Ukrainian community. From the first Ukrainian immigrants arriving in Canada in 1891 and on, members of the community started participating in the municipal, provincial and federal political life of the country. Each political success was viewed as a victory for the entire community.

How can the son of Ukrainian immigrant parents rise within the Canadian political establishment and reach the position of a cabinet minister? What were the steps in this political "ladder" to Ottawa? How did the Oshawa community contribute to Starr's political career? And after his appointment to the federal cabinet, how did Starr's new position benefit Oshawa, the larger Canadian population and, especially, the Ukrainian Canadian community? The answers to these questions can be traced to Starr's early years, his parent's arrival in Canada and, also, to their country of origin.

In the Ukrainian villages of eastern Galicia, in the Austro-Hungarian Empire prior to the First World War, difficult political, social and economic conditions encouraged emigration. Its semi-feudal political regime, the growing problem of land shortage, and severely limited economic opportunities compelled many Ukrainians to search for a more hopeful future in a new land. Stories about free land in Canada were spread across Galicia by agents of the Canadian federal government; Canada soon came to symbolize hope and the promise of a better life throughout small and impoverished Ukrainian villages. Between 1891 and 1914 Canada admitted over 100,000 peasant farmers from the Austro-Hungarian provinces of Galicia and Bukovyna. Among this large influx of Ukrainian immigrants was a young agricultural labourer who shared in the Canadian dream of a better life.

---

1. *Daily Times Gazette*, June 21, 23, 1957.
2. Since 2015, this portfolio has been named the Minister of Employment, Workforce Development and Labour.

Born on April 17, 1888, in Ivane-Puste, a small village near the Dniester River, Matthew Starchewski[3] spent his early years working as an agricultural labourer for the local landowners in the Borshchiv region of Galicia, then a province of the Austro-Hungarian Empire.[4] Everyday life in the local Ukrainian villages was difficult and he had only the dismal prospect of a hard peasant's life before him. The great majority of peasant families in this region had less than five hectares of land.[5] During the years 1896-1900 at least fourteen families left Ivane-Puste and joined the mass migration to Canada.[6] The discontent with the economic situation was also manifested in the first agrarian strikes organized by agricultural workers in the Borshchiv district in 1897, and the strikes rapidly spread to other areas of Galicia. There were more agrarian strikes in the region in 1900, 1902 and 1906.[7]

In 1907 Matthew may have followed the wave of immigrant families to Canada, but he had a very personal reason for emigrating: his father had recently died, leaving his mother to manage their small landholding. As in many similar cases, she married a local villager named Huculiak to assist her with the farm work. Huculiak may have adopted Matthew but any hope Matthew had about inheriting the small family landholding disappeared. Knowing he did not have much of a future in Ivane-Puste he left for Canada via Antwerp, departing Europe on April 24 aboard the Canadian Pacific ship *Lake Michigan* and arriving in Quebec City on May 9, 1907. He was described on the passenger manifest as Matij Huculiak, a "general labourer" whose destination was Montreal. The ship transported 2,189 passengers—Galicians, Hungarians, Italians, Russians—all of whom were in steerage. Matthew would begin his life in Canada as an agricultural labourer, the only occupation he knew.

However, Matthew did not continue his journey to western Canada, where most Ukrainian immigrants hoped to claim a homestead. As many single men without resources, he revised his dreams, stayed in eastern Canada, and began working at a series of agricultural and industrial jobs. During his first year he worked for a short time on a farm in Quebec, then made his way to northern Ontario, walking for some distances along the railroad tracks. He worked in the woods of northern Ontario as a lumberjack and later found work as a mining smelter worker at the International Nickel smelter in Copper Cliff near Sudbury, Ontario.[8] While working in Copper Cliff, Matthew met Mary Matechuk. She, too, was a recent immigrant from eastern Galicia. Mary was born on June 16, 1888, in Pecharnia, a village in the Ternopil region of the Austro-Hungarian Empire about forty kilometres from Ivane-Puste. Mary arrived on the ship, *Volturno,* in Halifax on June 30, 1909, destined for

---

3. The surname was also spelled as "Starczewski," "Starczeucke," "Starchewski." Obituary: *The Daily Times Gazette*, April 23, 1951. In some documents, he is listed as "Michael Matthew Starchewski."
4. Interview with Mike Starr by Leo LaClare, October 9, 1973. Sound Archives, Library and Archives Canada (LAC).
5. Stella Hryniuk, "A Peasant Society in Transition: Ukrainian Peasants in Five East Galician Counties 1880-1900," PhD diss., University of Manitoba, 1985, p. 233.
6. V.J. Kaye, *Dictionary of Ukrainian Canadian Biography, Pioneer Settlers of Manitoba, 1891-1900*, Ukrainian Canadian Research Foundation, Toronto, 1975, p. XXI.
7. Orest T. Martynowych, "The Ukrainian Bloc Settlement in East Central Alberta, 1890-1930: A History," Occasional Paper No. 10, Historic Sites Service, *Alberta Culture*, Edmonton, 1985, pp. 34–35.
8. Ukrainian Canadian Research and Documentation Centre, "Memoirs of the Honourable Michael Starr," 1998.

Copper Cliff, Ontario, as a domestic.[9] Matthew and Mary met at the boarding house where she was working and, in 1909, they were married.[10] By this time, Matthew had reverted to his deceased father's name, Starchewski.

Michael (Mike) Starchewski was born in Copper Cliff on November 14, 1910.[11] When Michael was a year old, Matthew moved with his family to Montreal, where he was able to find work in a meat packing plant. The Starchewski family lived in the Point St. Charles area of Montreal, where there was a small Ukrainian community including recent immigrants from Ivane-Puste. Life for recent immigrants—and the Starchewski family in particular—became a struggle for survival. The family had to depend entirely on their own resources and physical abilities to survive. Mary Starchewski opened a small candy store on Centre Street to augment her husband's meagre wages.[12] She also grew vegetables in her own small kitchen garden. When Michael was six years old, he too began contributing his share by selling newspapers on streetcars.[13] Until he was nine years old, Michael attended the Sarsfield School, where one of the languages of instruction was Ukrainian.[14] The family spoke Ukrainian at home and were active members of the local Taras Shevchenko Prosvita Society (reading association). Prosvita was the cultural centre for the Ukrainian families and everyone from grandparents to small children attended its meetings and events. It was, in fact, a "home" for many of the early Ukrainian immigrants who came to Montreal without any knowledge of English or French, without any family and, in the case of Michael's parents, relatively young. Ukrainian language, culture and traditions were taught in a warm family environment. Matthew was familiar with the Prosvita Society because a similar reading association was founded in Ivane Puste, his home village, in 1890.[15] As a result, Ivane Puste was known for being "nationally conscious" about Ukrainian identity.[16] As active members of the Prosvita Society in Point St. Charles, Matthew and his family met other recent Ukrainian immigrants from Galicia and Bukovyna and further developed their sense of Ukrainian cultural identity.

When Michael was nine years old he participated in his first public event along with other children: reciting a poem to the Prosvita Society in honour of the Ukrainian national poet Taras Shevchenko. Thirty-four-lines long, he learned it like a prayer but, once on stage, Michael remembered only Taras Shevchenko's name and place of birth and forgot everything else. Upset over having to be prompted to finish, he left the stage in tears. However unsuccessful, it marked his first involvement in Ukrainian community activities.[17] Later in

---

9. Ancestry (Canadian Passenger Lists, 1865-1935). Her surname was also spelled as "Matyczuk" and "Matijchuk."
10. Interview by Leo LaClare, October 9, 1973, Sound Archives, LAC.
11. Province of Ontario, The Vital Statistics Act, Delayed Statement of Birth, February 23, 1970, (502691). The surname was originally registered as "Starczewski" but later amended by Mike Starr, on February 6, 1969, to "Starr."
12. Lovell's Montreal Directory for 1914-1915, John Lovell and Son Ltd., Montreal, 1914, p. 1977: "Starczerskyi, M., Candy Store, 369 Centre."
13. *Toronto Star*, August 7, 1968.
14. Interview with Mike Starr by Leo LaClare, October 9, 1973, Sound Archives, LAC.
15. Stella Hryniuk, op.cit., p. 193.
16. Ibid., p. 439, footnote 52.
17. Myhailo Star, "Shcho Ia Zavdiachuiu Prosviti," in *Zolotyi Iuvilei Tovarystva 'Prosvita' im. Tarasa Shevchenka v Montreali-Point St. Charles 1913–1963*, pp. 35–36.

life, Michael often thought about this event and hoped he would one day return to the same stage to successfully recite his poem.

The Starchewski family would live in the Point St. Charles area for eight years. They suffered a personal tragedy when Wasyl Starchewski, born in 1913, passed away in Montreal during these years.[18] Among the surviving children were Michael, Paul born in 1911, Ann born in 1914, Stella born in 1915, Pearl born in 1919 and Mary, born in 1920 in Toronto.[19] The First World War did not directly affect them, nor did the internment of recent Ukrainian immigrants—men of military age deemed to be "enemy aliens"—who were sent to the internment camp at Spirit Lake in northwestern Quebec. .

In 1919, William Davis Co., the meat-packing firm where Matthew worked, transferred him to Toronto. Michael continued his education in Toronto, where he was enrolled in an English-language school. Mary Starchewski found acquaintances from her home village in nearby Oshawa and, after a year and a half, Matthew moved the family to Oshawa where he found work in a leather factory. He later worked in a foundry, a picture-frame firm and, eventually, after several years found employment at General Motors.

As was often the case with most immigrant women of this period, Mary Starchewski never had the opportunity to learn to read or write, even in Ukrainian. She understood some English but did not speak the language. She continued to make and sell candy from her home. Matthew, on the other hand, had been able to teach himself to read and write in Ukrainian and in Canada, through his experience working in factories, was more fluent in English.[20]

During these early years, the Starchewski family lived in the semi-rural Lakeview area of south Oshawa that was within walking distance to many of the factories and plants that hired immigrant labourers. Matthew had purchased four acres of land near Oshawa Creek and built a four-room house. One of Michael's early chores was taking the family cow to pasture on a rope, an age-old tradition from Ukrainian village life. Among Michael's favourite activities as a young boy was picking mushrooms with his father in the woods around Oshawa, another old Ukrainian village tradition the family perpetuated in Oshawa.[21]

In 1921, the Ukrainian community in Oshawa numbered 338 people in a population of 11,940. This can be considered as a minimal figure since many Ukrainians were listed by the census-takers as Austrians, Poles and Russians.[22] The first Ukrainians settled in

---

18. Ancestry, Quebec Vital and Church Records (Drouin Collection), 1621–1968, Wasyl Starchewski, baptized February 15, 1913.
19. Ancestry, Quebec, Canada, Vital and Church Records (Drouin Collection), 1621-1968; Census of Canada, 1921; East Whitby.
20. Interview by Leo LaClare, October 9, 1973, Sound Archives, LAC.
21. Thomas Van Dusen, *The Chief*, McGraw-Hill Company of Canada Limited, 1968, p. 14; conversation with Mrs. Anne Hercia at her home in Windsor, Ontario, on June 9, 1988.
22. William Darcovich and Paul Yuzyk (eds.), *A Statistical Compendium on the Ukrainians in Canada 1891–1976*, University of Ottawa Press, Ottawa, 1980, p. 82; *Otvorennia Ukrainskoi Pravoslavnoi Tserkvy Rizdva Presviatoi Bohorodytsi v Oshavi, Ont, 1916–1953* (November 1, 1953, Oshawa, Ontario). Some of the early immigrants came from Kamianets-Podilskyi and Kyiv, then part of the Russian Empire. They established an Orthodox Church parish in 1916 but the early clergy were from the Russian Orthodox mission until 1938, when the parish affiliated with the

Figure 1.1 Mike Starr (front row, far left) with the Ukrainian Choir. Starr's family was actively involved in Ukrainian community activities in Oshawa. As a young boy, Mike was a member of the local Ukrainian choir, dressed in the Ukrainian tradition. This choir performed at the Canadian National Exhibition in Toronto. Photograph: *The Oshawa Reformer*, September 1, 1926; image courtesy Walter Kish.

Oshawa in 1902 but it was only in 1911 that they formed their first community organization. The life of the community was centred on their various churches, halls and other institutions in the Bloor Street area of south Oshawa. The Prosvita Society, founded in 1917, was one of the earliest Ukrainian associations and quickly became a focus of the community's activities, with regular meetings, dramatic groups, dances and picnics. Oshawa's Ukrainian community had a rich and varied cultural life and was able to organize plays and other dramatic performances. From their first years in the city, the Starchewski family actively participated in the cultural life of the Ukrainian community.[23] Michael and the other members of his family performed in the local Ukrainian choir and, when he was twelve years old, his choral group competed at the Canadian National Exhibition in Toronto.[24]

Michael attended the local Cedardale Public School and, like many other children of immigrants, was soon made aware of the obvious and subtle differences between children of immigrants and of native-born Canadians. Although Michael would later claim that he

Ukrainian Orthodox Church of Canada. See also Laura Suchan, "Ukrainians in Oshawa, 1900–1955," Oshawa Historical Society, *Historical Oshawa*, Vol. VI.
23. Ukrainian Canadian Research and Documentation Centre, "Memoirs of the Honourable Michael Starr" (1998).
24. "Oshawa Ukrainian Choir to Sing at CNE Music Day," (includes photograph of choir with Michael Starchewski), *The Oshawa Daily Reformer*, September 1, 1926; interview with Mike Starr by Leo LaClare, October 9, 1973, LAC Sound Archives.

did not experience any overt discrimination, there were enough individuals with nativist attitudes in Oshawa to form a local branch of the Ku Klux Klan.[25] However, these differences at school only encouraged Michael to compete and study more diligently.[26] During these early years, Michael formed friendships with children from Ukrainian and other immigrant families from Central and Eastern Europe that endured for most of his life in Oshawa. Starr was ambitious from his earliest years and thought of becoming a lawyer.[27] Despite his interest in education, Michael left school at the early age of fifteen to financially assist his family, as did many sons and daughters of immigrant families. By this time there were two boys and four girls in the Starchewski family. In 1925, Michael began working as a printer's devil at the printing plant of the *Ontario Reformer*, the local newspaper. Tasked with melting metal that would be used as blocks for type, he worked five and a half days per week for $15.00.[28] One day, while working at the newspaper, a proofreader reviewing an article about prizes won by local students asked Michael why children of immigrants always received the best school prizes. Michael replied, "The Canadians are too busy going in for games and sports but we 'foreigners' go into it for business." After six months as a printer's devil, Michael began working with his father and brother Paul making picture frames. Michael, however, proved more ambitious and soon learned he could earn substantially more by working in a clerical position in an office. Thus he decided to return to school to complete his education but, since he could not afford more than one year in school, he crammed thirteen subjects into a one-year commercial course at the Oshawa Collegiate Institute. Michael did, indeed, mean business.[29]

There was no time to waste: seeing a newspaper notice for an office position at Pedlar People Limited as a cost clerk he "grabbed it quickly." Michael began working at the Oshawa company, which manufactured sheet-metal equipment, in mid-1928[30] as part of the office staff, and he signed a new contract of employment for every year he worked with this company. Michael showed initiative and interest in his new work and soon attracted the attention of his employer. The president of the company, Reginald Geikie,[31] interviewed him and told Michael he would soon have a responsible position in the firm. Michael was asked to shorten his surname to make it more pronounceable in English and therefore, more convenient for correspondence purposes. At eighteen years of age, and with his father's permission, Michael shortened his surname from Starchewski to Starr.[32] However, records show the family name continued to be spelled over the years as "Starczewski," "Starchewski" or "Starr."

As the oldest of six children in an immigrant's family, Michael's early life was shaped by thriftiness and hard work. Matthew supported his large family on modest wages but he was a constant reminder in Michael's formative years of the fundamental principles of his

---

25. *The Oshawa Daily Reformer,* October 2, 1925.
26. Interview with Mike Starr by Leo LaClare, October 9, 1973, LAC Sound Archives.
27. *Oshawa/Whitby This Week*, October 28, 1987.
28. *Oshawa News*, February 3, 1999.
29. Michael Starr Papers, MG 32, B 15, *The Mike Starr Story*, Vol. 1.
30. The papers of the Pedlar People Limited are held at Library and Archives Canada.
31. Walter Reginald Geikie was the son-in-law of George H. Pedlar of the Pedlar People Limited.
32. Interview with Mike Starr by Leo LaClare, October 9, 1973, Sound Archives, LAC.

family's life—good housekeeping and a frugal lifestyle.³³ These principles had a penetrating and permanent influence on Michael's character and outlook on life. Michael's early life was also influenced by political events not only in Oshawa but also in the land of his parents.

After the collapse of the Imperial Russian and Austro-Hungarian Empires, many Ukrainian Canadians supported the revolutionary events in Ukraine and the establishment of an independent Ukraine in 1917. After several years of civil conflict and foreign military invasions, the country was incorporated into the Soviet Union in 1922 as the Ukrainian Soviet Socialist Republic. Substantial segments of the Ukrainian population remained under the administration of neighbouring countries—Poland, Czechoslovakia and Romania. During these years, Ukrainian community politics in Canada were influenced to a large extent by events in Ukrainian lands in Eastern Europe. Community politics were also influenced by the difficult social and economic conditions in Canada especially on the resource and agricultural frontiers.³⁴ However, it was the question of support for or opposition to Soviet Ukraine and the Soviet Union that became the determining factor in the ideological orientation of Ukrainian individuals, organizations and institutions in Canada, including Oshawa.³⁵ This issue became the central theme in Ukrainian politics, literature and historiography, and continued to dominate Ukrainian Canadian community life from the end of the Second World War through 1991.

Matthew Starchewski was a Ukrainian nationalist and maintained a profound interest in Ukrainian politics as well as politics at the local community level. In 1926, Matthew became president of Oshawa's Mykhailo Hrushevsky Prosvita Society and, in 1930–31, he was the organization's recording secretary. Mary Starchewski joined her husband as a member of Prosvita.³⁶

Owing to its large concentration of Ukrainians, south Oshawa became a centre for Ukrainian left-wing political activity that polarized the community. A branch of the Ukrainian Social Democratic Party was organized in Oshawa as early as 1917.³⁷ This political group existed from May 1917 until the last weeks of 1918 because this political party—and its newspaper, *Robochyi Narod* (Labouring People)—was banned by the Canadian federal government. A number of Ukrainian "enemy aliens" interned in Kapuskasing had been sent to work in the Oshawa foundries during the First World War to ease the labour shortage. They provided the core of the small but growing Ukrainian left-wing group in Oshawa. In 1922, a branch of the Ukrainian Labour Farmer Temple Association (ULFTA) was established and the construction of a hall began in 1923. News about Ukrainianization policies in Soviet Ukraine in the 1920s attracted a large segment of the Oshawa community

---

33. *Sudbury Star*, September 13, 1961.
34. For a left-wing interpretation of the Ukrainian Canadian experience during these years, see Peter Krawchuk, *Our History: The Ukrainian Labour-Farmer Movement in Canada 1907–1991*, Logus Publications, Toronto, 1996.
35. For a detailed study of the various factions in the Ukrainian Canadian community, see Orest T. Martynowych, *Ukrainians in Canada, The Interwar Years, Book I*, CIUS Press, 2016.
36. Ontario Archives, Ukrainian National Federation Collection, Oshawa Branch.
37. *Friends in Need, The WBA Story*, WBA, Winnipeg, 1972, pp. 109–111; also, *Ukrainian Life*, September 25, 1963.

supporting the local ULFTA. The new Soviet government in Ukraine publicized its efforts to create Ukrainian-language institutions, universities and government agencies to develop support for the Bolshevik regime among the population. Propaganda spread across Ukrainian communities throughout Canada via meetings and the left-wing press attracted supporters. In 1924, the Oshawa branch of the ULFTA claimed seventy members and had a mandolin orchestra, string orchestra, children's school, and a women's branch with fifteen members. Among the first instructors at the Ukrainian school was Ivan Sembay, who recently arrived from Europe to assist with the building of the pro-Soviet movement among Ukrainians in Canada. The ULFTA drew crowds of over one hundred for concerts and other cultural events.[38]

In 1924, a branch of the Canadian Sitch Organization was established in Oshawa.[39] This association supported a monarchist political program, was anti-communist and had the support of the Ukrainian Catholic clergy. The Ukrainian Presbyterian Church was also politically active in the Ukrainian community and the pastor published a newsletter on community events in the 1930s.[40] By 1930, the Ukrainian community with their halls organized a much more active cultural life than the larger English community surrounding it, staging approximately 150 plays and about 20 concerts each year.[41] These activities helped to maintain family and community solidarity and to survive the Depression, and Starr later commented that the Ukrainian community in Oshawa lived a rich cultural life during his youth and was able to preserve some of the cultural traditions of the community. However, he felt more efforts should have been made at that time by the Ukrainian community to integrate with the larger Oshawa community.[42]

During his formative years, Michael frequently witnessed heated fundamental political debates and arguments between members of the Ukrainian community about the benefits and weaknesses of socialist versus market economies; these experiences were an important part of his early political education. The left-right political debates had their origins in the recent political history of Ukraine and the struggle for Ukrainian independence during the years 1918–1921.[43]

---

38. LAC, CSIS, RG146, Box 62, Vol. 3788 (97-A-00063). AUUC, Oshawa, Report April 11, 1929; *Almanakh Tovarystva Ukrainskyi Robitnycho-Farmerskyi Dim v Kanadi, 1918-1929*, Winnipeg, 1930, pp. 108–110; Slavny istoriiu maie zhinochyi viddil TOUK v Oshavi, *Ukrainske Zhyttia*, May 9, 1962,
39. Archives of Ontario, Ukrainian Sporting 'Sitch' Association, Branch no.3, Oshawa Records, 1940-63, Reel 257 (from 1923) Knyha Chleniv III Kosha KSO v Oshavi. Branch had forty members in 1923; Michael H. Marunchak, *The Ukrainian Canadians: A History*, UVAN, Winnipeg, 1982, p. 394; *Iliustrovanyi Kaliendar Kanadyiskoho Ukraintsia na Rik 1926*, Winnipeg, 1926, pp. 108–109.
40. Michael H. Marunchak, *The Ukrainian Canadians: A History*, UVAN, Winnipeg, 1982, p. 493.
41. McIntyre Hood, "Night in Oshawa's Little Ukrainia Reveals Marvellous Expression of Dramatic Power of the Ukrainians," *The Oshawa Daily Times*, January 20, 1930; Michael Petrowsky, "The Little Theatre and Cultural Life of Oshawa," *The Oshawa Daily Times*, February 10, 1930; "Ukrainians Excel in Presentation of Play in Oshawa," *The New Canadian*, May 1930.
42. Ukrainian Canadian Research and Documentation Centre, "Memoirs of the Honourable Michael Starr" (1998).
43. A similar political polarization developed in the Finnish community in Canada. See Oiva W. Saarinen, *Between a Rock and a Hard Place: A Historical Geography of the Finns in the Sudbury Area*, Wilfred Laurier University Press, Waterloo, Ontario, 1999.

In the 1920s Oshawa was a middle-sized community, not yet the commuter suburb of Toronto it later became. Those living there tended to work there as well. It was also a market centre for the surrounding farming area, but its primary industry was—and remains—the automobile industry, dominated by the large General Motors plant. There was an informal division of labour in Oshawa with the recent immigrants from Central and Eastern Europe working in the foundries and tanneries and native-born Canadians, primarily of British origin, working at General Motors. In addition to the Ukrainian community, south Oshawa was also the neighbourhood for other recent immigrants from Europe—Poles, Hungarians, Germans—among others.

Oshawa was, in many ways, a one-industry town: the automobile industry. The family of Samuel McLaughlin, president of General Motors of Canada, maintained a paternalistic attitude towards Oshawa residents and closely monitored local social and political activities. The McLaughlins also owned a significant interest in the local newspaper.[44] Samuel's brother, George, who was chairman of the Citizens Advisory Relief Committee,[45] surveyed local community activities from his small downtown-Oshawa office. As one historian wrote, "A sparrow did not fall in Oshawa without George having some say in it; he belonged to every organization that wasn't specifically Ukrainian or Catholic . . ."[46] Although George McLaughlin did not officially monitor the social and political activities of the local Ukrainian community, it should be noted that the Royal Canadian Mounted Police did maintain its surveillance of left-wing communities in Oshawa through the 1960s.[47]

The Depression of the 1930s had profound consequences in Oshawa: the unemployed were numerous and welfare cases increased. The municipality and voluntary groups attempted to implement various programs to help the unemployed and those on welfare[48] but some of the recent immigrants were afraid to apply for welfare, fearing deportation. According to *The Oshawa Daily Times*, 500 aliens who were not naturalized were registered in Oshawa as unemployed and a large percentage were on relief.[49]

The issue of deporting "unnaturalized aliens on relief" was debated in the Oshawa municipal government, which raised a storm of opposition within immigrant communities.

---

44. Charlotte Yates, "From Plant to Politics: The Canadian UAW 1936–1984," PhD thesis, Carleton University, 1988, p. 43.
45. *The Oshawa Daily Times*, July 2, 1932.
46. Heather Robertson, *Driving Force, The McLaughlin Family and the Age of the Car*, McClelland and Stewart, Toronto, 1995, p. 251.
47. LAC, CSIS, RG146, Volume 3788, Box 62 (97-A-00063), AUUC, Oshawa, Report: "Myron Momryk, The Royal Canadian Mounted Police and the Surveillance of the Ukrainian Community in Canada," *Journal of Ukrainian Studies*, Volume 28, No. 2, 2003. It is interesting to note that in 1939 Michael Petrowsky from Oshawa, in his role as a special constable became the RCMP expert on the Ukrainian community in Canada. His papers are preserved at Library and Archives Canada.
48. A good description of the Depression years in Oshawa is found Heather Robertson's *Driving Force*, pp. 243–287.
49. *The Oshawa Daily Times*, August 11, 1932. It should be noted that many immigrants were not naturalized because they came to Canada as sojourners to earn some money and had planned to return to their country of origin, where their families lived and where they still held property. The Depression prevented their return.

The Finance Committee passed a unanimous resolution recommending the deportation of recent immigrants on relief and recommended action by the Oshawa City Council. Alderman Louis S. Hyman, who was absent at this Finance Committee meeting, opposed this resolution. About twenty-five men were liable to be deported but those who were in Canada over five years would not be deported. Some unemployed men returned to Europe voluntarily. Meetings were called within the Ukrainian community to discuss this resolution. Representatives of the Ukrainian Greek Catholic Church, Greek Orthodox Church, the Presbyterian Church and eight secular organizations met on August 24, 1932, at St. George's Hall. Also present were some local politicians. Attendees were told ". . . aliens have nothing to fear."[50] One recommendation resulting from these meetings was the establishment of the Public Welfare Board.[51]

Between January 1932 and March 1933 at least thirteen Oshawa residents who were not naturalized were deported for being "Public Charges" or "Medical Charges."[52] The unemployed, including many of British descent, began to organize and meetings were held in the ULFTA hall in the "Red" or "foreign" section of Oshawa.[53] Fights broke out among individuals for the leadership of the unemployed movement. In one case, John Farkas, a Hungarian immigrant and member of the Communist Party of Canada, was arrested after a fight in a local park. Sentenced to be deported back to Hungary in December, 1932, he managed to escape to the Soviet Union.[54] In 1933, Nick Sawchuk, another activist from Oshawa, went on strike in a relief camp and for his efforts was deported to Poland.[55]

Reflecting on this period in the history of Oshawa's Ukrainian community, Starr was fully aware of the social and economic conditions that were the push factors encouraging emigration to Canada from Galicia. Ukrainians in Galicia lived a subsistence existence, managing as best they could under the prevailing social and economic conditions. During the Depression, the standard of living in Oshawa may have been low but Ukrainians there managed to survive by accepting odd jobs; almost every family had a kitchen garden. Even during the most difficult years of the Depression, conditions in Oshawa were better than those in the Ukrainian villages in Galicia.

On September 9, 1933, Michael, now twenty-two years old, married Anne Zaritsky, an eighteen-year-old Ukrainian girl whom he had been courting for some time.[56] Anne was born on May 1, 1915, in Montreal but moved to Toronto with her parents as a child of three

---

50. Lara Campbell, *Respectable Citizens, Gender, Family and Unemployment in Ontario's Great Depression*, University of Toronto Press, 2009, p. 180; *The Oshawa Daily Times*, August 19, 20, 23, 25, 1932; *Toronto Daily Star*, August 22, 1932.
51. *The Oshawa Daily Times*, August 26, 1932.
52. LAC, RG26, Volume 16, File: "Public Charges Deports 1931–1937."
53. *Oshawa Workers Tribune*, December 30, 1932.
54. See Myron Momryk, "From the Streets of Oshawa to the Prisons of Moscow: The Story of Janos Farkas (1902–1938)," *Hungarian Studies Review*, Vol. 38, Nos. 1–2, (2011). Farkas was executed in 1938 during the Stalin purges in Moscow.
55. *Canadian Labour Defender*, Vol.4, No..5, August 1933.
56. Ontario, Canada, marriages 1933–1934, Michael Starchewski (Starr), Greek Catholic, and Anne Zaritsky, Greek Orthodox, were married in the Greek Orthodox Church in Toronto. Starr reported his occupation as a mechanic.

Figure 1.2 Mike Starr and Anne Zaritsky were married on September 9, 1933, in the midst of the Depression and began their life in Oshawa facing an uncertain future, as was the case for many young couples during this era. According to the custom at that time, the wedding party included family, friends and acquaintances from Oshawa and Toronto who also traced their roots to ancestral villages in Ukraine. Image courtesy of Walter Kish.

years old and was educated there. Her family and the Starchewski family were close friends from the Montreal years and this friendship continued when the Starrs moved to Oshawa; Anne visited many times with her family. Both families were delighted when Anne and Michael decided to marry.[57] Together they began the task of establishing a home in Oshawa during the most difficult years of the Depression. Compared to many young men during these years, Michael considered himself fortunate to be working at Pedlar People Ltd. In 1933 Starr earned $33.00 a month and, after careful expenditures, he and Anne had $2.00 left until the next month.[58] However, there were occasions when their difficult financial situation obliged Michael to seriously consider working at the General Motors plant, where he could earn much more once there was an increased demand for new automobiles. They lived a modest life and for entertainment played cards, listened to the radio and visited the local Ukrainian halls. Later in retirement, Starr reminisced that they led a happy life.[59]

57. LAC, Michael Starr Papers, MG 32, B 15, *The Mike Starr Story*, Vol. 1.
58. Ukrainian Canadian Research and Documentation Centre, "Memoirs of the Honourable Michael Starr" (1998).
59. Ibid.

Figure 1.3 Ukrainian softball team, Oshawa 1935 (Michael Starr is seen standing far right, in white shirt). During the 1930s, Mike Starr was actively involved with the Ukrainian softball team in Oshawa. He held several positions on this team and this experience aided Starr to develop his leadership skills that later became useful in organizing election campaign teams. He maintained his interest in softball for many more years. Image courtesy Walter Kish.

Starr was among the first of the Canadian-born and Canadian-educated generation of Oshawa's Ukrainian community. He spoke English and Ukrainian equally well, which meant his family and friends often turned to him for advice and information when dealing with official and legal matters. Many Ukrainian immigrants were unfamiliar with local institutions and preferred to seek the assistance of community leaders such as Starr in their dealings with municipal and government officials at all levels. This practice was fairly common among other immigrant groups for many years. During the early 1930s, Starr began developing an aptitude for public speaking and community leadership. He spoke at service-club functions and other public events. He took an active part in the cultural life of the local Ukrainian community and was regularly invited as master of ceremonies at various cultural events. During the provincial and federal elections, he was persuaded to campaign on behalf of the Conservative candidates and, when necessary, addressed audiences in Ukrainian.

In the summer of 1927, Starr organized a softball club called the Ukrainian Athletic Club and the M. Hrushevsky Prosvita Hall sponsored the club. In 1928, the club entered the Oshawa City Industrial League and Starr played three positions: pitcher, first base and outfield. He doubled as the coach and manager. The team played every summer and, in August 1932, it travelled to Toronto to participate in the Ukrainian Field Day. They played other local teams, including the Polish team from Starr's Oshawa neighbourhood. In September 1933 Starr's team won Oshawa's city championship. The Women's Section of the local branch of the Sitch held a tea evening for the softball team because the sports team "brought glory to the Ukrainian community."[60] In 1935, the team was affiliated with the Oshawa Branch of the Ukrainian National Youth Federation and Starr was one of the coaches. The team won the Eastern Ontario championship in 1935, 1936 and, in 1937, the Oshawa championship.[61] The team continued to play until 1940 when the members became involved in the war effort. The team attracted large Ukrainian audiences as community organizations reduced their activities during the summer. Starr was on the executive of the softball team and was one of the early organizers of the Oshawa and District Softball Association. He maintained his interest in softball for many more years.[62]

Throughout this period Starr was encouraged by his employer to become more actively involved in local community affairs.[63] It was one of Pedlar People's management policies to encourage employees to take an active interest in local politics.[64] For example, Frank L. Mason, who joined the company in 1894 and went on to become a director and purchasing agent of the firm before he retired in 1941, served on the Oshawa Municipal Council for twelve years, became warden of Ontario County in 1917, and mayor of Oshawa in 1918. He was also a past president of the South Ontario Agricultural Society and a member of the first Public Utilities Commission elected in Oshawa, in 1930.[65]

By 1931, Oshawa counted over 900 Ukrainians from its total population of 23,439.[66] Those fortunate to be employed worked in the foundries and the leather industry. The increasingly desperate economic situation during the Depression and the growing political instability in Europe caused the Ukrainian community to polarize even further along political lines. The local branch of the Ukrainian Labor and Farmer Temple Association increased its membership to new levels. On February 4, 1934, the Prosvita Society became a branch of the Ukrainian National Federation which supported a pro-nationalist policy opposing the Polish administration of eastern Galicia and, especially, the Soviet Union.[67]

60. Archives of Ontario, Ukrainian Sporting "Sitch" Association, Reel 257, Minute Book, III Kosha (Oshawa) minutes of meeting, September 25, 1933, pp. 126–127.
61. UNYF of Oshawa, 35th Jubilee, May 15-16, 1971, UNF Hall, 68 Bloor Street.
62. K.W. Sokolyk, *Their Sporting Legacy, The Participation of Canadians of Ukrainian Descent in Sport, 1891–1991*, The Basilian Press, Toronto, 2002, pp. 117, 119, 125; *The Globe and Mail*, January 3, 1949.
63. The Geikie/Pedlar family were supporters of the Conservative Party for many years. Alexander Fraser, *A History of Ontario*, The Canada History Company, Montreal/Toronto, 1907, Vol. 2, p. 1227. See the entry on George Henry Pedlar; also, Ukrainian Canadian Research and Documentation Centre, "Memoirs of the Honourable Michael Starr" (1998).
64. LAC, Peter Stursberg Papers, MG 31, D 78, Vol. 16, p. 5.
65. M. McIntyre Hood, *Oshawa, "The Crossing Between the Waters"; A History of Canada's Motor City*, McLaughlin Public Library Board, Oshawa, 1968, p. 105.
66. Rick Salutin, *Kent Rowley, The Organizer: A Canadian Union Life*, Toronto, 1980, p. 409. According to this source, 9.5 per cent of the population was of Eastern European origin.
67. W. Fedorowycz, "The Ukrainian National Federation of Canada: Its Presence in Ontario," *Polyphony, The Bulletin of the Multicultural History Society of Ontario*, Volume 10, 1988 (Ukrainians in Ontario), pp. 135–136.

The Starchewski family were originally members of the Ukrainian Greek Catholic parish in Oshawa. However, in 1935, the parish became involved in a fundamental dispute regarding clerical celibacy. Father Andrew Sarmatiuk, who had served the parish since 1931, was asked by Bishop Vasyl Ladyka, the head of the Church in Winnipeg, to leave his wife if he wished to continue as the parish priest. Fr. Sarmatiuk refused and was suspended by the bishop.[68] Despite having served as a priest for twenty years, Fr. Sarmatiuk had been married for fourteen years. Being married after his ordination was contrary to the Greek Catholic Church tradition, where marriage was allowed but only for those candidates married prior to their ordination. A petition with 400 signatures was sent to Bishop Ladyka demanding he retain Fr. Sarmatiuk as the parish priest. When this failed approximately 80 per cent of the parish left the Ukrainian Greek Catholic Church in protest.[69] The division became public knowledge among the larger community; even the *Toronto Star* covered the story. The dispute extended to questions about the ownership of the Church building and its property.[70] Fr. Sarmatiuk was obliged to leave the Church and the parish residence and founded the St. John Ukrainian Greek-Orthodox Church.[71] The Starchewski family became members of Fr. Sarmatiuk's new Ukrainian Orthodox Church parish that supported the principle of a married clergy, an ancient tradition in Ukraine. Bishop Ladyka assigned Fr. Ivan (John) Pereyma as the new pastor to the Oshawa parish, who began to rebuild the parish, however this dispute divided the Ukrainian community in Oshawa for many decades.

Starr's growing interest in politics developed during a crucial period in Oshawa's—and Canada's—labour history. At the beginning of April 1937, General Motors employees went out on strike,[72] a move that would have national repercussions: as a result of this strike, the United Automobile Workers (UAW) Union was founded in March and April of 1937. The strike action, and the formation of a union at the plant, provoked strong and emotional responses. Members of the Communist Party of Canada (CPC) had an active role in the labour conflicts and the establishment of the UAW union. The local ULFTA hall was used as a headquarters for union activities. The ULFTA in Toronto sent members to Oshawa to recruit for the union. This situation created a dilemma for the pro-nationalist Ukrainians who also sought to improve their economic situation but were aware that the leadership of the union movement included members of the CPC.[73] For this reason, many Ukrainian and Polish workers refused to attend union meetings and pay membership dues.[74] This successful strike marked the birth of industrial unionism in Canada and stimulated the growth of a new political party, the Co-operative Commonwealth Federation (CCF), in

---

68. *Toronto Daily Star*, January 30, 31, 1935. Also, Julian Beskyd (ed.), *Eparchy of Toronto, A Quarter of a Century on the Episcopal Throne 1948–1973*, Nasha Meta, Toronto, 1975, p. 331.
69. *Toronto Daily Star*, February 4, 1935.
70. Ibid., June 28, 1935.
71. "Oshawa Ukrainians Open New Church." *Globe and Mail,* October 4, 1935. This incident is described in the book by Orest T. Martynowych, *Ukrainians in Canada: The Interwar Years. Book I*, Canadian Institute of Ukrainian Studies Press, Toronto, 2016, pp. 129–135.
72. "G.M. Employees Strike," *The Oshawa Daily Times*, April 8, 1937.
73. Heather Robertson, *Driving Force*, pp. 226, 293. Bill Gelech was fired from his job at General Motors in March, 1937 for making a pro-union speech in Ukrainian.
74. LAC, CSIS, RG146, Vol. 3788, Box 62 (97-A-00063); AUUC Oshawa; Report 29/7/1938. The ULFTA hall was also used in 1940 in local strikes.

Ontario.[75] It also increased the strength and morale of local labour activists and supporters. According to one report, Starr had walked the UAW picket line during the strike.[76]

On December 23, 1937, with the encouragement of his firm, friends and neighbours, Michael Starr decided to run for alderman in the 1938 Oshawa municipal election. "Ukrainian to be Candidate," announced the local newspaper.[77] He was also the youngest of the forty-six candidates declaring themselves in the election. Starr was encouraged to run as a labour candidate but he declined. Instead he was nominated by a representative committee and not by any particular political group. Starr introduced himself to the electorate as a member of Oshawa's so-called foreign section and claimed he represented 800 city taxpayers. The local newspaper stated he had the support for voters of Ukrainian, Polish and Russian descent in the south end of Oshawa.[78] His election campaign focussed on improving city sanitation, sidewalks and public services generally. During the campaign, Starr emphasized his concern with the high rate of real estate taxes and their negative effect on local prosperity.[79] During this campaign, as in all his other electoral campaigns, Starr received financial support from his employer. He also received support and encouragement from various segments of the Ukrainian community including some left-wing group members. For example, in the December 24, 1937, issue of the Ukrainian-language left-wing newspaper, *Narodna Hazeta*, Nikolai I. Melekh, who signed himself as "Head, Pre-election Committee, Oshawa," wrote in an article that Michael Starchevsky "... always and devotedly fought for workers' concerns and for all taxpayers." He stated that if the municipal elections in Oshawa were held according to the ward system, it would have been possible to elect two or three Ukrainians as representatives on City Council. But the voting was city-wide, and since only the top ten were elected, this was difficult. Melekh added that "[w]e Ukrainians help other candidates but not our own. We have a responsible candidate in Michael Starr. When we elect one, we can elect others. Starr promised to fight for our working people ... All Slavic organizations should support him without regard to political or religious differences."

The municipal election held on January 4, 1938, was a labour victory. Starr was not elected but he had obtained a total of 1,334 votes from the North-East and South-East Wards which were heavily populated by Ukrainians and other Slavic ethnocultural groups.[80] The mayor and six aldermen were labour candidates and a labour representative was also elected to the school board. The new municipal council immediately began implementing its election promises. The Welfare Board was reorganized and one of the appointees was Volodymyr (Walter) Bilsky, an active member of the Oshawa ULFTA. A motion submitted

---

75. James Alexander Pendergest, "Labour and Politics in Oshawa and District, 1928–1943," MA thesis, Queen's University, 1973, See also Irving Abella, *On Strike, Six Key Labour Struggles in Canada, 1919–1949*, James Lewis and Samuel, Publishers, Toronto, 1974. See chapter on Oshawa, 1937, by Abella, p. 93.
76. *Ottawa Citizen*, September 21, 1957; Bob Ford, president of the Ottawa District Trades and Labour Council, stated that he and Mike Starr walked the picket line in Oshawa in 1937.
77. LAC, Michael Starr Papers, MG 32, B 15, *The Mike Starr Story*, Part One, first page.
78. Ibid.
79. *Oshawa Daily Times*, December 28, 1937.
80. During these years, Oshawa was organized into the following polling subdivisions: Northwest Ward, Southwest Ward, Northeast Ward, Southeast Ward and Cedardale

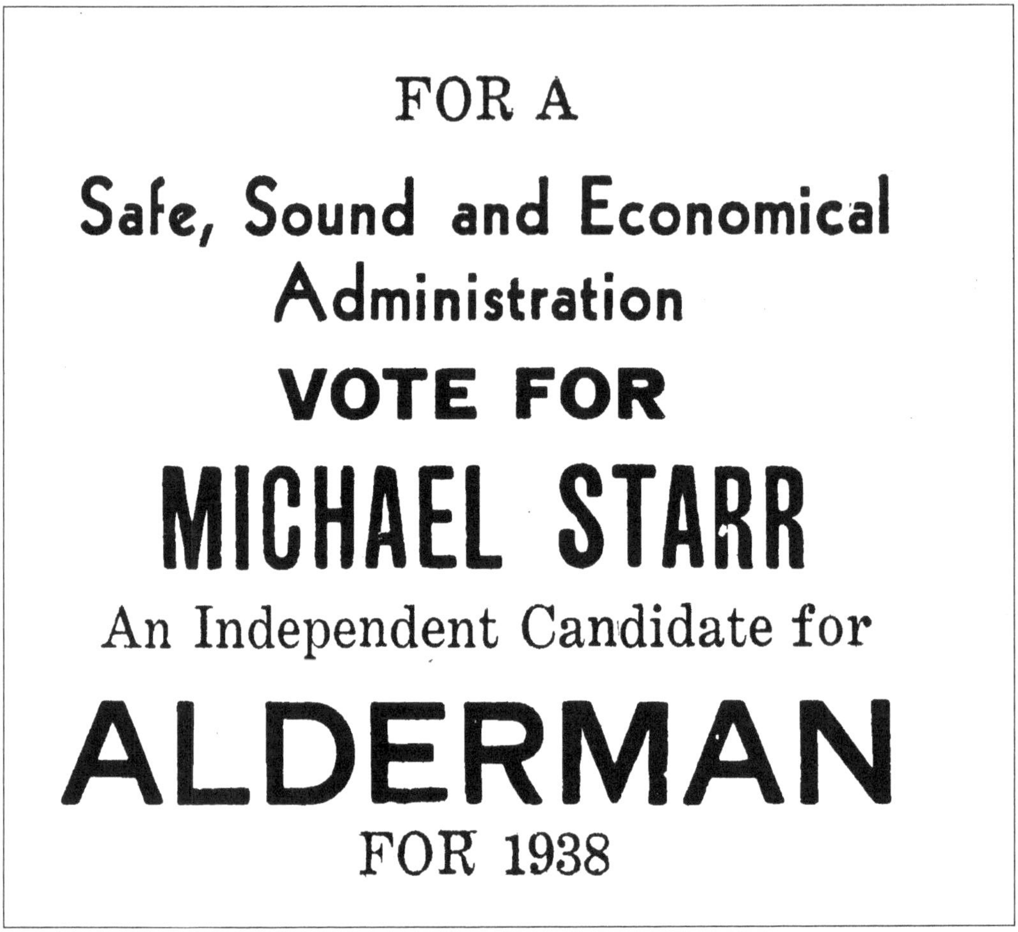

FOR A
Safe, Sound and Economical Administration
VOTE FOR
MICHAEL STARR
An Independent Candidate for
ALDERMAN
FOR 1938

Figure 1.4 Starr for Alderman, 1938. This election poster was distributed for Starr's first attempt as a candidate for the position as alderman. He was unsuccessful in this municipal election and campaigned again, until he was ultimately elected in 1944. Image courtesy of Walter Kish.

to City Council "that Mr. Bilsky be appointed to the Welfare Board as a representative of a large body of citizens of many nationalities who predominate in the South end of our City" was carried.[81] When the news was announced in the local press, Ukrainian nationalists immediately launched a strong protest. A meeting was called on January 23, 1938, in the Ukrainian National Federation (UNF) Hall, and four speakers including Fr. Ivan Pereyma, the local Ukrainian Catholic priest, spoke against this appointment before an audience of 400 people.[82] A resolution against Bilsky was passed and presented to the City Council. On January 30 and February 6, meetings were held at the ULFTA Hall to support the appointment of Bilsky.[83] Accusations were made that "the Ukrainian National Hall (UNF) was a

---

81. Ontario Archives, Oshawa, City of Oshawa Council Minutes, MS 671, January 17, 1938, p. 188.
82. "Oshawa Ukrainians Protest Against Appointment of 'Red' on Relief Body," *The New Canadian*, January 29, 1938; *The Globe and Mail*, January 24, 1938, "Appointment is Protested."
83. *Narodna Hazeta*, February 3, 1938; also, Ontario Archives, Oshawa, City of Oshawa Council Minutes, MS 671, February 7, 1938, p. 191.

fascist organization" and the meetings were called "by agents of fascism and Trotsky-ites."[84] The administrators of the local Sitch Hall were accused of renting their building for a meeting of the Canadian fascist leader Tom Farr and his "Blue Shirts" in July 1938.[85] The political debates and accusations between the pro-nationalists and pro-communists continued throughout the year and later.[86]

Starr ran for alderman in the 1939 municipal elections and again was not elected. Accusations were made in *The Oshawa Labor Press* that the *Oshawa Times* was spreading racial hatred and undemocratic ideas and also used the Communists as "red herring" to discredit the labour movement.[87] Frank Towers, a CPC member in Oshawa, said Starr was not a labour candidate for alderman.[88] However, in this election only four labour aldermen were elected to a City Council of ten members. Bilsky ran for a position on the Municipal Board of Education but was not elected.[89] The labour representatives no longer dominated the municipal government and accusations were made in the left-wing newspaper, *Narodna Hazeta* (People's Newspaper), that this was the result of voting irregularities. Starr's candidacy in municipal elections attracted the attention of municipal authorities and, on January 16, 1939, he was appointed to the Oshawa City Welfare Board.[90] As a member of this board, he had to spend many long evenings considering which citizens were eligible for welfare; approximately twenty per cent of Oshawa citizens were receiving welfare. Starr's work with the Welfare Board and his various community involvements further stimulated his interest in municipal affairs.

The outbreak of the Second World War in September 1939 had a dramatic effect on Oshawa and the Oshawa Ukrainian community. Rationing was introduced for sugar, coffee, butter and gasoline, and tokens were obtained from the Post Office. Industries retooled for war production: General Motors' 6,200 employees started building one-third of all trucks, tanks, jeeps and other mechanized military vehicles that would be produced by wartime Canada; Starr's employer, Pedlar People, made millions of shell cases; Robson Leather made leather for soldiers' shoes; Fittings Limited and Ontario Malleable Iron Co. also produced military-related material. Every factory worked three shifts and women were employed by the thousands. There were so many people working that, to the west of Oshawa, a new town—Ajax—was built to house workers.[91]

Not surprisingly, the number of relief recipients began dropping. In September 1938, 4,453 people in Oshawa received support, and 4,130 in September 1939; by September 1940 those numbers were down to 665, and to 400 in March 1941.[92] The Depression was definitely over by December 1941, when the United States entered the war and American orders for military material flooded in.

---

84. *The Globe and Mail*, January 31, 1938.
85. *The Oshawa Labor Press*, June 13, 1940.
86. *The Oshawa Labor Press*, June 15, 1939, "Bilsky Defends Temple Association."
87. *The Oshawa Labor Press,* December 29, 1938.
88. Ibid.
89. Ontario Archives, Oshawa, City of Oshawa Council Minutes, MS 671, January 4, 1939.
90. Ontario Archives, Oshawa, City of Oshawa Council Minutes, MS 671, January 16, 1939.
91. Harold N. Pascoe, *Take My Hand*, Harold N. Pascoe Publisher, 1978, pp. 27–29, 68–69.
92. LAC, RG27, Volume 2119, Oshawa Welfare Cases, NES NRB National Registration of Relief Recipients – Monthly Summary, Oshawa, September 1938–March 1941.

In February 1938, a Ukrainian Flying School was established in Oshawa through the efforts of the National Executive of the Ukrainian National Youth Federation.[93] It was opposed by some members of the local labour movement who described the school as having "fascist leanings."[94] The school taught flying and parachuting; forty-five students graduated before the outbreak of war. Most of the graduates joined the Royal Canadian Air Force (RCAF) and the school's training plane and other equipment were donated to the RCAF. Ukrainian nationalist organizations from across Canada supported the war effort and their national executives communicated their support to the Canadian government. The support of the Ukrainian nationalists for the Canadian war effort was also due to the recent signing of the Nazi-Soviet Pact, on August 23, 1939, which made the Soviet Union a "partner" of Nazi Germany and, therefore, a perceived enemy of Canada.[95]

The Ukrainian nationalist community in Oshawa held a meeting on December 29, 1939, "to raise our voice in aid of our former kinsmen in Europe." They sent a letter of protest to the Prime Minister, against the occupation of Ukraine by the Germans and also by the Soviet Union. They declared that ". . . all Ukrainians are prepared to fight on the side of the democracies to establish a decent order in Europe based on the principles of self-determination and ethnographic rights." The letter was signed by representatives of the Ukrainian National Federation, Ukrainian Greek Orthodox Church, Ukrainian Greek Catholic Church, Ukrainian Presbyterian Church, Ukrainian Sitch Sport Association and the Ukrainian Orthodox Church.[96]

On April 5, 1940, these Ukrainian community organizations and churches held a meeting to establish a Ukrainian Canadian Committee. Mike Starr was elected secretary of the new umbrella association.[97] He also held the position of secretary of the St. John Ukrainian Orthodox Parish in Oshawa.

The local branch of the ULFTA was caught in a difficult situation. The Canadian federal government suspected and feared the activities of pro-communist organizations in Canada, which were perceived as detrimental to the war effort. Prominent members of the CPC were arrested and interned.[98] On June 4, 1940, the federal government declared the ULFTA and several other organizations illegal and their halls were placed under the control of the federal government's Custodian of Enemy Property. The ULFTA Hall in Oshawa was closed

---

93. *The Globe and Mail*, January 25, 1938; Thomas M. Prymak, The Ukrainian Flying School in Oshawa, *Polyphony, The Bulletin of the Multicultural History Society of Ontario*, Vol. 10, 1988, (Ukrainians in Ontario) pp. 149–152.
94. *The Oshawa Labor Press*, May 11, 1939, "Flying School has Fascist Leanings." A reply was published on June 1, 1939.
95. An announcement was made that Fr. Ivan Pereyma, the Ukrainian Catholic parish priest, was appointed chaplain in the Canadian Army, however, he did not serve. *The New Canadian*, December 1939.
96. LAC, RG25, Vol.1896, File 165-39c, pt.1, Treatment of Ukrainians in Poland and Activities of Ukrainians in Canada, 1935-1940.
97. Archives of Ontario, Ukrainian Sporting "Sitch" Association, Reel 257, Minute Book, III Kosha (Oshawa) minutes of meeting, April 5, 1940, p. 146.
98. *The Oshawa Labor Press*, April 18, 1940, "Frank Towers held in Whitby jail."

and their overt political activities ceased.[99] In 1941, the hall was rented by the local branch of the Polish Friendly Alliance Association.[100]

Starr ran for alderman in the 1940 municipal elections and was again unsuccessful. He was not discouraged and ran in the municipal elections of 1941 and 1942. Again he was an unsuccessful candidate, but he continued to receive substantial support in the North-East and North-West and South-East Wards in Oshawa.

During the early war years, Starr became even more active in Oshawa community affairs. Pedlar People Ltd., where Starr worked as a cost clerk, was now involved in war-related work producing anti-aircraft cartridge cases for the United States military. Starr continued as a member of the Welfare Board and also was a member of the executive committee of the local Red Cross Society. He served as a member of various Oshawa city boards, including the Salvage Board and the Vocational School Advisory Committee of the Board of Education. Starr was a member of the War Loan Committee and had organized the local civil defence program.[101] He was also responsible for the rationing of gasoline for private vehicles in Oshawa. Anne Starr worked as a bookkeeper in a cleaning business and developed her aptitude in business matters.

The Second World War brought prosperity to Oshawa. The factories produced war-related products, munitions and vehicles that greatly expanded the work force. These workers came from the rural areas surrounding Oshawa and from other parts of Ontario, including other provinces. The war stimulated a large shift in population from western to eastern Canada. Among this large migration were many Ukrainian families that sought to escape the devastating effects of the Depression on the Prairie provinces. Some of these families settled in the Oshawa area and Mike Starr was often the first local Ukrainian community member that they encountered. Starr was president of the Ukrainian Orthodox Parish from 1940 to 1943 and in this capacity introduced many new members to the parish and the larger Ukrainian community.[102]

During the war, a determined effort was made to organize unions within the various Oshawa plants. The Steel Workers Organizing Committee (SWOC), a pro-communist organization, targeted Oshawa workers from various immigrant groups. Lodge 1817 of the SWOC published the newspaper *The Melting Pot* in four languages—English, Polish, Ukrainian and Hungarian—but this newspaper was published for only a few months before the CPC leadership and organizations were banned by the federal government.[103] Plans to organize unions in Oshawa included factories like Pedlar People, leaving Mike Starr with a particular dilemma: the union organizer for his factory in 1943 was Michael Fenwick,[104]

---

99. *The Oshawa Labor Press*, June 13, 1940, "Police Raid Labor Temple but Flying Club Unmolested."
100. LAC, RG146, Vol. 3788, Box 62 (97-A-00063); AUUC, Oshawa, Report 21/8/1941. The report stated that the Polish association purchased the hall, however later reports suggest that the hall was rented from the Custodian of Enemy Property.
101. *Toronto Telegram*, March 19, 1958.
102. *Fortieth Anniversary, St. John's Ukrainian Greek-Orthodox Church in Oshawa, Ontario, 1935-1975*, Harmony Printing Ltd., Toronto, Ontario, pp. 46–49.
103. *The Melting Pot*, Oshawa, SWOC Lodge 1817. The paper was printed in Toronto.
104. Michael Fenwick (1911-1983) was born in Ukraine. He later became an active member at the national level with the United Steelworkers of America. In 1965, he was appointed to the Hall-Dennis Committee on Education in Ontario.

whose real name was Mychailo Fenyk. Fenwick's father was a Ukrainian immigrant who was an active participant in the One Big Union movement and the Winnipeg General Strike in 1919. Although his family returned to Soviet Ukraine, Fenwick returned to Canada in 1929 and became an active member of the CPC.[105] Starr's attitude to unions and union organizers were shaped to a certain extent by his contacts with Fenwick. Even though Fenwick claimed he had left the CPC in 1939 over its editorial policies, he remained a suspected Communist agent who was working for the Communist Party of Canada.

Starr ran again in the 1943 municipal elections campaigning on his record of community service. He stated, "I have served you for the past three years on the Welfare Board and now stand as a candidate for alderman for a more unified and united front in our war effort for 1943."[106] He was again unsuccessful, placing eleventh out of fourteen candidates. However, he received the largest share of votes of any candidate in the South-East Ward. As in previous elections, the majority of Starr's support came from the largely immigrant-populated North-East and South-East Wards.[107]

Nazi Germany's surprise attack on the Soviet Union on June 22, 1941, produced a rapid change in attitudes among the Canadian federal government, the general Canadian population and, locally, among former ULFTA supporters in Oshawa. The Soviet Union was now, for all practical purposes, an ally of the British Empire, including Canada, against Nazi Germany. Within a short time, a local branch of the pro-Soviet organization was formed—the Ukrainian Association to Aid the Fatherland. This association and others gave their full support to the Canadian war effort and raised funds to assist the Soviets in their struggle.[108] In January 1942, Oshawa unions sponsored a concert for the Red Cross Russian Relief Drive. The Ukrainian pro-nationalist community refrained from participating in this event and, when a member of the local branch of the Ukrainian Self-Reliance League of Canada donated $5.00 to the campaign, the pro-Communist newspaper alleged he was threatened with expulsion from the organization.[109] Sympathy towards the Soviet Union in their struggle against Nazi Germany grew and in December 1942 a committee of prominent citizens including Col. R.S. McLaughlin was formed in Oshawa to provide aid to the Soviet Union.[110] In January 1944, the federal government's Custodian of Enemy Property began returning confiscated ULFTA Halls to their previous owners.

Starr tried once again in the 1944 municipal elections. In this campaign, Starr stressed that Oshawa required "a sound business administration ... with a sound outlook for the future progress of the community."[111] Starr emphasized his ability to speak several European languages that were familiar to a large number of Oshawa citizens, and that he was actively

---

105. His papers are at the Library and Archives Canada, Michael J. Fenwick fonds (MG31 B17); obituary, *Toronto Star*, December 27, 1983.
106. *Times Gazette*, December 29, 1942.
107. Ibid.
108. LAC, CSIS, RG146, Vol. 3788, Box 62, (97-A-00063), AUUC, Oshawa, Reports 16/1/1942, 11/6/1942, 4/2/1943, 31/5/1944.
109. *Canadian Tribune*, January 3, 1942. The Ukrainian nationalists were described as "pro-Nazis" in this article from the CPC newspaper.
110. *Canadian Tribune*, December 5, 1942.
111. *Times Gazette*, December 29, 1943.

Figure 1.5 Election poster for 1944 municipal elections. Starr ran for the position of alderman in Oshawa every year from 1937 until he was successfully elected in 1944. With limited financial resources, he could afford only a modest advertising campaign. Image courtesy of Walter Kish.

involved in various community organizations.[112] He was endorsed this time by the Oshawa Non-Partisan Voters' Association, which attempted to increase voter turnout at the polls, although they were opposed by the Labour Progressive Group (Communists). Only three of eight candidates supported by the Oshawa and District Labour Council were elected. However, six of the seven candidates endorsed by the Oshawa Non-Partisan Voters Association were elected. Starr's sisters assisted the campaign by providing encouragement, offering baby-sitting, and organizing food and drinks.[113] In the 1943 municipal elections, only twenty per cent of eligible voters cast their ballot but it was enough to finally elect Starr as alderman: his first electoral victory. He received 2,471 votes and ranked tenth out of the twenty-one candidates. As in previous elections, the majority of Starr's support came from the largely immigrant-populated North-East and South-East Wards.[114] It was a learning experience enabling him to identify his core supporters, sympathetic community organizations, and friendly neighbourhoods—useful insights for future elections.

---

112. Ibid.
113. Conversation with Mrs. Anne Hercia at her home in Windsor, Ontario, on June 9, 1988.
114. *Times Gazette,* January 4, 1944.

Chapter 2
Oshawa Municipal Politics, 1944–1952

On January 10, 1944, Starr was appointed to the Board of Works, Finance, Fire Protection, City Property and General Purpose Committees[1] of the City Council; seven days later he resigned from the Welfare Board.[2] Two months later he was appointed as the council's representative to the Oshawa Chamber of Commerce.[3] The expanding work force in Oshawa required housing, one of the more important issues during Starr's first year as alderman. He supported a wartime housing proposal to build two hundred houses but it was defeated in council by a vote of five to four.[4] Starr decided to solve his own housing problem by building his own home on Olive Avenue, where he had purchased land in 1943. With the assistance of family and friends—and a pick and shovel—Starr excavated the basement of his new house over a ten-week period in 1944. Then, in his spare time, he built his one-and-a-half-storey house with the assistance of a carpenter, an electrician and a concrete pourer. This would be Starr's family home for the rest of his life.[5]

During Starr's first year, the Oshawa City Council appointed Michael Jacula to the Oshawa Welfare Board and William Andrusky to the Town Planning Commission. Starr supported Mr. Jacula's appointment because he felt the board required someone who knew more than one language to administer the business of the board, a view based, no doubt, on Starr's experience with the Welfare Board.[6] He was re-elected as alderman in the 1945 municipal elections, continuing to receive the majority of his electoral support from the North-East and South-East Wards. On January 8, 1945, Starr was appointed vice-chairman, Board of Works, and continued his membership on the other committees.[7] He was later appointed to represent the mayor on the Welfare Board.[8]

The end of the war in 1945 brought changes to Oshawa. The Ontario Regiment, which drew many of its recruits from the Oshawa area, had served as the 11th Canadian Regiment of the 1st Canadian Armoured Brigade in Sicily, Italy, France, Holland, Belgium and Germany. Among the fatal casualties from Oshawa were three soldiers from the small Ukrainian Presbyterian Church in the city.[9] Returning soldiers required suitable employment and housing; both became urgent matters. Most veterans sought employment in the cities and

---

1. Ontario Archives, Oshawa, City of Oshawa Council Minutes, January 10, 1944.
2. Ibid., January 17, 1944.
3. Ibid., March 20, 1944.
4. LAC, Michael Starr Papers, MG 32, B 15, *The Mike Starr Story,* Vol. 1.
5. *Oshawa News*, February 3, 1999; *Durham Post*, March 24, 2000.
6. LAC, Michael Starr Papers, MG 32, B 15, *The Mike Starr Story,* Vol. 1.
7. Ontario Archives, Oshawa, City of Oshawa Council Minutes, January 8, 1945.
8. Ibid., March 5, 1945.
9. Two members of the Ukrainian National Youth Federation were also casualties during the war: Morris Krasutsky and Eugene Salmers.

Figure 2.1 Michael Starr as a municipal politician (circa 1950). As an alderman, Starr was a member of several municipal committees and took an active part in promoting the growth of Oshawa in the post-war years. Library and Archives Canada, Mikan 3221331, copy negative PA-047574 (Arthur Roy Fonds).

avoided farm work. Pedlar People, where Starr worked in the office, retooled for a peacetime economy and began manufacturing agricultural and construction products. However, the Aircraft Division of General Motors closed and nearly 2,000 employees were laid off. In total, there were 4,893 people unemployed in Oshawa in December, 1945.[10]

From 1946 to 1948 Starr served as chairman of Oshawa's Board of Works. The city was still a small, typical Ontario town where Starr could ride a bicycle around the streets looking for potholes and thereby demonstrate his personal concern to fellow citizens.[11] During these years, Starr turned the Board of Works into a modern and efficient department of the City of Oshawa.

Starr suffered a personal loss when his younger brother, Paul Starchewski, passed away from cancer in 1948. Paul had been born in Montreal in 1911 and worked at General Motors. He was survived by his wife and three children.

In Oshawa's municipal politics, the traditional route to the mayor's office was through the position of finance chairman. Starr knew the current chairman planned to run for mayor but had not yet announced his intentions.[12] At the urging of his many friends and neighbours, Starr, too, was being encouraged to run for mayor. Some of his friends, however, doubted he would be successful because his Ukrainian background would be a negative factor. Starr discussed his election plans carefully with his wife before he finally arrived at his decision. Starr waited until the city estimates were submitted and the budget and mill rate established.[13] He then, in April 1949, announced he would campaign for mayor. In announcing his candidacy Starr stated: "I have worked long and hard on Council and I know I have the experience needed for the position of Mayor. I feel I am deserving of promotion after all these years in Council."[14]

---

10. Charlotte Yates, "From Plant to Politics: The Canadian UAW 1936–1984," PhD thesis, Carleton University, 1988, p. 69.
11. Thomas Van Dusen, *The Chief*, McGraw-Hill Company of Canada Limited, 1968, p. 14.
12. LAC, Peter Stursberg Papers, MG 31, D 78, Vol. 16, p. 3.
13. Ibid.
14. *Daily Times Gazette*, November 18, 1948.

At each City Council meeting, Starr would propose new projects, such as city lighting, but his plans would be voted down because they hadn't been budgeted. Despite these defeats, Starr's plans always became headline news in Oshawa; more and more Oshawa citizens began considering him as a serious mayoral candidate.[15] Starr had added other responsibilities to his regular municipal duties and his record of experience: he served on the Board of Health, the Library Board and he was also a director of the South Ontario Agricultural Society and the Canadian Red Cross Society.[16]

The entire Starr family helped in the 1949 mayoral campaign: his children, Joan and Robert, painted posters and attended political meetings; Anne answered the telephone, while Starr knocked on doors and built his campaign on his municipal record. He campaigned with confidence because after five years' experience he was generally recognized as one of the most dedicated members of City Council.

Starr was elected Mayor of Oshawa, with 3,627 out of 6,889 votes cast, winning a clear majority of 366 votes over the combined votes of his two opponents. The voter turnout was 46.1 per cent of the electorate. The Albert Street polling station in his neighbourhood gave him 72.2 per cent of the vote. As in previous elections, Starr received the majority of his votes in the North-East and South-East Wards.[17]

He was the first mayor of Ukrainian descent of any major Canadian city. After his election Starr told the press,

> I feel pretty wonderful about it. However, there's something bigger about it to me than just becoming Mayor. It's convinced me that Canada is fast reaching the point they've attained in the States where Racial origins have been melted down into one term "American" and that's the way we all want it. People may well be proud of their ancestry and native traditions whether Scotch, Irish, Dutch, Czech or anything else, but they should concentrate on being "Canadians first" [. . .] Anglo-Saxons and people of other racial origins perhaps do not mix enough and get to understand one another. There's fault on both sides. There's often not enough effort on the Anglo-Saxon's part to [show] interest minorities in the Canadian way of life and the minorities themselves don't show enough interest.[18]

This election justified Starr's faith in Canadian democracy and proved wrong the naysayers who told him his Ukrainian origins would prevent him from becoming mayor. Starr immediately became a household name across Canada, especially in Ukrainian communities: the Canadian and Ukrainian-language press cited his election victory as another first of which all Ukrainian Canadians could be proud.[19] At this time, Starr believed in the

---

15. LAC, Peter Stursberg Papers, MG 31, D 78, Vol. 16, p. 4.
16. *Daily Times Gazette*, November 18, 1948.
17. Ibid., January 3, 1949.
18. *Globe and Mail*, January 3, 1949.
19. Ibid., "Mr. Mayor Mike, Chief Magistrate Son of Ukrainian Parents;" Ukrainian Canadian Research and Documentation Centre, "Memoirs of the Honourable Michael Starr" (1998); LAC, V.J. Kaye Fonds, MG31 D69, Volume 48, File 5, article by V.J. Kaye, "Participation of Ukrainians in the Political Life of Canada" (1957).

Figure 2.2 Starr was elected Mayor of Oshawa in 1949 and held this office until he was elected as a Member of Parliament to the House of Commons in 1952. According to Starr, his election as Mayor of Oshawa enabled him to continue his record of municipal service and was the most important step in his political career. Image courtesy of Walter Kish.

melting-pot concept, that the integration of immigrants in the host society encouraged a better understanding among all groups in society. When reviewing his political career, Starr believed his election as mayor really opened the doors to his further political career.[20]

An "Old Home Week" was held from June 30 to July 4, 1949, to celebrate Oshawa's Silver Jubilee. Mayor Mike Starr participated in the events as did the honourary patron, Col. R.S. McLaughlin. On the evening of Saturday, July 2, a program involving new Canadians was organized at the band shell in central Oshawa: there were Slovak, Hungarian and Ukrainian performers and Michael Jacula was the master of ceremonies.[21]

This was a dream come true for Mike Starr's father, Matthew. He had come to Canada as a young immigrant from Ukraine and his son was now mayor of a large Canadian city. He had reached this responsible position—one that Matthew himself could not even dream of attaining in his country of birth—entirely through his own efforts. Mike's victory came just in time: less than two years later, on April 22, 1951, Matthew died after a long illness.[22]

The new mayor faced many urgent civic problems. The Oshawa municipal government had been very careful about spending public funds due to the Depression and the Second World War. Now, after years of growth coupled with municipal penny-pinching, Oshawa required a new city hall (Mayor Starr did not have his own office and had to sign documents on the windowsill in the city clerk's office[23]), a police station, a fire station, and a sewage-disposal plant. On top of that, the annexation of a large section of East Whitby to the City of Oshawa was pending and soon there would also be negotiations for the annexation of East Whitby; Starr was largely responsible for these being successfully concluded. After the annexation of East Whitby, the population of Oshawa reached 40,000.[24]

20. Ukrainian Canadian Research and Documentation Centre, "Memoirs of the Honourable Michael Starr" (1998).
21. Old Home Week, Programme, Oshawa Silver Jubilee, June 30–July 4, 1949, Oshawa Old Home Week Committee.
22. Obituary: Michael M. Starchewski, *The Daily Times Gazette*, April 23, 1951. He was buried in St. Gregory's Cemetery, Simcoe Street North, Oshawa.
23. *This Week*, March 6, 1974.
24. *Daily Times Gazette*, January 3, 1949.

Starr also campaigned for street paving and for tracks from the Oshawa Railway Company to be removed from King Street. On February 17, 1949, Starr headed a delegation to Ottawa that presented a brief to Transport Minister Lionel Chevrier concerning the King Street tracks,[25] which had effectively divided the city and stopped traffic for long stretches of time whenever trains were travelling back and forth along the tracks.

On March 26, 1949, Prime Minister Louis St. Laurent received an enthusiastic welcome while on an official visit to Oshawa. He was very impressed with Starr's popularity among citizens after seeing children run beside his official car shouting "Hiya Mike," although Starr's popularity among children was largely out of gratitude for the school holiday they were given to mark the occasion of St. Laurent's visit. The prime minister was accompanied by J.W. Pickersgill,[26] who was also impressed by Starr's charm and popularity and, after making a quick inquiry, Pickersgill was informed Starr was not committed to any political party. When he returned to Ottawa, Pickersgill urged the Liberal Party to persuade Starr to become Oshawa's Liberal candidate in the next federal elections. However, another prospective candidate, Walter Thomson, had already been approached.[27] At the time it was not generally known that Starr had been a Conservative Party supporter since he was eighteen years old, largely because his employer, Pedlar People, and most of the employees were Progressive Conservative supporters.[28] Without doubt, Starr would have declined Liberal Party offers to run as a candidate.

During Labour Day of each year, the mayor had the opportunity to convey his best regards to the labour movement. In September 1949, Starr complimented Oshawa's unions for their ". . . conduct as well as business-like ability to iron out disputes," an ability that created harmony between labour and industry. He stressed the need for the co-operation of organized labour, industry, business and other community organizations to produce ". . . a bigger and better community of which we all will be proud."[29] Despite his sentiments, 5,200 workers took part in a wildcat strike on October 26, 1949, in Oshawa[30] after four UAW union stewards and officials were suspended by the company. The strike was settled on November 20, 1949, after concessions were made on both sides.[31] Lloyd Peel, the local UAW committeeman and an active member of the Labor Progressive Party was suspended from work for six months.

---

25. Ibid.
26. J.W. Pickersgill was at that time special assistant to the Prime Minister and later a prominent Liberal Party MP
27. J.W. Pickersgill, *My Years with Louis St. Laurent, A Political Memoir*, University of Toronto Press, Toronto, 1975, p. 89.
28. LAC, Peter Stursberg Papers, MG 31, D 78, Vol. 16, p. 5; Peter C. Newman, in his book *Renegade in Power, the Diefenbaker Years*, McClelland and Stewart Limited, Toronto, (1964), suggests on page 95 that Starr attended the Progressive Conservative 1948 leadership convention, but there are no records of Starr participating in this convention and Starr later claimed that he did not attend. See also LAC, Progressive Conservative Party of Canada fonds, MG28 IV 2, Volume 245, File: Delegates 1948 Convention.
29. *Labour Day*, Oshawa and District Labour Council, 1949, "Michael Starr, Oshawa Proud of Labor," p. 5.
30. Charlotte Yates, "From Plant to Politics: The Canadian UAW 1936–1984," PhD thesis, Carleton University, 1988, p. 96.
31. *The Globe and Mail*, November 21, 1949.

In 1948 and 1949, European displaced persons, including many Ukrainians, began arriving in Oshawa to fulfil their obligations under their one-year contracts. Adelaide House, a community institution, welcomed the new immigrants. As mayor, Starr presented new immigrants with Department of Labour certificates upon completion of their contracts.[32] He also helped immigrants find housing, jobs and generally aided their adaptation to life in Oshawa.

The Ukrainian displaced persons were, for the most part, young people who survived the Second World War and spent the period until their emigration to Canada in displaced persons camps in Germany. Their experiences during the war under Soviet and Nazi rule greatly politicized this generation. In the displaced persons camps, these former forced labourers, concentration-camp inmates, prisoners of war, ex-soldiers and political refugees had the opportunity to form political organizations and cultural associations that reinforced their national and political consciousness. They felt the trials and tribulations they endured since the outbreak of the Second World War were due to the lack of a Ukrainian state that could defend them and look after their interests. Almost without exception, this third wave of Ukrainian immigration arriving in Canada between 1946 and 1952 was anti-Communist; a large percentage were militant Ukrainian nationalists. Many who had been sent to work in the mines and lumber industries in northern Ontario and Quebec eventually gravitated towards the industrial centers in southern Ontario. Oshawa was among the manufacturing centers where they found work. There was some opposition to the immigration of the Ukrainian displaced persons to Oshawa. Individual members of the Oshawa community wrote letters to the local newspaper describing the Ukrainian displaced persons as "quislings" and "traitors" who should be deported to the Soviet Union. The leadership of the Association of United Ukrainian Canadians (AUUC) also sent letters to Ottawa denouncing these immigrants.[33]

In Oshawa, the displaced persons joined the older Ukrainian community, boosted the membership of the Ukrainian churches, and also founded their own cultural and political organizations. In local community politics, they quarrelled bitterly with supporters of the pro-Soviet Association of United Ukrainian Canadians.[34] Their relative youth and energy greatly stimulated local Ukrainian community life. Within a short time they extended their interests to local, provincial and national politics. The issues and political questions that interested them most were those brought from Europe. Among the new Ukrainian political organizations that were established at that time was the Ukrainian Youth Association (SUM) and they held their first meeting on December 26, 1948. They continued to hold their

---

32. LAC, Michael Starr Papers, MG 32, B 15, *The Mike Starr Story*, Vol. 1.
33. Canadian Museum of History, Archives, Prokop (Prokopchak) Family fonds, Volume 2, File 15, Displaced Persons (Documents); "Letters to Editor Claim 'Displaced Ukrainians' Traitors to Allied Cause," letter to the *Oshawa Times*, November 29, 1945. For information on federal government policy regarding the arrival of Ukrainian displaced persons, see Myron Momryk, Ukrainian DP Immigration and Government Policy in Canada, 1946-1952, in Wsevolod W. Isajiw, Yury Boshyk and Roman Senkus (eds.), *The Refugee Experience: Ukrainian Displaced Persons After World War II*, CIUS Press, Edmonton, Alberta, 1992.
34. LAC, CSIS, RG146, Volume 3788, Box 62 (97-A-00063) AUUC, Oshawa, Report 1 June, 1951; "Report on a fight between a Displaced Person and AUUC members that was not reported to the local police," *The Times-Gazette*, February 8, 1950.

meetings in Hetman Hall until 1955.[35] An affiliated organization was the League for the Liberation of Ukraine and a branch was also established in Oshawa. Within a short time the league was organizing anti-Russian meetings in Oshawa with representatives of the Ukrainian Catholic Church, the Ukrainian Orthodox Church and also representatives of the Slovak and Hungarian communities.[36] The league remained a "core" Ukrainian organization in Oshawa for many years to come.

Oshawa also received a large number of displaced persons from other central and east European nations—Czechs, Slovaks, Hungarians, Belarussians, Serbs, and Croats. Many Poles who had served in the Polish Army under General Wladyslaw Anders decided to remain in England after the war rather than return to a Soviet-dominated Poland. They were among the first immigrants to Canada after the war and many had to work as farm labourers before settling permanently in other parts of eastern Canada. The Belarussian immigrants in Oshawa soon founded a newspaper in their native language, the *Belaruski Emigrant*, which was in circulation from 1948 until 1954.

By the end of his first year as mayor, Starr had helped City Council draft by-laws for a new city hall, police station and fire station. While many of Starr's friends and supporters were hesitant about the plans, Starr was a proud citizen and felt that the city's buildings should be a focus of civic pride. Also, on December 19, 1949, the City Council under Starr's guidance passed an anti-discrimination by-law empowering city officials to refuse the issue of a business licence to anyone found guilty of discrimination.[37] There was no opposition to his candidature for a second term as mayor and he was elected by acclamation.[38]

On January 10, 1950, by-laws were passed to raise $575,000 for the new buildings. All the by-laws Starr supported were passed with overwhelming majorities except the library by-law.[39] His leadership on City Council was to a large extent responsible for progress on long delayed civic projects and most Oshawa citizens were proud of his achievements in completing these civic projects.

Starr also arranged to provide aid to communities in other parts of Canada. In 1950, the disastrous Red River floods in Manitoba destroyed many homes, and strong winds swept a terrible fire through the towns of Cabano and Rimouski in Quebec, destroying dozens of homes. With the Rotary Club, Starr established a fund to assist these communities and $23,000 was raised and sent to these disaster areas.[40]

In 1951, Starr was again elected to a third term as mayor by acclamation. Although he served conscientiously as mayor it was not officially a full-time job and he continued working a full day as manager of the order department at Pedlar People. Citizens, recent immigrants, and friends with grievances and various problems often came to consult with Starr both at home and at the office.[41] Starr's home on Olive Avenue became an informal drop-in centre for friends, visitors and acquaintances. Some of these meetings evolved into

---

35. Mykola Figol (ed.), *25 Years of SUM Canada, 1948–1973*, Toronto, 1973, pp. 274–283.
36. *Homin Ukrainy* (Ukrainian Echo), October 27, 1951.
37. *Daily Times Gazette*, December 20, 1949.
38. Ibid., November 25, 1949.
39. Ibid., December 31, 1949.
40. Frank Chappell, *Oshawa Rotary in Retrospect, 1920–1952*, p. 88.
41. *Daily Times Gazette*, November 24, 1950.

Figure 2.3 United Steelworkers of America (USWA) meet at Eastern Ontario Council meeting in Oshawa, Ontario, in 1950. From left to right: National director C. H. Millard, CCF MPP for York West Riding; Mayor Michael Starr of Oshawa; and T. D. Thomas, CCF MPP for Ontario Riding. Library and Archives Canada, PFA-500, Mikan 3369997, PA-120676.

marathon poker sessions in Starr's basement, where local and federal politics alike were discussed at length.

Local problems, however, were always Starr's priority. In most cases, Starr was responsive to the needs of individuals who called on his services and, in some cases, Starr spent much more time and effort than was generally warranted. On one occasion Starr received a phone call from a woman complaining her garbage had not been picked up by the garbage truck as it passed down her street. Starr wrote down her name and address and drove to her home. At first, he could not see her garbage pail but as he approached her house he noticed a small pail behind a large tree on her front lawn. It was obvious that the truck driver could not see the pail from the street. Starr knocked at her door and introduced himself. He then advised the woman to place her garbage pail in a more visible location. Starr took the pail in his car and drove it to the municipal dump. He emptied the pail, drove back to the woman's home and returned it. He knew electors would always remember these gesture at election time.

Starr soon became known as "mayor of all the people" through his close contacts with all sections of the population and he began his third term as mayor (during these years, Oshawa's municipal elections were held annually) by continuing this tradition. He attended openings of public buildings, new churches and social events in both the Canadian-born and immigrant communities. In January 1951 he officially opened the Polish National Union Hall and took part in laying the cornerstone of the new United Automobile Workers Hall. He turned the first sod for the parsonage built by the congregation of the Albert Street United Church.[42]

---

42. *Daily Times Gazette,* January 2, 4, and 8, 1951.

The Second World War produced a tremendous industrial boom in the Oshawa area. This prosperity had a variable quality as Oshawa was very dependent on the automobile trade. In 1951, approximately 7,800 industrial workers of a total of 11,722 workers in Oshawa were employed in manufacturing. Of this number, two-thirds were employed by General Motors, with many more in feeder industries.[43]

In 1951, Starr was persuaded to run as a Progressive Conservative candidate for the Oshawa riding seat in the Ontario provincial legislature by Leslie Frost, the Premier of Ontario, who offered him a cabinet position if Starr was elected.[44] Starr, always the sensible politician, also ran for a practical reason. He said, "Honestly speaking there is no doubt in my mind that the Frost government is going back into power. So the logical conclusion is that if you want to serve the riding best you should be in Parliament on the side that is going to be in power."[45]

Starr wanted to conduct a simple campaign by pledging to provide his best service on behalf of all people in the riding if elected. It was a believable pledge: Starr had won many friends and supporters through his work on the executives of various community organizations and voluntary groups. For example, he was honorary vice-president of the Oshawa branch of the Canadian Red Cross Society, an executive member of the Chamber of Commerce and the Greater Oshawa Community Chest and a director for Ontario of the Brotherhood of Christians and Jews.[46]

Starr was, however, faced with one serious problem. The Progressive Conservative riding association and election organization was practically non-existent. The Oshawa riding had been a Co-operative Commonwealth Federation Party and UAW union stronghold for many years. The CCF candidate, Thomas D. Thomas, was born in Cardiff, Wales, on February 19, 1899, and had emigrated to Canada in 1929. Thomas worked at General Motors in Oshawa as a toolmaker and was a founding member of Local 222 of the UAW. He served on the East Whitby Township council and was elected reeve in 1946 and 1947. Since 1948 he had been the member of the Legislative Assembly of Ontario representing Ontario riding.[47] The Conservatives had not had an electoral victory in the area for many years. Yet, despite this impressive CCF record, Starr entered the electoral campaign and tackled traditional CCF themes: social issues, old-age pensions, construction grants, educational opportunities, and advanced labour laws.[48] When Starr received the Progressive Conservative nomination, Oshawa trade-union delegates announced they would withdraw their support from Starr in future mayoralty campaigns. Faced with this situation, Starr made his position clear, declaring that "he would not be tied down to any Conservative Party line where the general benefit of the people of the riding was concerned."[49] Starr stated that the Conservative government could represent labour and that "the old parties

---

43. *Regional Studies Program, Research Publications, Number Three, Population C.O.J.P.B.*, Oshawa, 1967, Ontario, p. 36.
44. LAC, Peter Stursberg Papers, MG 31, D 78, Vol. 16, p. 5.
45. *Daily Times Gazette*, October 18, 1951.
46. Ibid., November 3, 1951.
47. T. D. Thomas, obituary, *Toronto Star*, July 31, 1980; *The Globe and Mail*, July 31, 1980.
48. *Daily Times Gazette*, November 8, 1951.
49. Ibid., November 14, 1951.

should have some new blood injected into them so that they could see the other side of the picture."[50] Starr also addressed some political meetings in Ukrainian and, as a result, had access to a larger part of the electorate. The other political parties also made use of speakers from various ethnocultural groups to gain the support of "new Canadians."[51]

In previous elections, the Oshawa riding had elected a Liberal, Conservative and CCF member, but there had been a large increase in the riding population since the previous provincial election. This increase had added uncertainty to the election outcome. In spite of Starr's efforts, T. D. Thomas was re-elected to the Ontario legislature. The votes were distributed as follows:[52]

Candidate	Party	Votes	Votes (%)
T. D. Thomas	CCF	12,000	40%
M. Starr	PC	9,869	33%
W. C. Thomson	Lib.	7,789	26%
E. M. Bateman	Ind.	254	0.85%

Starr received most of his support in Port Perry, Reach Township, Whitby and Whitby Township; all essentially outside of the Oshawa urban area. The rural and semi-rural areas of the riding were populated by descendants of pioneers who settled the area from the British Isles and tended to vote along traditional political preferences for the Progressive Conservative Party. Starr had conducted a one-man campaign without a well-structured riding organization and despite his best efforts and the support of the local newspaper, *The Daily Times Gazette*, was unsuccessful. Starr, however, gained some satisfaction that he received more votes than W. C. Thomson, the Liberal candidate.

Starr returned to municipal politics and, in the 1951 municipal election, ran again for mayor. This time he campaigned by promising to not increase city taxes and to complete the work on municipal projects in progress. Starr repeated in his speeches that the unusual expenditures in the municipal budget were due to the tremendous growth of the city and the increase in the population from 28,000 to 40,000 in a few years.[53] Since Starr had run as a Progressive Conservative candidate in the provincial elections, he feared the mayoralty contest might become overly politicized, but the municipal election took place without any major incident.

On December 11, 1951, Starr was re-elected mayor of Oshawa. He received most of his support from the newly annexed area of East Whitby and, also, from his traditional areas of support in the North-East and South-East Wards of Oshawa.[54] The local branch of the AUUC gave their support to the Labor Progressive Party candidates in the municipal elections.[55]

---

50. Ibid.
51. Ibid., November 3, 1951.
52. Ibid., November 23, 1951.
53. *Daily Times Gazette*, December 5, 1951.
54. Ibid., December 11, 1951.
55. The pro-Communist ULFTA was reconstituted after the Second World War as the Association of United Ukrainian Canadians (AUUC). LAC, CSIS, RG146, Volume 3788, Box 62 (97-A-00063), AUUC, Oshawa, Report, December 19, 1951.

Starr was viewed favourably by friends and peers alike. His local Rotary Club colleagues were especially proud of his achievements. Frank Chappell wrote in the club's history that Starr, in his fourth year in office, "is lauded on all sides as a good mayor, a faithful servant of the people who fills the chair with dignity and assurance. But his fellow Rotarians take equal pride in the fact that Mike Starr is an able, clear-thinking, conscientious member of the club."[56]

---

56. Frank Chappell, *Oshawa Rotary in Retrospect, 1920–1952*, p. 98.

Chapter 3
Election Campaign for Ontario Riding, 1952

On March 21, 1952, news was received that Walter C. Thomas had resigned his seat in the House of Commons in order to contest the riding as leader of the provincial Liberal Party. That meant a federal by-election would be held in Ontario riding.[1] Then, on April 12, 1952, Starr announced he intended to seek the Progressive Conservative Party nomination for the riding. Anne Starr originally objected to her husband's electoral plans, however, federal Conservative leader George Drew phoned Starr and persuaded him to run. To help Starr overcome any hesitation he might have had after his recent provincial defeat, Drew promised Starr that the federal Progressive Conservative Party would assist in organizational work in the riding.[2] Allister Grosart, a public-relations specialist, was assigned to assist Starr with his campaign.[3] On April 18, 1952, Starr was unanimously chosen as the Progressive Conservative candidate at the riding nomination meeting held at the Whitby town hall. Starr reflected on his recent experience in conducting election campaigns and said he intended to

> take the gloves off and fight by the rules of the game I was taught during my recent campaign when I was an unsuccessful provincial candidate. I have learned in the last provincial election that it does not always pay to act like a gentleman in these contests. Accordingly, in this election, I am going to pull no punches and while I will not go as far as the machines which were behind my opponents in the provincial contest still I am going to use all the tricks and devices, within the bounds of honesty, that I have learned.[4]

During his election campaign, Starr kept repeating that the Liberal Party was no longer responsible to the electorate because it had been in power for so long, and he argued the time had come for a change. Starr's Liberal opponent was John Lay, a nephew of William Lyon Mackenzie King, the former Liberal prime minister. Lay had been selected as Liberal Party candidate without consulting the local Liberal riding president, who had been on

---

1. *Daily Times Gazette*, March 21, 1952.
2. LAC, Peter Stursberg Papers, MG 31, D 78, Vol. 16, p. 6.
3. LAC, The Hon. Allister Grosart fonds, MG32 C65, Volume 2, File: Daily Journal 1952; Volume 9, File 5, Grosart, Allister, 1983, 1985; For information on Allister Grosart's career, see chapter 12 in Peter C. Newman, *Renegade in Power: The Diefenbaker Years*, McClelland and Stewart Ltd., Toronto, 1963.
4. *Daily Times Gazette*, April 19, 1952.

holiday in Florida, an action that alienated many local Liberals who then shifted their support to Starr.[5]

Starr also raised an important local issue, arguing Oshawa was one of the largest collectors of Canadian government revenue in the form of customs—yet the post-office facilities through which these revenues were collected were an embarrassment. On other issues, Starr alleged the federal government had done nothing about immigration and unemployment problems. Together with delegates from the Labour Council, he helped to prepare a brief on both questions, however, there was no action after it was sent to the federal government. Starr said to the press,

> People are walking about destitute and they are the people who were led to believe that they were coming to a land of plenty and opportunity. Their children have to go barefoot and the families are thrown on municipal social welfare because the federal government feels that it does not have any responsibility towards them.[6]

Starr continually emphasized his concern for new Canadians and stated how anxious he was to foster principles of "Canadianism" among minority groups. During his campaign, Starr was able to obtain the active support of John Yaremko, the newly elected member of Ukrainian origin from Toronto. Yaremko, speaking on behalf of Starr's candidature, was introduced to the electorate of the Ontario riding as "the man who whipped the Commies in Toronto."[7] Starr received Yaremko's support not only because both campaigned for the same political party but also because their respective wives were cousins, and the family connection reinforced Yaremko's support.

Starr took the initiative to establish a Ukrainian Professional and Businessmen's Club in Oshawa. On May 2, 1952, a meeting was held at the Genosha Hotel where copies of the new club's constitution were distributed to members.[8] Its goals were to represent the Ukrainian community in Oshawa; further cultural activities in the Ukrainian community; promote better relations with other Canadians; and promote projects that would benefit the entire community.[9] Having begun its work with forty-six members, many would maintain their membership for decades. The meetings were held at the Genosha Hotel because Starr wanted to take the Ukrainian voluntary organizations into the mainstream of Canadian society and out of the parish and community halls where they had traditionally conducted their affairs.

The issues and problems raised by Mike Starr in this election campaign were the very same interests and preoccupations that had marked his municipal political career and they would continue to form the basic guidelines and framework for Starr's future political statements, interests and actions. On May 14, 1952, Starr spent twelve hours barnstorming the riding with George Drew. He then gave a speech in which he criticized the local Labour

---

5. LAC, Peter Stursberg Papers, MG 31, D 78, Vol. 16, p. 9.
6. *Daily Times Gazette*, May 14, 1952.
7. Ibid., May 10, 1952.
8. Archives of Ontario, Ukrainian Professional and Businessmen's Club, Oshawa.
9. *Ukrainian Canadian Review* (Voice of the Federation of Professional and Business Men's Clubs of Canada), Winter 1966-67, p. 10.

Council for its biased view of the election and refuted allegations that he was an enemy of labour. Starr stated to the press that

> Nobody has laboured so much for a living as I have, nobody can say that in my capacity as either alderman or Mayor of Oshawa that you have ever had a Mayor so friendly to labour and who has worked so hard to bring everyone into the fold, including labour, to play their parts in the administration of this great city of Oshawa. The allegation was set up to poison voters' minds.[10]

On the same day, Starr attended a meeting of Progressive Conservative Party workers composed largely of Ukrainians from his own neighbourhood, the Oshawa south end. At this gathering, Starr said,

> I don't care how early I have to get up as long as I bring this matter to the people. I think the voters like to know their candidates for public office. And certainly they have a right to. Nowadays people are reaching the point where they want their politics brought to them. I don't say that's right, but they're coming to expect it. And I think it's pretty important that we go along with them.[11]

Starr campaigned at the grass-roots level in rural areas, climbing fences, talking with farmers in the fields and at home. Starr also campaigned on the local radio with his program "Mike Starr and Friends." His radio friends were an alderman, a store clerk and a General Motors factory worker.[12] These arrangements to speak on the radio were made by Starr's political advisor, Allister Grosart.[13] During his campaign, Starr stressed again the need for local government facilities. He said,

> I am running for office so that I can lift my voice in protest to get for the people of this riding the things that should have been forthcoming. My record is such that you know I will not sit idly by if these things are not rectified. I will be fighting for the things the people should have.[14]

However, Starr did not claim responsibility for the Progressive Conservative Party's actions in the past, especially during the Depression; he did not want to resurrect bitter memories of the Bennett Conservative government. When elected, Starr promised that he would introduce new political ideas and "instil things into the members' minds."[15]

As promised by George Drew, the federal Conservative Party machine descended on Oshawa to help Starr. Members of Parliament arrived regularly to campaign and Conservative Party women from Kingston, Peterborough, Lindsay, Toronto and Kitchener arrived by bus

---

10. *Daily Times Gazette*, May 14, 1952.
11. Ibid.
12. *Toronto Telegram*, May 19, 1952.
13. LAC, The Hon. Allister Grosart fonds, Volume 2, File: Daily Journal, 1952.
14. *Daily Times Gazette*, May 14, 1952.
15. Ibid.

to help canvass.[16] Recent Ukrainian immigrants from Toronto travelled to Oshawa to help Starr by transporting campaign workers in their cars and by distributing posters. Starr's home on Olive Avenue became a hive of political activity. On May 12, 1952, future Tory Prime Minister John Diefenbaker spoke on behalf of Starr before an audience of 600 people in Oshawa's United Auto Workers Hall. At this meeting, Diefenbaker said the Liberals had been in power for so long that they thought they ruled by divine right:

> Liberals had lost all independence of thought in a House where they had such a steam-roller majority. They did just what the Cabinet ordered. In the secrecy of the ballot room you can give your answer to the government. You can give a message from the ordinary man and woman.

According to Diefenbaker, the Conservatives campaigned for a national labour act, improvements in the National Unemployment Insurance Act, the establishment of parity prices and a state of affairs where "...agriculturalists and labouring men could march forward together." He emphasized that the election of Mike Starr would effectively register the protest of the ordinary citizen.[17] This visit by Diefenbaker was Starr's first opportunity to meet with the famous politician and orator from western Canada.

On May 27, 1952, Mike Starr was elected in the Ontario riding. The votes in this by-election were distributed as follows:[18]

Candidate	Party	Votes	Votes (%)
Mike Starr	PC	12,275	41.15%
John Lay	Lib.	9,091	30.48%
Roy Scott	CCF	8,464	28.37%

In the city of Oshawa, Roy Scott's 6,403 votes came within 70 of Starr's total of 6,473 votes, compared to the Liberals' 4,295 votes.[19] The rural communities of the riding gave their overwhelming support to Starr. Starr's family shared in the joy of his election victory: his four sisters, his mother-in-law and especially his mother, were jubilant. After his victory, Starr stated:

> I will serve conscientiously and just as well at Ottawa in looking after your interests as I have as Mayor. My home is open to you ... and if it lies at all within my power to look after your interests then I will do so.[20]

Starr was scheduled to take his federal seat in Ottawa on June 12, 1952. He flew to Saskatoon to give last-minute support to the campaign of John Hnatyshyn, a Progressive Conservative candidate who was running in a by-election for the provincial legislature. Starr's presence

---

16. LAC, Peter Stursberg papers, MG 31, D 78, Vol. 16, p. 9.
17. *Daily Times Gazette*, May 21, 1952.
18. Elections Canada, *History of the Federal Electoral Ridings since 1867*.
19. *Daily Times Gazette*, May 27, 1952
20. Ibid.

Figure 3.1 John Diefenbaker with Michael Starr at Ontario reception.

was a last-minute effort to divert the Ukrainian voters from their traditional support for the Liberal Party. Most of the Ukrainian pioneers came to Canada during the Liberal administration of Sir Wilfrid Laurier during the years 1896–1911 and had not forgotten the Liberal Party at each subsequent federal election. Starr spoke to Ukrainian audiences in support of Hnatyshyn but when the final results were counted, Hnatyshyn was not successful. However, in this series of by-elections, the Progressive Conservatives won four of six seats and these results greatly encouraged the federal party.

Starr decided he would remain as mayor of Oshawa until his term expired at the end of 1952 but would not stand again for municipal office.[21] Most Oshawa citizens continued to be proud of Starr's accomplishments during his many years on city council. However, he had difficulty obtaining approval to build a municipal library. Col. Sam McLaughlin, Oshawa's most prominent citizen, phoned Starr to congratulate him on his efforts to provide city services but said he was concerned about the lack of a municipal library. He offered to donate the library if the city would purchase the land on which it would be built.[22] The library was built, and over the years expanded, and is now one of the many monuments to the generosity of Col. McLaughlin in Oshawa.

---

21. Ibid. May 27, 1952.
22. Ontario Archives, Oshawa, City of Oshawa Council Minutes, July 21, 1952.

Figure 3.2 Starr and wife, Anne Starr: Anne Starr was an invaluable partner and assistant to Starr throughout his political career in Oshawa. She served amongst other roles as his most faithful and trusted advisor, campaign worker, secretary, receptionist and archivist. Image courtesy Walter Kish.

In the local press, it was generally recognized that Starr had many advantages over his political opponents. He had a record of nine years of municipal service in Oshawa and he had already campaigned in the provincial election. Starr had an impressive record as mayor and electors acknowledged his accomplishments. He had conducted a strong and aggressive campaign and had loyal and devoted supporters. John Lay and Roy Scott were relatively unknown in the riding and had a tough campaign in their attempts to reach the voters. It was generally agreed among local political observers that this electoral victory was more of a personal triumph for Starr than for the Progressive Conservative Party.[23]

Starr's election as a federal member resulted in a few changes in his home life. When Starr had to leave for Ottawa, Anne Starr said that she had no desire to move to the capital. She added, "We love our home and the children are happy here and even if Mike is away we shall

---

23. *Daily Times Gazette*, May 27, 1952.

have weekends all together to look forward to."[24] When Starr left for Ottawa, Anne Starr assumed additional duties in local community organizations. She held the position of honorary vice-regent of an Imperial Order of the Daughters of the Empire chapter and membership in hospital auxiliaries. With a loan from Mike, Anne Starr purchased a cleaning business on Simcoe Street South. She had gained valuable business experience during the war years administering a cleaning business and the new business quickly grew until she had seven employees.[25]

Starr's election to Ottawa created a sensation among the Ukrainian community in Canada. His victory was not only widely reported in the national Ukrainian newspapers, news was also carried to Europe and particularly to Soviet Ukraine. Starr was invited to send his greetings to Soviet Ukraine during the opening transmission of the Ukrainian Section at CBC Radio International on July 1, 1952. In this transmission, there were also greetings from Lester B. Pearson, John Decore and two Ukrainian Canadian clergymen. Starr said,

> We, Canadian Ukrainians, deplore that you, our brother Ukrainians in Ukraine, do not have the right to a full political, national and personal life such as we enjoy in Canada. But do not lose courage, brothers, for the free world has not forgotten you. The time will come when the spirit of freedom penetrates the Iron Curtain of oppression, the prison of nations crumbles and the regime of terror disintegrates under the blows of the victorious forces of freedom and democracy.[26]

Starr's speech made the officials at the Department of External Affairs cringe with the expectation of serious protests from the Soviet Embassy in Ottawa. This incident launched a policy debate within the Department of External Affairs regarding the ultimate purpose of the Ukrainian Section of the CBC Radio International; the debate would continue for several years.

Starr maintained his involvement with the local branch of the Ukrainian Professional and Businessmen's Club. At a meeting held on September 3, 1952, he spoke about municipal affairs and, at a November 10, 1952, meeting, Starr supported a proposal to sponsor a half-hour radio program on Ukrainian Christmas, to air on January 6, 1953.[27]

Celebrating his election victory, Starr visited neighbouring ridings and on one occasion expressed his increasing concern with the apparent growing influence of socialism in Canada. Speaking to the annual meeting of the Peterborough Young Progressive Conservative Association, Starr was critical of the CCF and socialism in general. He described socialism as a failure in Europe, which should not be attempted in Canada. In the case of the provincial socialist government in Saskatchewan, Starr described the government as essentially "a good conservative government."[28]

In December 1952, Starr was in Ottawa and prepared to make his first speech in the House of Commons.

---

24. Ibid.
25. Ibid.
26. Bernard Hibbitts, "CBC International Service as a Psychological Instrument of Canadian Foreign Policy in the Cold War, 1948–1953," MA thesis, Carleton University, 1981, p. 87.
27. Archives of Ontario, Ukrainian Professional and Businessmen's Club, Oshawa.
28. *Peterborough Examiner*, October 30, 1952.

Chapter 4
Member of Parliament, 1952–1957

On December 2, 1952, Mike Starr delivered his maiden speech in the House of Commons. He began by describing himself as the son of a poor immigrant from Ukraine. Starr said:

> My presence here, I venture to say is to some Canadians a readily understood symbol of the reality of Canadian democracy. I refer first of all to my fellow Canadians in Ontario constituency who know me as a plain man working at an everyday job. I refer also to an even larger group of my fellow Canadians whom it is in current fashion to call "new Canadians" for I am one of these, though having the honour and good fortune to be born in Canada . . . . I am humbly aware of the fact . . . that my own experience in the many problems that confront governments is limited strictly to the local field of municipal self-government.[1]

In the House of Commons, Starr devoted himself to his areas of special concern, municipal affairs and defending the interests of the small-wage earners, ordinary people and the individual homeowner, who, according to Starr, were the backbone of the country. Because of his municipal political experience, Starr adapted easily to Ottawa federal politics. Starr carried on a personal campaign in the House of Commons to abolish the excise of luxury tax on passenger cars. He persisted in this campaign in the hope that the elimination of this tax would increase car sales and therefore boost car production at the General Motors plant in Oshawa, the largest employer in his riding. He complained about the increase of the tax burden on the ordinary homeowner and called on the federal government to follow "old-fashioned family virtues of not spending money which their taxpayers cannot afford to pay."[2]

Starr was the first in the House of Commons to suggest on March 10, 1953, that "a suitable memento . . . which would be distributed to all children of school age in the country" be issued to commemorate the coronation of Queen Elizabeth during that year. He felt this memento would be an economical gesture to celebrate the event. Starr respected the monarchy because he believed the Queen stood as a symbol of freedom to all Canadians. This proposal was accepted by the Liberal government and coronation medallions were distributed to school children across Canada.

When Starr was mayor of Oshawa, he regularly received people looking for employment and citizens with all types of problems and grievances. But in Ottawa, Starr began to feel that he could lose contact with his constituents and began organizing his daily schedule to ensure he kept "in touch" with voters.[3] Within a short period after his arrival in Ottawa, Starr received

---

1. *House of Commons Debates, Session 1952–53*, Vol. I, p. 258.
2. Ibid.
3. LAC, Michael Starr Papers, MG 32, B 15, *The Mike Starr Story*, Vol. l.

Figure 4.1 "Starr blasts Ottawa over Municipal Aid" – coverage of Starr's maiden speech in Parliament. As alderman and then mayor of Oshawa, Mike Starr knew that the municipalities required federal government aid to build municipal institutions and schools in order to reduce the tax burden on the ordinary citizen and taxpayer. As Minister of Labour, he would later initiate a number of federal government programs to aid the municipalities and to reduce winter unemployment. Image courtesy of Walter Kish.

job applicants, businessmen, immigrants, representatives of various ethnocultural groups and organizations and others. Also, at his Oshawa home, the phone never stopped ringing for Starr to help solve some problem or provide advice. At the national level, Starr had been designated by George Drew as a key figure in attracting the votes of immigrants and descendants of immigrants, especially those from Eastern Europe. Both Starr and Drew opposed the threat of communism and the influence of the Labor Progressive Party in Canada. In a speech made at the University of Ottawa during spring convocation in 1948, Drew spoke of the need to get rid of "this treacherous Fifth Column." Without the Communist threat, Drew believed a foundation could be laid for effective co-operation and good will between labour, management and government. He stated that, "it is the one sure way to create that measure of domestic security and stability which is the desire of every loyal Canadian."[4]

The Progressive Conservative Party was particularly interested in increasing their electoral support among the voters in Western Canada. During his visits and speeches among

---

4. Dr. George Drew, "On the Menace of Communism," *Revue de l'Université d'Ottawa*, Vol. 18, No. 1, January–March 1948, p. 13.

ethnocultural groups, Starr spoke out against the Communist regimes of Eastern Europe and even accused Lester Pearson, the Minister of External Affairs, of conducting a wavering policy in regards to communism. Starr's most important assignment was to represent George Drew at the Fourth All-Canada Congress of the Ukrainian Canadian Committee (UCC) held on July 10, 1953, in Winnipeg. Starr was introduced to the UCC delegates as the official representative of Col. Drew. Starr spoke to the delegates in Ukrainian, informing them that he was from Oshawa, where he was involved with the local UCC when he had the time. He explained that although he had been officially elected as a delegate, his official duties prevented him from participating in the sessions. Since Col. Drew could not attend personally, he had asked that Starr represent him at the congress and extend his best wishes. Starr added that Col. Drew had visited Ukraine during that year, where he saw the people suffering from famine and that he was even arrested in Moscow.[5] At this conference, he addressed the fundamental question that dominated the congress since its formation and said: "We are greatly concerned in the welfare of our kin behind the Iron Curtain and for that reason we must not forget them. We wish them well and trust that their aspirations for freedom and independence may soon be realised."[6] Starr added that he saw communism as the greatest threat to the world. Although Ukrainian Canadians were fortunate to live in Canada, he felt the Communist threat was growing and eroding the free world. Starr continued,

> In our work we have to be very careful about our relations with the communists. Let us not forget that there are many communists in our midst especially in Winnipeg where despite our efforts, they elected their candidate to the provincial legislature. This is also our fault because we do not pay enough attention to our community affairs especially by our low voter turnout at elections which is about 45%. We support democracy but we do not know how to benefit from it .... A most important matter is the fate of our brothers behind the Iron Curtain, which we should never forget.

Starr referred to the speech he made during the first Ukrainian broadcast on CBC Radio International to Soviet Ukraine. He said a newspaper criticized his statements and commented that Canadians should not promise freedom to other countries. Starr replied that Ukrainians in Canada should do all they could to assure their brothers in Soviet Ukraine that Ukrainians in Canada had not forgotten them and wished for their freedom. Starr continued,

> Although the Soviet Union signed the United Nations Charter in 1945, the nations under their control are still not free. As long as there are nations not independent there will be no peace in this world ... But these are long term goals, today we have more immediate goals ... to be good Canadians and to take part in community and political life. And we will accomplish this only when we are good Ukrainians.[7]

---

5. *The Fourth Ukrainian Canadian Congress*, Winnipeg, Manitoba, July 8–10, 1953, p. 73.
6. *Fortieth Anniversary of the Proclamation of Independent Ukraine, 22, 1, 1918–22, 1, 1958*, Ukrainian Canadian Committee Headquarters, Winnipeg, p. 6.
7. Ibid., p. 74.

Figure 4.2 After several years as a Member of Parliament, Starr honed his experience in campaigning and used every opportunity to personally meet with electors in every part of the riding. Image courtesy of Walter Kish.

When speaking to ethnocultural groups, especially those from Eastern Europe, Starr assured them the only way to control Communist activities in Canada was through a Conservative victory.[8] Starr also spoke at a celebration on February 22, 1953, in Windsor, Ontario, commemorating the proclamation of the thirty-fifth anniversary of Ukraine's independence sponsored by the Windsor UCC. Paul Martin, the Liberal cabinet minister and Windsor MP, also participated in this event. In his speech, Starr urged all Ukrainian Canadians to join the UCC and support its objectives. *The Canadian Tribune*, representing the opinion of the Labour Progressive Party, expressed their annoyance and stated that Starr had "shouted for the dismemberment of the Soviet Union. He and his like will be repudiated and spurned by the people."[9]

The next federal elections were to be held on August 10, 1953. Starr was nominated as the Progressive Conservative candidate on July 6, 1953. His campaign was essentially a continuation of his first election and he focused his attention on excessive government spending, government inefficiency, and waste. Starr also held a series of radio talks with local people on various riding issues.[10] Starr promised the Conservative Party would reduce

---

8. LAC, Michael Starr Papers, MG 32, B 15, *The Mike Starr Story*, Vol. 2, July 22, 1953.
9. *Canadian Tribune*, March 2, 1953.
10. *Daily Times Gazette*, July 15, 1953.

all hidden taxes and, in this way, reduce high prices. His campaign was based on personal contact with the voters and a series of picnics were immediately organized in the rural areas of the riding. Starr was also able to obtain the support of other prominent Conservative politicians to speak on his behalf. The Hon. Earl Rowe stated at an election rally that Starr was too modest in speaking of his own work in the House of Commons. According to Rowe, Starr had made a greater mark in six months than many members do in four years of office. He said Starr had always made his presence felt, he was always in place in caucus, and he had never spoken unless he knew what he was talking about.

At this time, Starr was a member of the Standing Committee on Labour and Employment and also on Miscellaneous Private Bills in Parliament. Rowe predicted that Starr would be a prominent member of the cabinet in the next Conservative government.[11] At the local level, Starr's election strategy of emphasizing personal contacts with the voters was one of the main CCF criticisms. The CCF criticized Starr's attempts to appeal to the electorate on a personal basis while keeping his political affiliation with the Conservative Party well in the background.

In accordance with Starr's successful electoral strategy proven in previous electoral campaigns, he ran on his record.[12] Starr reminded voters that he obtained a better postal service for Ajax, first suggested the coronation medals for students, and protested the "taxgrabbing" policies of the federal government.[13] On August 10, 1953, Starr was able to hold the Ontario riding for the Progressive Conservative Party. The votes were distributed as follows:[14]

Candidate	*Party*	*Votes*	*Votes (%)*
Michael Starr	PC	12,482	42.05%
John Lay	Lib.	11,285	38.02%
Wesley Powers	CCF	5,524	18.61%
Lloyd Peel	LPP	393	1.32%

Starr received majorities in nearly all voting districts. In the city of Oshawa, he had a 910-vote victory over Liberal candidate John Lay. The strong decline in the CCF vote was attributed to the timing of the election, which coincided with the industrial holiday period. But Starr fought a strong electoral campaign and he also campaigned for the Conservative Party in western Canada. After his electoral victory, Starr continued his well-known tradition and again invited constituents to discuss their problems with him personally; he was available at any time to look after their interests.[15] Starr already had a solid record with assisting constituents and enjoyed a growing reputation for successfully obtaining action on questions relating to employment, immigration, citizenship and taxation.

11. Ibid., July 27, 1953.
12. *Daily Times Gazette*, July 29, 1953.
13. Ibid., August 7, 1953.
14. Elections Canada, History of the Federal Electoral Ridings Since 1867; Also *Daily Times Gazette*, August 11, 1953.
15. *Daily Times Gazette*, August 11, 1953.

The local Ukrainian community also celebrated Starr's victory and the Ukrainian Professional and Businessmen's Club held a testimonial dinner and dance for him on September 26, 1953, at the St. John's Parish Hall. Over 250 people attended from Oshawa and Toronto and as far away as Hamilton and Port Hope. Starr's mother, Mary Starchewski, and Mrs. Zaritsky, the mother of Anne Starr, also attended.[16] Starr's victory provided the necessary encouragement for other members of the Ukrainian community in Oshawa to enter politics. Starr's success was rubbing off: in November 1953, Michael Jacula and Michael Wladyka, both members of the Ukrainian Professional and Business Club, announced their decision to enter municipal politics and run for the position of alderman.[17]

The period of 1954 to 1956 were good years in Oshawa. In 1954, General Motors, located in the south section of Oshawa near Lake Ontario, undertook the greatest expansion in their history. The assembly plant along with the distribution warehouse soon covered over sixty acres.[18] In Oshawa, the water-filtration plant was completed, the new post office, new city hall and new McLaughlin Public Library were built and opened. New churches, schools and homes were built and more were planned; new homes were being constructed at a rate of approximately 650 annually. These developments were influenced by the increase in population from 28,759 to 50,136 in six years.[19]

By the mid-1950s, the various neighbourhoods in Oshawa were more or less well established. The managers and executives from General Motors and the other factories lived in the central and northern neighbourhoods of Oshawa. The majority of immigrants and ethnocultural groups from Central and Eastern Europe continued to live in south and east Oshawa. South Oshawa was traversed by two railways from east to west, and the 401 highway was completed from Toronto to Newcastle by the end of 1952. Other ethnocultural residents included Maltese, Italian, Hungarian, German, Dutch, and Irish among others. Within a short distance from Starr's home on Olive Avenue were the Ukrainian churches: the new St. George Ukrainian Catholic Church built in 1955, the St. John Ukrainian Orthodox Church, the Ukrainian Presbyterian Church and the Holy Mary Virgin Ukrainian Greek Orthodox Church and their respective community halls. The parishes grew with the baby boom of the post-war years. Starr formed a close friendship with Fr. John Pereyma, pastor of the Ukrainian Catholic Church and attended church services and community activities at the Catholic and Orthodox parishes. There was also the Ukrainian Club and the Ukrainian Hall called Dnipro.[20] On Bloor Street were the Ukrainian National Hall and the Ukrainian Labor Temple. Olive Avenue, running east to west, was known as the center of the Polish community, with the Oshawa Polish Hall and St. Hedwig's Roman Catholic Church, officially opened in 1953, overlooking southeastern Oshawa. This church also served, at various times, Italian, Slovenian and Portuguese congregations. The largest Polish community in Canada was located in Oshawa at that time. Oshawa attracted a large number of Polish post–Second World War settlers and former soldiers who had endured prisons in the Siberian gulags and then fought in Anders' Army, the Polish Armed Forces under the

---

16. Archives of Ontario, Ukrainian Professional and Businessmen's Club, Oshawa.
17. Ibid.
18. L.R. Barrand (compiler), *City of Oshawa, Municipal Manual*, 1957, p. 12.
19. Ibid., p. 13.
20. Dnipro is the largest river in Ukraine.

command of General W. Anders, in Italy and in northwestern Europe. They were known collectively as the "Sybiraki" (Siberians) and the Polish veterans were dedicated anti-Soviets.[21] Nearby was the Polish Alliance (Branch 21), Polish National Union Hall (Branch 7), the Slovak National Hall and the Hungarian Cultural Club.[22] The Hungarian community was reinforced with the arrival of approximately 600 Hungarian refugees in 1956–1957 after Soviet tanks suppressed the Hungarian uprising.[23] The Slovak community built the Slovak Greek Catholic Church in 1955 not far from Starr's home. Stores, bakeries, barbershops and small businesses were catering to ethnocultural communities, General Motors was hiring new immigrants, including members of the Ukrainian community. Within General Motors, there were even informal networks of Ukrainian workers facilitating the employment of other Ukrainian workers. General Motors paid well, and its wages and benefits allowed members of ethnocultural groups to aspire to a middle-class lifestyle: owning their own homes and sending their children to university. The Ukrainian Professional and Businessmen's Club of Oshawa continued to promote interest among the Ukrainian community in Canadian politics. On March 7, 1955, the club sponsored a two-day bus trip to Ottawa for students of Ukrainian origin to visit Parliament Hill and Ottawa and also to meet Members of Parliament of Ukrainian origin.[24]

In the House of Commons, Starr continued raising questions of particular interest to him and his Ontario riding. He campaigned for the removal of the luxury tax on automobiles, a move that could create over 4,000 new jobs in Oshawa. He asked questions relating to the importation of malleable iron pipefittings into Canada and other matters concerning local Oshawa industries. The Ontario Malleable Iron Company was a major employer in Starr's neighbourhood in Oshawa and the importation of malleable iron products would have competed with the production of the local foundry. He also asked questions about Communist publications printed in Canada and directed at recent immigrants. He made speeches in support of increased insurance benefits and he also favoured an increase in personal income-tax exemptions in the lower- and middle-income brackets. Whenever possible, Starr defended the interests of municipalities, stating that they required a larger share of the tax dollar. He also asked for the revision of all labour laws but in co-operation with management, labour unions and the government. According to Starr, the main aim of the federal Department of Labour should be one of ensuring steady work and pay throughout the year. He believed there were two great problems facing Canadians—unemployment and inadequate family income. Starr was particularly concerned about the Canadian tradition of seasonal unemployment, and repeated that this was a national and federal problem and not a local responsibility.

21. Helen Bajorek MacDonald, "The Power of Polonia: Post WWII Polish Immigrants to Canada; Survivors of Deportation and Exile in Soviet Labour Camps," MA thesis, Trent University, 2001; see in particular the chapter "Oshawa Polonia—The Imagined Village: A Community of Memory," pp. 284–306.
22. *Vernon's City of Oshawa Directory for the Year 1955*, Vernon Directories Ltd., Hamilton, Ontario (1955)
23. Sharon Young, *Oshawa Folk Arts Council, 1961–1981*, Oshawa Folk Arts Council, 1982, p. 119.
24. Archives of Ontario, Ukrainian Professional and Businessmen's Club, Oshawa.

In Parliament, Starr was an active member of the Standing Committee on Industrial Relations. When the Unemployment Insurance Act was discussed for possible amendments in 1955, Starr became an especially active member of this committee. Starr argued to make more benefits available, increase supplementary benefits along with extensions of time to receive the benefits. During this period, Starr also had the opportunity to meet with John Diefenbaker in Parliament on a regular basis and grew to admire his knowledge and expertise in political and historical matters. Starr began to believe Diefenbaker, as leader of the Progressive Conservative Party, could win the next federal election.[25]

Christmas in Oshawa in 1955 was not particularly happy. A strike at General Motors that began on September 19, 1955, remained in progress. It ended on February 15, 1956, and the huge plant went back into production, meaning the local economic climate soon improved with increased pay cheques, full employment, and a larger local working population.[26]

In Parliament, Starr continued to raise questions about issues of local concern in Oshawa: the automobile excise tax, the importation of automobiles and motor-vehicle parts from the United States, municipal grants, repairs to the Oshawa armoury and the perennial unemployment problems. In Ottawa, Starr was active as a member of the Special Committee on Estimates and the Standing Committee on External Affairs. He also mentioned in the House his presence at a Canadian citizenship ceremony held at the Whitby County Court where seventy-four new citizens received their citizenship certificates. He was impressed how the ceremony was conducted with dignity and stressed the value of Canadian citizenship. Starr also mentioned the participation of community voluntary organizations and suggested that this citizenship ceremony could serve as a model for others to follow.

Allister Grosart, now president of the Ontario Riding Conservative Association, organized a Mike Starr-Doc Dymond[27] picnic on July 21, 1956. Organized as a campaign event with advertisement, publicity, radio, platform decorations, ground signs, badges and press tables, it was popular and successful and became an annual event. Constituents, friends, and supporters had the opportunity to meet Starr and Dymond, their federal and provincial representatives, in a friendly and informal setting.[28] Allister Grosart continued drafting notes and speeches for Starr that he delivered in the House of Commons and at various political events.

Starr rose several times in the House to warn that municipalities faced bankruptcy if Ottawa burdened them with too large a share of the aid-to-jobless program. Starr repeated that this federal government should be directly responsible for the unemployed. Municipalities at the time had other ways to spend their money: with the early cohort of baby boomers entering schools, the Oshawa Board of Education had to raise funds for building five new

---

25. LAC, Peter Stursberg Papers, MG 31, D 78, Vol. 16, p. 1.
26. L.R. Barrand (compiler), *City of Oshawa, Municipal Manual*, 1957, p. 14.
27. Matthew Dymond (1911-1996) was a medical doctor who was the member for the Ontario riding in the provincial legislature from 1955 until 1975. He served in the Ontario cabinet as Minister of Transport and later as Minister of Health. Obituary: *The Globe and Mail*, February 23, 1996.
28. LAC, The Hon. Allister Grosart fonds, MG 32, C 65, Vol. 2, Daily Journal 1956 (entry for July 7, 1956).

schools, borrowing the money to do so at high interest rates. He suggested the need for a federal fund from which hard-pressed municipalities could borrow money at low interest rates. Starr was also interested in international politics and took the opportunity, in September 1956, to be the official observer for the Progressive Conservative Party at the opening of a new session of the United Nations in New York.

On September 21, 1956, Starr heard that George Drew resigned as leader of the Progressive Conservative Party. He quickly contacted Allister Grosart, the president of the Ontario Riding Conservative Association, in Pickering, who had provided important advice and information to Starr during his electoral campaigns and also wrote some of his speeches.[29] In 1949, Grosart had managed George Drew's campaign for leadership of the Progressive Conservative Party; one of the other candidates in that race was John Diefenbaker. Starr now attempted to enlist Grosart to manage Diefenbaker's campaign for leadership of the Progressive Conservative Party. Starr strongly believed Diefenbaker was the only candidate capable of winning the next federal election for the Conservatives. He was convinced that Diefenbaker would attract "the huge reform vote" to the Conservatives.[30] Starr threatened never to speak to Grosart again if he did not support Diefenbaker. He even phoned Diefenbaker from Grosart's home to inform him of his personal support. Starr also told Diefenbaker that he knew of at least twelve other Members of Parliament who supported him. Starr said over the phone, "John, you're a babe in the woods politically; they'll take you again." Starr added, "I'll support you but you have got to have Allister Grosart run your campaign." Starr had been keeping Grosart informed of Diefenbaker's positions on various issues in the House and now, because of his friendship with Starr, Grosart agreed to help Diefenbaker. A meeting was arranged between Grosart and Diefenbaker at the Royal York Hotel in Toronto, after which the Diefenbaker leadership campaign was launched in earnest.[31]

Grosart was, by profession, an advertising executive, and those skills were helpful in managing and winning Diefenbaker's leadership campaign on December 10, 1956. Starr supported Diefenbaker at the national Progressive Conservative convention and proudly wore a Diefenbaker button throughout the campaign. Most Conservative Members of Parliament supported Diefenbaker in his leadership campaign.

In the Speech from the Throne, the Liberal government promised reforms relating to municipal grants. In his reply to the speech, on January 17, 1957, Starr supported federal government grants to municipalities to pay in lieu of taxes for federal property and buildings located within their boundaries; a matter he had brought to the government's attention on many occasions. In Oshawa, these grants would contribute an additional $40,000 to the municipal budget. Starr added that there was a need to restructure taxation powers among federal, provincial and municipal authorities so the tax burden on the small homeowners was reduced in the municipality.[32] Starr said, "It is an acknowledged principle of our way of life that the strong must help the weak and that the rich must assist the poor." On

---

29. LAC, The Hon. Allister Grosart fonds, MG32 C65, Vol. 2, Daily Journal, November 29, 1952.
30. Patrick Nicholson, *Vision and Indecision*, Longmans Canada Limited, Don Mills, 1968, p. 5.
31. LAC, Peter Stursberg Papers, MG 31, D 78, Vol. 16, p. 2.; The Hon. Allister Grosart fonds, MG32 C65, Volume 8, File 5, Campaign Committee for John Diefenbaker, October 5, 1956.
32. *House of Commons Debates*, January 17, 1957, pp. 379–380.

Figure 4.3 The information on this newspaper clipping from June 6, 1957, summarizes the main reasons to re-elect Starr. He was campaigning on his record and also on his ability to be available to all constituents. Image courtesy of Walter Kish.

February 7, 1957, Starr's long campaign in Parliament to remove the excise tax on automobiles was rewarded when the Minister of Finance announced that excise tax would not be paid until ownership of the automobile was passed to the dealer. This measure stimulated car sales and automobile production in Oshawa.[33] According to Starr, the automobile had become a basic necessity because more and more people had to drive to work.

Starr suffered a personal loss when his mother, Mary, passed away on March 27, 1957.[34] Survived by Mike, his four sisters and their children, she had seen Starr's political career grow from the Ukrainian halls of Oshawa to the halls of Parliament in Ottawa.

The twenty-second Parliament was dissolved on April 12, 1957. A federal election was called and the date for the election was June 10, 1957. From the beginning of the election, Starr was confident about a Conservative Party victory. The local CCF candidate was W. John Naylor and the Liberal candidate was Dr. Claude H. Vipond.[35] During his campaign Starr emphasized his five-year record in Parliament and asked to be re-elected on the strength of this record. He informed voters that he was the first to speak on the issues important to the riding and the country: the need for a greater share of the tax dollar for the municipalities, the first to suggest the distribution of coronation medallions to school children, the abolition of the luxury tax on automobiles, the revision of health-insurance laws and the improvement of labour legislation.[36] Starr said the Conservative Party stood for improved unemployment-insurance benefits, full employment, limited hours and vacations with pay, and he reminded voters that the first labour unions, the first labour minister, and the first labour legislation had been incorporated by and under a Conservative administration.[37]

To prepare for the election, fifteen members of the Ukrainian community in Oshawa met during the first week of May 1957 to form the South End Branch of the Progressive Conservative Committee. Belonging to various Ukrainian community organizations, they gathered at the Ukrainian Sitch Hall on Merritt Street. The Ukrainian Committee was particularly active among the post-World War II immigrants who arrived in Oshawa between 1948 and 1952. All immigrants had applied for Canadian citizenship soon after their arrival and for many new citizens, the 1957 federal election was their first opportunity to vote. The Ukrainian Committee ensured that their first vote would be for Mike Starr. This group played a crucial role in mobilizing support for Starr among Oshawa's ethnocultural communities and continued their efforts in all of Starr's electoral campaigns.[38]

In Western Canada where the Liberal Party continued to receive strong support, the Ukrainian newspapers *Vilne Slovo*, *Canadian Farmer* and *Ukrainskyi Holos* predicted a Liberal victory. The newspapers focussed their attention on the Edmonton East riding where Mayor

---

33. *House of Commons Debates Session 1957*, Vol. I, pp. 1046–1047.
34. Mrs. Mary Starchewski was buried beside her husband in St. Gregory's Cemetery, Simcoe Street North, Oshawa.
35. *Daily Times Gazette*, May 8, 1957; Dr. Claude Hibbert Vipond graduated in medicine from Queen's University in 1943 and served overseas with the Canadian Army during the Second World War. As a doctor, he practiced with Oshawa Clinic and at the Oshawa General Hospital. (obituary: *Queen's Alumni Review*, Issue 1, 2017).
36. Ibid., May 29, 1957.
37. Ibid.
38. LAC, Michael Starr Papers, MG 32, B 15, *The Mike Starr Story*, Vol. 2.

William Hawrelak and Ambrose Holowach were candidates. *Ukrainskyi Holos* informed its readers that one of the candidates would more than likely be appointed to a cabinet post. The Ukrainian voters of Edmonton East were reminded they had an opportunity to contribute to the making of history of Ukrainian Canadian politics and "this should guide them in their decision at the polls."[39] *Vilne Slovo* stated that "it should be clear to every Ukrainian Canadian that it would be more advantageous to have a member in the Cabinet than a mayor of a city or a member representing a minority party."[40]

Starr thoroughly covered his Ontario riding and, within the first few days of the election campaign, had personally spoken to hundreds of voters and had addressed numerous rallies and gatherings. Starr and his campaign manager visited every subdivision in the riding and organized a complete constituency organization.[41] In the last weeks of the campaign, Starr was especially active at the gates of Oshawa industrial plants. He conducted an intensive door-to-door campaign ringing doorbells and meeting with voters in the shops and factories.

On June 10, 1957, the results of the federal election campaign in the Ontario riding were as follows:[42]

Candidate	Party	Votes	Votes (%)
Michael Starr	PC	18,468	42.78%
John Naylor	CCF	13,806	31.98%
Claude Vipond	Lib.	10,896	25.24%

Starr had comfortable majorities in every polling subdivision except for the city of Oshawa, where John Naylor won the city with 9,576 votes; Starr received 8,322 votes and Vipond obtained 5,376 votes. The main reason for the strong CCF showing in the city of Oshawa was the role of the United Automobile Workers Union that had over 11,000 members in Oshawa at that time and actively supported the CCF. Continuing his well-established tradition Starr said: "I will continue to look after your interests on a personal and collective basis. I am here to do a job for you. Please don't fail to look me up at my home, or at my office, if you have any problems."[43]

However, across Canada the Conservative victory produced a minority government. The federal election had failed to elect a majority to the House of Commons for the first time since 1925. The seats in the House were distributed as follows:

Party	Seats
Progressive Conservatives	111
Liberals	105
CCF	25

---

39. *Press Digest*, Vol. 13, No. 7, July 1957, p. 1.
40. Ibid., Vol. 13, No. 6, June 1957, p. 4.
41. *Daily Times Gazette*, June 8, 1957.
42. Elections Canada, *History of the federal Electoral Ridings Since 1867*; see also *Daily Times Gazette*, June 11, 1957.
43. *Daily Times Gazette*, June 11, 1957.

Social Credit	19
Independents	4

Although Mike Starr and Paul Martin sat on opposite sides of the House of Commons, they remained good friends outside the House in the best parliamentary tradition. Both represented electoral ridings whose economy was based on the automobile industry and had many constituents from the various ethnocultural groups. Soon after the 1957 federal election, Starr and Martin met while walking across Parliament Hill. Their conversation soon turned to the recent election results. Martin admitted that the Progressive Conservative election victory had surprised him and the Liberal Party. Martin added: "It's a sorry day for us. One man is to blame for this. Just the one man Diefenbaker beat us. We've got to destroy him if it's the last thing we do, so we can get back into office." Starr replied: "You must be kidding, Paul."[44]

---

44. Quoted in Patrick Nicholson, *Vision and Indecision: Diefenbaker and Pearson*, Longmans Canada Limited, Don Mills, 1968, pp. 62–63.

Chapter 5
Appointment as Minister of Labour, 1957

When Mike Starr was attending the funeral of Dr William G. Blair, a Conservative Member of Parliament from Perth, Ontario, the new Prime Minister, John Diefenbaker called and asked to see him in Ottawa.[1] Starr arrived in Ottawa but was told to wait and reassured that Diefenbaker had something important to tell him. He waited two days. It was only then, on June 21, 1957, that he was informed of his appointment as Minister of Labour—and then, only three hours before he was due to be sworn in by the Governor General. Starr was a bit nervous during his trip to Rideau Hall. He lit a cigarette in the taxi but arrived at Rideau Hall before actually smoking it. He extinguished the cigarette and placed it in his pocket. Only after being sworn in, and exiting Rideau Hall did he retrieve the cigarette and relight it. Unfortunately, the press noticed Starr relighting his half-burnt cigarette and to his wife's dismay a photo of this frugal gesture made the newspapers.[2]

During the swearing in ceremony, Diefenbaker kept repeating to Starr that this was an historic moment. He was the first prime minister who was neither of English nor French descent and Starr was the first cabinet minister of Ukrainian descent. At cabinet's first meeting after the ceremony, the clerk of the Privy Council, Robert B. Bryce, briefed new cabinet ministers on procedures and Diefenbaker reminded them of their oaths of secrecy. Starr was appointed to the Treasury Board. Chaired by Finance Minister Donald Fleming, this most powerful of cabinet committees monitored government expenditures. Starr's membership on this committee provided him with an excellent opportunity to promote his own programs and priorities. Among the other historical firsts was the appointment of Ellen Fairclough as Secretary of State as the first woman appointed to the federal cabinet.[3]

Despite earlier rumours, the appointment of Starr as Minister of Labour surprised everyone. Although he had served on the Industrial Relations and Unemployment Insurance Committees in the House of Commons, the press and political observers didn't see Starr as the Conservative Party's official expert on labour. Starr had never belonged to a union and at Pedlar People Limited he was generally considered as management staff, although he did on occasion describe himself as a "white-collar" worker.[4] Yet, according to Diefenbaker, Starr was the obvious choice. He felt Starr knew labour problems from personal experience as an employee and as employer, not to mention that his riding was home to the large General Motors plant, with its large union membership. Although Starr was born in Canada,

---

1. LAC, Peter Stursberg Papers, MG 31, D 78, Vol. 16, p. 14.
2. Ibid. p. 17–18.
3. Among the first Canadian Cabinet Ministers of non-British and non-French origin was Joseph T. Thorson, born in 1889 in Winnipeg, who was of Icelandic descent. He was appointed Minister of National War Services in 1941-1942 during the Second World War. His biographic note is in *The Canadian Parliamentary Guide,* 1945, Ottawa (1945), p. 659.
4. *Toronto Star,* July 8, 1957.

Figure 5.1 Starr was loyal to John Diefenbaker throughout his political career in Ottawa. He was profoundly grateful to Diefenbaker for appointing him as Minister of Labour in 1957 and for giving him the opportunity to serve his country.

Diefenbaker saw him as part of the waves of immigration that arrived in Canada from Europe to become Canadians.[5] Starr had already gained some recognition by identifying "with the cause of the little people who have made Canada known throughout the world as the land of opportunity blessed with a high standard of living."[6]

Starr's cabinet appointment created a sensation not just in the Ukrainian community but throughout ethnocultural communities across Canada. The American-published Ukrainian newspaper *Svoboda* (Liberty) said Starr's appointment pleased not only Ukrainian Canadians but all Ukrainians throughout the free world.[7] The Ukrainian weekly *Ukrainsky Holos* (Ukrainian Voice), published from Winnipeg, wrote that Starr's appointment was the most important political achievement of Ukrainian Canadians during 1957. The newspaper stated that Starr's name would be recorded in Ukrainian Canadian history as a pioneer in the field of politics.[8] In an editorial, *Novy Shliakh* (New Pathway) wrote that there was still a long way to go before Ukrainian Canadians were completely integrated into Canadian life and therefore "...the more active part we play in every walk of life the faster we are going to contribute to the improvement of our own lot and the well-being of Canada. At the same time, we will be in a better position to assist in the liberation of Ukrainians in Europe."[9] The pro-Communist newspaper *Ukrainske Zhyttia* (Ukrainian Life) also mentioned that Starr was the first Ukrainian appointed to the federal cabinet but without any further comments.[10] The *Toronto Star* and the *Globe and Mail* published the names of the new cabinet ministers and when Starr's name was mentioned, they also included that he was "... the first person

---

5. John Diefenbaker, *One Canada, Memories of the Right Honourable John G. Diefenbaker, The Years of Achievement 1952–62*, Macmillan of Canada, Toronto, 1976, p. 46.
6. *The Labour Gazette*, July 15, 1957, p. 802.
7. *Press Digest*, Department of Citizenship and Immigration, Vol. 13, No. 8, August 1957, p. 6.
8. Ibid., Vol. 14, No. 2, February 1958, p. 5.
9. Ibid., Vol. 13, No. 8, August 1957, p. 5.
10. *Ukrainske Zhyttia (Ukrainian Life)* June 26, 1957. The newspaper did mention that the first Ukrainian to hold ministerial office at the provincial level was Alex G. Kuziak, Minister of Telephones and Minister in Charge of Government Finance Office, appointed on October 24, 1952 in the CCF government of Tommy Douglas in Saskatchewan. (Pierre G. Normandin, *The Canadian Parliamentary Guide*, 1954, Ottawa, 1954).

of Cabinet rank in Canada of Ukrainian extraction"[11] and "a representative of the Ukrainian people."[12] In listing the members of the new cabinet, *Time* magazine described Starr as the former mayor of Oshawa, where "he owned a cleaning business" and that he was the "first Ukrainian-descended minister of [a] federal cabinet."[13]

Cliff Pilkey, president of UAW Local 222 in Oshawa said:

> We are happy that Mike Starr has received the appointment in so much as he represents Ontario Riding. The labour movement in Oshawa will be watching very closely the actions of Mr. Starr to see if the labour legislation is forthcoming as promised ... Mr. Diefenbaker promised to revise the National Labour Act and it will be up to Mike Starr to carry out these promises.[14]

After the swearing-in ceremony, Starr went home to Oshawa for the weekend. When he returned to Ottawa the following Monday, he drove to the offices of the Department of Labour, found the parking space designated for the Minister of Labour and left his car there. But not everyone recognized the new minister: he returned in the evening only to discover the RCMP had ticketed his car. This continued for several days until the situation was clarified.[15]

Since its establishment in 1900, the federal Department of Labour has been responsible for a number of statutes affecting Canadian workers employed on contracts by the federal government and in certain designated industries largely of the interprovincial nature, such as railways, shipping, radio broadcasting and other types of transportation and communication. The department was established to aid in preventing and settling labour disputes and to collect, compile and publish statistical and other relevant information. It was also responsible for the administration of a number of statutes, including the Conciliation and Labour Act (1935), the Unemployment Insurance Act (1940), the Vocational Training Co-ordination Act (1946), the Industrial Relations and Disputes Investigation Act (1948), the Canada Fair Employment Practices Act (1953) and the Female Employees Equal Pay Act (1956). On March 31, 1957, there were 619 persons on staff at the department in addition to the staff of the Unemployment Insurance Commission and the National Employment Service, with a combined total of 8,773.[16]

Although the Conservatives won their minority victory in the 1957 election during an economic recession, this economic problem was not the only central issue. The main concern was growing inflation. During the election, the Conservatives raised the additional

---

11. *The Globe and Mail*, June 22, 1957.
12. *Toronto Star*, June 21, 1957.
13. *Time* (magazine), July 1, 1957.
14. *Daily Times Gazette*, June 24, 1957; Morden Lazarus, *Up From the Ranks, Trade Union VIP's Past and Present*, Regent Press, 1977, biographical note on Clifford Pilkey, pp. 102–103. Clifford Pilkey, born in 1922, was an autoworker in Oshawa and, in 1957, Pilkey was elected president of the Oshawa and District Labour Council and held this office for ten years. For more on Pilkey, see the obituary, *Globe and Mail*, December 12, 2012.
15. LAC, Peter Stursberg Papers, MG 31, D 78, Vol. 16.
16. Department of Labour, *Annual Report for the Fiscal Year Ended March 31, 1957*, Ottawa, 1957, p. 8. See also *Canada Year Book 1957–58*, Dominion Bureau of Statistics, Ottawa, 1958, p. 744.

issues of high taxes and low social-security benefits. But the Conservative Party built its support on the appeals for nation-building and economic development. As the new Minister of Labour, Starr said his main purpose would be to do all that is "humanly possible" to implement the Conservative platform on labour policies. The platform contained the following points: an immediate review of all federal labour legislation by the combined efforts of government, management and labour; co-operation with the provinces with a view to reform labour laws; adequate representation for labour on government boards dealing with matters of interest to labour; improvement of unemployment-insurance legislation to widen coverage, increase benefits and eliminate "discrimination against married women."[17] Starr planned a rapid examination of federal labour legislation with a view to some possible revisions but had no major changes in mind. He said:

> I intend to review all federal labour legislation and to see what changes are needed with the cooperation of all those affected including the unions and the employers. I have no intentions of being dictatorial. I'm going to consider the ideas of all those who might be affected by any changes.[18]

In Ottawa, Starr was regarded with nervous suspicion by some of the public servants who had worked for twenty-two years under a Liberal administration. Starr made it clear from the beginning that he intended to be fully responsible for the Labour Department.[19] Starr added, "But I'm mighty green at this big job and it's going to take me some time to feel around and get my footing."[20] Starr was able to obtain the services of Thomas Van Dusen as his executive assistant. Van Dusen was a former Ottawa journalist and Progressive Conservative candidate who knew his way around Parliament Hill and was able to provide invaluable assistance to Starr during his years as minister.[21]

Soon after his appointment, Starr was interviewed by Jack Williams, the director of public relations of the Canadian Labour Congress. The interview was printed in the July 1957 issue of *Canadian Labour*, which claimed that Starr ". . . has already undertaken to bring about improvements in the handling of conciliation boards and other reforms in legislation and procedure along lines advocated by the Congress." Starr told Williams, "The programme of our party and the programme of your Congress are very closely in line" and he also mentioned his plans for a thorough review of federal government labour legislation, how he'd like to see close co-operation between labour, management and government, to renounce compulsory arbitration as a method of settling disputes, revise the Unemployment Insurance Act, and ensure adequate representation for labour on all appropriate government bodies and commissions. Starr said he had never held a union card because he had never worked at a job that was organized. But, he added, his father and brother were both members of UAW Local 222 and ". . . with my background, if anyone says I do not understand labour problems, they are wrong." According to Bob Ford, president of the Ottawa and District

---
17. *Daily Times Gazette*, June 26, 1957.
18. Ibid.
19. Thomas Van Dusen, *The Chief*, McGraw-Hill Company of Canada Limited, 1968, p. 29.
20. *Daily Times Gazette*, June 26, 1957.
21. The Thomas Van Dusen fonds (R11596-0-4-E) is located at the Library and Archives Canada.

Trades and Labour Council, he and Mike Starr had walked the UAW picket line in 1937, and that Starr was "a regular fellow."[22]

Starr announced to his staff that he would answer each letter from the unemployed, which were arriving at the rate of 150 letters a day. He began implementing this pledge and he also gave orders to the National Employment Service to look into each individual case and report back to him within ten days. If no report was forthcoming after ten days, Starr phoned the local National Employment Service office to inquire about the delay. From the beginning, Starr insisted the unemployed be treated with courtesy. This was part of Starr's human approach to labour, something he did not regard as an abstract commodity. Rather, he believed, ". . . labour means men and women, bringing up families, educating children, paying taxes, supporting the community."

At the cabinet meeting held on June 25, 1957, Starr reported that unemployment forecasts for the coming winter were "alarming." It was being predicted that as many as 750,000 individuals might be unemployed and it was therefore important that the government should attempt everything possible to reduce these numbers. A number of reasons were discussed for the high unemployment rates and it was suggested that the large number of recent immigrants along with the tight-money policies of the Bank of Canada were possible causes. Plans were made to reduce the number of immigrants entering the country for the balance of the year and to establish a cabinet committee to review the general unemployment situation and present a report to cabinet on "practical counter measures."[23] In 1954, under the Liberal administration, the Department of Labour and the Unemployment Insurance Commission had established a working committee and an Interdepartmental Committee on Winter Employment to explore ways of increasing winter employment.[24] During the winter of 1955–56, a national program was specifically designed to increase employment for those out of work due to seasonal factors. However, the Liberal government's efforts were considered only as an introduction to encourage support from business and industry.[25] A nationwide publicity campaign—Why Wait for Spring? Do It Now!—was initiated to promote maximum employment during the winter months. Newspapers, radio, television, film, pamphlets and circular letters were used to encourage winter employment. The slogan "Why Wait for Spring? Do It Now!" was included on all kinds of federal government media, including Canadian Post Office cancellation stamps. This slogan was questionably received in some foreign countries. The Hungarian Foreign Ministry sent a diplomatic protest to Canada and actually interrupted shipment of Canadian mail in the belief that Canada was urging Hungarians to resume their uprising of November 1956.[26] According to the protest made through the British legation, this stamp gave ". . . evidence that the Canadian Government is not led by the desire to develop peaceful relations but would welcome new counter-revolutionary activities and bloodshed in Hungary." The foreign ministry in Hungary requested that the Canadian government ". . . halt these activities."

---

22. *Ottawa Citizen*, September 21, 1957.
23. LAC, RG2, Volume 1892, June 25, 1957.
24. Department of Labour, Annual Report for the fiscal year ended March 31, 1957, p. 7.
25. Department of Labour, Annual Report for the fiscal year ended March 31, 1956, p. 50.
26. *The Globe and Mail*, March 9, 1957, February 7, 1958.

On Sunday, June 30, 1957, a mass meeting was held in Toronto by Ukrainians to commemorate the fortieth anniversary of the Ukrainian national revolution of 1917. This event was organized by the Canadian League for the Liberation of Ukraine. Starr was one of six speakers addressing over 10,000 Canadians of Ukrainian descent gathered at the Canadian National Exhibition Bandshell. In his speech Starr said "The Revolution we commemorate today is still going on. Some day, by God's help the revolution of the people of the Ukraine will be successful. Some day, some blessed day, the land of our forefathers will take its proud place beside those nations which we call the free world."[27] He added, "We here represent those millions of Ukrainians driven by despair to find new lands. But we will not forget those left behind." He also recalled that Ukrainian pioneers did much to help open the Canadian prairies and easily adapted as a group to Canadian society. He reminded the audience that he was the first Canadian of Ukrainian origin to become a federal cabinet minister and promised the crowd that "... there will be others."[28] The other speakers at this event were Dr. J. W. Kucherepa, Member of Parliament for High Park who introduced Starr and Arthur Maloney, MP, John Yaremko, MPP, A. Grossman, MPP, and Con. W. R. Allen.

On July 11, 1957, Starr and George Hees, the Minister of Transport, met with representatives of the railway unions regarding a proposal by the Canadian National Railway (CN) management to lay off over 1,000 railway workers as an economy measure and due to the transfer from steam to diesel engines. They listened to the union representatives sympathetically but were non-committal. The next day, they met with Donald Gordon, the president of the Canadian National Railway Company. They suggested to Gordon that the announced layoffs be postponed until the entire employment situation was reviewed. Gordon replied that these requests would be very difficult to implement since the lay-offs were planned some time ago but delayed because of the federal elections. Starr and Hees pointed out to Gordon that, although the federal government did not operate the railways, the Canadian public believed that the Canadian National Railway was under the direction of the government when, in fact, it was the responsibility of the CN board of directors. These meetings were reported to the cabinet and concern was expressed about the gravity of the situation.[29]

In a letter dated August 12, 1957, Starr wrote to the principal labour and management organizations in Canada requesting their views on the amendment of the Industrial Relations and Disputes Investigations Act.[30] Shortly after his appointment as Minister of Labour, Starr was persuaded by departmental officials that the Industrial Relations and Disputes Investigations Act required amendments. This act outlined the basic rules regarding labour-management relations in industries within the legislative jurisdiction of Parliament. Starr soon received reports and proposals from labour and management. However, their recommendations were generally incompatible.[31] As a result, no amendments were

---

27. *Daily Times Gazette,* July 2, 1957.
28. *Toronto Star,* July 2, 1957.
29. LAC, RG2 Volume 1892, July 11, 12, 1957.
30. *Labour Gazette,* September 15, 1957.
31. David Kwavnick, *Organized Labour and Pressure Politics: The Canadian Labour Congress, 1956-1968,* McGill-Queen's University Press, Montreal, 1972, pp. 168–169, 199.

submitted to Parliament and the act remained unchanged during the tenure of the Diefenbaker government. Despite this initial setback, Starr continued promoting the need for improved labour-management relations as essential to any solution of Canadian economic problems. In his first six weeks Starr had to learn a vast amount of information and problems arose from the fact that he attempted to absorb too much all at once. Starr admitted he had much to learn and he quickly learned to pace himself. He also visited the various offices and branches with whose operations he had to be familiar.[32]

The pattern of Starr's home life, and the regular commuting to Oshawa, did not change. Anne Starr said, "Things will go on as they always have. Ottawa is not such a great distance that I cannot visit the capital whenever necessary."[33] Starr visited Oshawa on weekends when his schedule allowed. Starr, however, resigned from Pedlar People, where he had worked for twenty-four years successively as cost clerk, invoice clerk and, finally, as manager of the order department. On two occasions, between parliamentary sessions, he was special products sales manager and was responsible for training new sales personnel. The firm stated that, if required, Starr could always return to work at Pedlar People.

In his Labour Day message printed in *The Labour Gazette* of August 15, 1957, Starr stated he intended to

> always keep before me the interests of the working people of this country in all questions of importance, and your government intends to see that organized labour is adequately represented on government boards dealing with matters of direct interest to labour. Organized labour has reached a degree of maturity and strength which entitles it to consideration in all matters affecting those for whom it speaks.

He emphasized that he was particularly concerned with "such problems as the difficulty of people past 40 getting employment, rehabilitation and employment of the disabled, discrimination in employment because of race, colour or creed and unemployment resulting from cold weather in the winter." The agricultural tradition established during the pioneering era of Canadian development of suspending outdoor work during the winter season was continued in several other urban trades such as construction. This tradition was responsible for a significant increase in unemployment during the winter months.

In September 1957, Starr addressed the annual convention in Toronto of the International Stereotypers' and Electrotypers' Union of North America. He promised that the total resources of the National Employment Service would be used to find jobs. The insurance aspect would be regarded as an emergency or alternative measure only when every effort was exhausted in finding suitable employment.[34] Speaking at a seminar in Toronto sponsored by the International Confederation of Free Trade Unions, Starr said that Canadian unions ". . . have made economic gains for their numbers, have encouraged them to cooperate with management in making possible greater production and thus even greater prosperity and have helped them gain in security and in self-reliance." Starr added that he could think of few things more conducive to the achievement of greater freedom and better living

---

32. LAC, Michael Starr Papers, MG 32, B 15, *The Mike Starr Story*, Vol. II, September 1957.
33. *Daily Times Gazette*, June 26, 1957.
34. *Labour Gazette*, October 15, 1957, p. 1161.

standards for the peoples of the world than free, strong, democratic trade-union movements firmly established in all the countries of the world.[35]

In September 1957, Starr was named "Ukrainian of the Year" for North America and received a bronze plaque from the Ukrainian Professional Society at the close of its convention in Detroit.[36] This honour was one of many confirming Starr's status as one of the most prominent Ukrainians in North America. Starr was regularly invited to speak at numerous Ukrainian community events, where he was frequently honoured for his contributions to Ukrainian Canadian political life.

During his first year, Starr's main problem as cabinet minister was the serious unemployment situation, particularly during the winter season. In addition, Canada was entering one of the most serious economic recessions in the post–Second World War period. The prosperous years starting with the Second World War, and continuing with the Marshall Plan and the Korean War, were beginning to stall. Japan, Germany and the various European countries ruined by the Second World War were re-entering the world economy, and were often equipped with the most modern factories and equipment. They began to effectively compete with Canadian industry and the annual average percentage of unemployed workers in Canada rose from 3.4 per cent in 1956, to 4.6 per cent in 1957, then to 7.1 per cent in 1958.[37] Already, political observers were able to point to the annual winter unemployment crisis as the Conservative government's greatest problem. This annual problem was compounded by an increase of almost a quarter-million new people in the labour force from the previous year. Some political observers and economists expressed their fear that an unemployment rate between 7 per cent and 10 per cent could have an overwhelming effect on the total economy. Also, they believed that any expensive nation-wide program by the federal government to reduce unemployment would result in uncontrolled inflation.[38] In addition, the Conservatives knew that the Liberals would do their best to identify them with former Prime Minister R. B. Bennett's Progressive Conservative regime and the Depression of the 1930s. Starr, who lived through the Depression in Oshawa, knew very well the possible consequences and this memory guided his thoughts and actions as Minister of Labour. With a minority Conservative government, the Liberals also knew that a federal election was a strong possibility and planned to attack the government whenever the opportunity arose to locate any weaknesses.

The first session of the twenty-third Parliament opened on October 14, 1957. A few days later, on October 16, 1957, Starr said in the House of Commons:

> Mr Speaker, we are aware that there will be seasonal unemployment this winter. We have stepped up our winter program to take care of winter unemployment. We have also advised our national service offices to step up their tempo in obtaining jobs for people as soon as they become unemployed . . . we have curtailed for the balance of

---

35. Ibid. p. 1163.
36. *Daily Times Gazette*, February 6, 1958.
37. Frank T. Denton and Sylvia Ostry, *An Analysis of Post-War Unemployment*, Economic Council of Canada, Queen's Printer, Ottawa, 1965, p. 3.
38. Jon W. Kieran, "Unemployment Crisis: How Will the Tories Weather the Winter?," *Saturday Night*, Vol. 72, No. 25, December 7, 1957, pp. 7, 41–42.

the year the influx of immigrants which swelled our total labour population. In addition, we have channelled $150 million into our economy for the construction of houses. These are the things the government has done so far in order to cope with unemployment this winter.

Starr was now rising regularly from his seat in the House of Commons to face the barrage of questions from the opposition political parties. As a member of an opposition party before 1956, Starr had often criticized the Liberal government's inability to solve the unemployment problem. Now as Minister of Labour, Starr was subjected to this same treatment. He was determined to permanently solve the winter unemployment problem. He sought solutions "based on a sound economic foundation." One program Starr strongly supported was winter construction, especially house building that could be continued all winter.[39]

Figure 5.2 The Honourable Michael Starr, Minister of Labour in the first Diefenbaker cabinet. Image courtesy of Library and Archives Canada (PA-114539).

On October 29, 1957, Starr introduced bills providing for annual paid vacations for public-works employees: the Industrial Relations and Disputes Investigations Act, the Fair Employment Practices Act and the Equal Pay Act.[40] On November 15, 1957, he presented a motion in Parliament to extend unemployment insurance benefits to married women, placing them on the same level as all the other claimants. Starr introduced a measure on November 25 to increase the length of seasonal benefit periods and the number of benefit payments for which applicants may qualify during those periods. As the unemployment situation grew in severity during the winter months, the government increased the number of subsidies and make-work schemes.

Construction projects and improvements to federal buildings in the Ottawa area during the winter months were one method of prolonging employment of tradesmen.[41] Starr said these measures were introduced because ". . . this government has no intention of sitting back and letting matters run their course."[42]

The national labour-union federations presented a brief or memorandum to cabinet and this event evolved into a solemn ceremony held in the Parliament buildings with all the members of cabinet present. The labour unions through this presentation confirmed their status as the "official" spokesmen of Canadian workers and cabinet received their

---

39. *Labour Gazette*, November 15, 1957.
40. *House of Commons Debates*, October 29, 1957, p. 503.
41. *Ottawa Journal*, October 23, 1957.
42. *House of Commons Debates,* November 27, 1957, p. 1570.

delegations because they were interested in the "voice of labour" and a large political constituency. In accordance with this tradition, Starr met with the representatives of the Canadian Labour Congress and the Canadian and Catholic Confederation of Labour. Starr said that he hoped that the suggestions received regarding amendments to the Industrial Relations and Dispute Investigations Act ". . . may be dovetailed into something that will be acceptable to both employers and employees." Starr spoke in English but revealed that he was making progress in his study of the French language and that he hoped to address the delegation in French at their next submission.[43]

In reply to Liberal accusations in the House that the Conservatives were doing little to fight the unemployment situation in the country, Diefenbaker blamed the Liberals for the economic recession. On January 20, 1958, he released a Department of Trade and Commerce report prepared by the previous Liberal government stating the economy was entering a period of economic recession.[44] Diefenbaker later admitted that he was initially reluctant to fully acknowledge the existence and extent of the recession because he felt that his government would be blamed for it.[45]

Building on the experience of the Department of Labour and the public servants who sought solutions to the winter unemployment problem from previous years, an active information campaign began on January 15, 1958, once again with the slogan, "Why Wait for Spring? Do It Now."[46] This message was spread through the public media every winter for most of Starr's tenure as Minister of Labour. In an attempt to provide a fundamental and permanent solution to the unemployment problem, Starr drew on his experience in municipal politics and initiated a historic piece of legislation. On January 29, 1958, Starr declared in Parliament:

> An agreement providing for the federal financial assistance to the provinces toward the construction and operation of vocational, technical and trade schools has been entered into by the government of Canada with each of the provinces, except the Province of Quebec, effective for a period of five years from 1 April 1957, under the authority of the Vocational Training Coordination Act and Order in Council P.C. 1957-23/367 of 31 March 1957. The Province of Quebec [has] not signed this agreement.

Premier Maurice Duplessis strongly protected the cultural autonomy of Quebec and he objected to federal interference in educational matters in any form. As a result, the province of Quebec lost millions of dollars to the great disappointment of many Quebecois, especially among the emerging nationalist youth. The question of financial relations later became a serious issue in federal-provincial politics. It should be mentioned that Quebec did not have an education ministry until 1964.

The Annual Vacations act was passed on January 29, 1958, and became effective by proclamation on October 1, 1958. This act provided for annual paid vacations for employees

---

43. *Labour Gazette*, November 15, 1957, pp. 1295, 1299.
44. Patrick Nicholson, *Vision and Indecision*, Don Mills: Longmans, 1968, p. 68.
45. J. Diefenbaker, *One Canada*, Volume II, Toronto, Macmillan, 1975, pp. 65–67.
46. Department of Labour, *Annual Report for the Fiscal Year Ended March 31, 1958*, Ottawa, 1958, pp. 43–44.

in federal works, undertakings and businesses.[47] Starr said, "... we are introducing an entirely new piece of labour legislation, one that has not been in existence in the federal field previously and that it was designed in advance of five other provinces that have existing legislation on ... vacations with pay."[48]

On January 31, 1958, Starr was the target of a speech in the House of Commons by Lester Pearson, the newly-elected leader of the Liberal Party. Starr had been insisting that a particular set of government figures represented unemployment, but Pearson reminded him that he had had a different viewpoint in opposition. Pearson reminded Starr of a Commons speech he delivered on March 31, 1955, when Starr used those registered for jobs with the National Employment Service to represent the total number of unemployed people. Pearson persisted in questioning Starr's figures despite Diefenbaker's intervention and the support of other Conservative MPs.

Cast in the role of the "Ukrainian representative" in the Canadian government soon after his appointment to cabinet, Starr naturally maintained his contacts with ethnocultural groups. On January 19, 1958, he flew to Chicago to celebrate the fortieth anniversary of the declaration of Ukraine's independence and on January 26, 1958, he and Diefenbaker spoke in Winnipeg to a Ukrainian audience about the anniversary.[49] Ukrainian and other ethnocultural organizations hurried to Ottawa with briefs and proposals on any number of government issues. The most important issue to many Ukrainians and other East European groups was Canada's foreign policy in relation to the Soviet Union and other Warsaw Pact countries. In turn, the Ukrainian Canadian pro-Communist newspapers criticized Starr and Diefenbaker for their participation and support of Ukrainian nationalist causes.[50]

Starr willingly, although sometimes reluctantly, became the spokesman of ethnocultural groups in Ottawa. He had the opportunity to visit most of the major ethnocultural population centres and meet with their leaders. He was able to persuade several community leaders to actively support the Progressive Conservative Party and, in some cases, to run for political office. Already there were mayors of other major Canadian cities from the Ukrainian community. William Hawrelak was first elected to the Edmonton city council in 1949 and, in 1951, he was elected mayor. Stephen Juba served in the Manitoba legislature in 1953–59 and was mayor of Winnipeg from 1956 to 1977. On his many trips across Canada, Starr would be invited to visit the homes of prominent leaders after the regular business of the day was completed. In this manner, he was able to establish friendly personal contacts with a wide spectrum of Canadians and make a substantial contribution to broadening the base of support for Progressive Conservatives.

At the national level, Ukrainian Canadians began distinguishing themselves in other areas of achievement. Some Ukrainian athletes gained star status in the sports field and contributed to the "white ethnic sports breakthrough." In the 1940s and 1950s, the National Hockey League had a number of famous hockey players who made the rest of Canada

---
47. Department of Labour, *Annual Report for the Fiscal Year Ended March 31, 1958*, Ottawa, 1958, p. 7.
48. *House of Commons Debates*, January 29, 1958, p. 4007.
49. LAC, Michael Starr Papers, MG 32, B 15, *The Mike Starr Story*, Vol. 1.
50. *Press Digest*, Vol. 14, No. 3, March 1958, pp. 7–8.

familiar with Ukrainian hockey stars and Ukrainian names—Turk Broda, Bill Barilko, Bill Mosienko, Terry Sawchuk, and many others. Starr's appointment as Minister of Labour was among the first examples of the "white ethnic political breakthrough" at the federal level.[51]

---

51. Bryan D. Palmer, *Canada's 1960s, The Ironies of Identity in a Rebellious Era,* University of Toronto Press, Toronto, 2009, p. 133.

Chapter 6
The 1958 Federal Election

On January 20, 1958, Opposition Leader Lester B. Pearson stood in the House of Commons and demanded the resignation of the Conservative government. On February 1, 1958, Diefenbaker obliged and called a federal election, to be held on March 31, 1958. Starr explained to his constituents that Diefenbaker had no choice; the minority government situation in the House of Commons was "intolerable." The government had to plan its actions on a day-to-day basis and was unable to make long-range plans because it was uncertain about support in the House.[1]

With his cabinet appointment in June 1957, Starr had assumed new political responsibilities at the national level. His political constituency extended from his riding to include all of Canada. It also raised his public profile and increased media attention. In preparation for the coming federal election campaign, Starr planned to travel across Canada speaking to Conservative riding associations at nomination meetings. During this period Starr's constituency organization was expected to campaign in his absence. Starr said, "I will devote all the time and effort to the people of Oshawa that I possibly can. My last few weeks before the election will be spent right here at home."[2]

Starr, who felt the Conservatives had accomplished much in a short time, said they would campaign on their political record since being elected in July 1957. He claimed the hundreds of millions of dollars the federal government had spent to stimulate employment was starting to produce results. Starr also claimed the party had been given an opportunity by the Canadian people to make some accomplishments and they had exceeded the voters' expectations. Starr was optimistic about the coming federal elections and knew his faith was shared by Conservatives across Canada.[3]

Dr. Claude Vipond, Starr's Liberal opponent in the Ontario riding, repeated the criticism Pearson had levelled at Starr in the House of Commons, accusing him of producing "confusing and misleading" figures on the unemployment situation. He added, "High as the unemployment figures are I would like to add one to that figure—namely the Hon. Mike Starr—and I think I can do that."[4] John Brady was nominated as the CCF candidate for the riding at the Oshawa Union Hall on February 13, 1958. He had previously received unanimous support at a meeting of the UAW Local 222 at General Motors attended by approximately 300 members.[5] John Brady stated:

---

1. *Daily Times Gazette*, February 3, 1958.
2. Ibid.
3. Ibid.
4. Ibid., February 14, 1958.
5. Ibid.

The Minister of Labour, Michael Starr, is busy stumping the hustings and not really concerned about the growing unemployment problem which the government admits is an all-time high. I ask the people of this riding to elect a man who really represents the whole of the people, not the few and wealthy.[6]

Once again, Starr was unanimously nominated as the Conservative candidate in his riding.[7] He advised his supporters that they would have to work especially hard for him since his status as a cabinet minister obliged him to campaign outside the riding until the last ten days of the election.

During the election campaign, Starr promised that the Conservative government would revise the Unemployment Insurance Act to deal more effectively with the economic situation. The Unemployment Insurance Commission would also be changed to secure a better placement service for applicants and deal more effectively with the seasonally unemployed problem. Starr said that it was "the government's business" as long as one Canadian was out of work and he pledged himself to find a solution to the problem. Starr added that one solution would be to encourage secondary industries to process products in Canada rather than continually export raw materials to other countries for manufacturing products that were later sold in Canada.[8] While campaigning in Montreal, Starr stated that the current unemployment crisis had ended sooner than the government expected. Starr claimed that the decline between January and February 1958 in the rate of increase in unemployment was due to government policies.[9] Starr also said that the Conservative government stimulated the slow house-building industry by injecting $300 million into housing projects that provided work for 90,000 men on housing projects and another 180,000 men in related industries.

The unemployment situation in Oshawa at the end of February had changed very little during the previous few months. According to the manager of the local Unemployment Insurance Commission office, there were 4,974 unemployed registered at the Oshawa office at the end of February compared with 4,179 at the end of January 1958. In comparison with the previous year, there were 4,208 unemployed registered at the end of February 1957 at the Oshawa office. Of these, approximately half resided outside the city.[10]

Starr said that if the Conservative government was re-elected, he would call a conference of labour, management and government representatives to provide specific proposals to solve the seasonal unemployment problems. He added that, in the future, the Conservative Party would be deeply concerned with three goals: the establishment of better relations between management and labour, the development of Canada's northland, and the processing of Canada's natural resources in the country. Starr explained these resources must be developed and processed in Canada to provide more opportunities for the young people of the country. He described the Conservative Party as a party of vision and of young men dedicated to improving the status of the working man in Canada.[11]

---

6. Ibid., January 21, 1958.
7. Ibid., February 22, 1958.
8. Ibid.
9. Ibid., March 20, 1958.
10. Ibid., March 6, 1958.
11. Ibid., April 23, 1958.

Figure 6.1 An original editorial cartoon depicting Diefenbaker as a father figure leading his "family" of ministers as dark "unemployment" and "recession" clouds follow behind them. Library and Archives Canada, Mikan 2889643.

Figure 6.2 An original editorial cartoon depicting a blind Diefenbaker standing before a rapidly rising unemployment graph while Labour Minister Starr looks into a crystal ball to predict its improvement. Library and Archives Canada, Mikan 2889651.

In Oshawa and across Canada, Starr campaigned as a representative of the "average citizen" in Ottawa and pointed to his record in shaping policies that had lowered income taxes, increased pensions, and improved unemployment-insurance measures.[12] During the election campaign, Starr was one of the most popular speakers in the Conservative Party. On one campaign trip alone, Starr made thirty-five speeches in fourteen days and often attended up to five meetings a day.

On February 24, 1958, Starr and Diefenbaker met in Ottawa with Mykola Livytsky, chairman of the executive committee of the Ukrainian National Council (Ukrainian government-in-exile). This meeting was widely reported in the Ukrainian press and a photograph was taken with Livytsky, John Diefenbaker, Mike Starr and Professor Paul Yuzyk.[13] The *Ukrainskyi Visti* commented that Mr. Livytsky's reception in Ottawa ". . . was stated to have included all the formalities of the reception of a head of state."[14]

Encouraged by Starr's political success, some members of the Ukrainian community made a determined effort to take an active role in the 1958 federal election campaign. For many of the post-war immigrants who recently received Canadian citizenship, it was their first experience with Canadian democracy. Starr assisted in bringing together over two hundred representatives of Toronto Ukrainian organizations at the Lord Simcoe Hotel for a weekend. The meeting was sponsored by the Ukrainian Canadian Committee to

---

12. Ibid., March 8, 1958.
13. LAC, Photo PA122226, February 24, 1958.
14. *Press Digest*, Vol. 14, No. 4, April 1958.

Figure 6.3 Visit of Mykola Levyckyj, Prime Minister of the Ukrainian government-in-exile, with Prime Minister John G. Diefenbaker and Minister of Labour Michael Starr, accompanied by Professor Paul Yuzyk, on Parliament Hill, February 24, 1958. Library and Archives Canada, PA-122226.

encourage a greater participation by Ukrainian Canadians in the Canadian political process.[15]

During the 1958 federal election campaign, Starr travelled across the Prairie provinces by car campaigning in the northern rural settlements and visiting old Ukrainian pioneer communities which had never seen a federal cabinet minister. In these small villages, the women cooked all morning to prepare a huge luncheon for Starr. When he spoke to them in English there was often little or no reaction from the audience. But when he spoke in Ukrainian there was an immediate and emotional response. At Vita, Manitoba, Canora, Saskatchewan, and Smoky Lake, Alberta, and other small towns, old pioneers stood at the back of the packed community halls with tears in their eyes as Starr spoke to them in Ukrainian.[16] A few old Ukrainian pioneers later came to Starr and told him that they could now rest in peace because there was a federal cabinet minister of Ukrainian descent. One of the dreams that the early Ukrainian pioneers brought with them—political freedom—had been realized. Starr was genuinely thrilled to meet with the old Ukrainian pioneers, many of whom came to Canada at the same time as his

---

15. *Toronto Telegram*, March 4, 1958.
16. Thomas Van Dusen, *The Chief*, McGraw-Hill Company Limited, 1968, p. 29.

parents and from the same part of western Ukraine. Starr, through his personal campaigning, was able to help elect several prairie Conservative candidates. He even helped elect a non-Ukrainian candidate in a predominantly Ukrainian riding whose political opponent was Ukrainian.

On his return to Oshawa, Starr thanked his local organization for the work done on his behalf during his absence. Although he spent only four days in the riding prior to election day, Starr hoped people didn't feel he was neglecting his own constituents. To remind them of his commitment to Oshawa, Starr kept repeating his traditional slogan, "Never have I refused to accept any problem of any individual or group in the Ontario riding and not done all in my power to solve it."

On April 1, 1958, the Progressive Conservatives won 208 of the 265 House of Commons seats, the largest election victory in the history of Canada's Parliament to that time. It was a complete electoral sweep based primarily on Diefenbaker's emotional appeal to the electorate. In Oshawa, the votes were distributed as follows:[17]

Candidate	*Party*	*Votes*	*Votes (%)*
Michael Starr	PC	26,887	58.44%
Dr. Claude Vipond	Lib.	10,848	23.58%
John Brady	CCF	8,023	17.44%
Helge Neilson	Ind.	248	0.54%

Starr won with the biggest majority in the history of the Ontario riding. Even though he was part of a landslide victory, Starr felt that he won this election because ". . . I did my best to serve the people of the Riding individually and collectively and I guess they recognized that fact." On election night, Starr led over 200 cars in a horn-blowing motor cavalcade throughout the riding. The cars were stopped several times when friends and supporters pulled him from the car, hugged and slapped him on the back and hoisted him on their shoulders. Cliff Pilkey, President of Oshawa's UAW Local 222 stated, "Although Starr knows virtually nothing about the labour movement in Canada, he's got a dynamic personality. It's the personality that won him the election." Dr. Vipond, the Liberal candidate, concluded, "He never antagonizes anyone because he doesn't have a strong conviction about anything. He's so damn equal he doesn't arouse anyone. I firmly predict he won't be a member of the cabinet in the next election."

The local press acknowledged Starr's tremendous victory was due to his personal popularity and the prestige he gained as a cabinet minister; constituents, too, recognized his sincerity and diligence as a Member of Parliament and Minister of Labour. Starr's personal victory was also part of the great Conservative landslide that swept across the country.[18] Soon after the election, Starr repeated his promise to the electorate:

> I will still be Mike Starr to all the people of Ontario Riding. My obligation is to every individual, to every group in this Riding, not alone to those who support my political

---
17. *Twenty-Fourth General Election 1958, Report of the Chief Electoral Officer*, Queen's Printer, Ottawa, 1959, p. 139.
18. *Daily Times Gazette*, April 2, 1958.

theories. I want to repeat what I said on this very platform last June when I was re-elected and that is that I want you people to bring your problems to me if you think I can help in any way.[19]

---

19. Ibid., April 1, 1958.

Chapter 7
Minister of Labour, 1958

Mike Starr's tenure as Minister of Labour was marked by numerous complex problems competing simultaneously for his attention and demanding immediate action. Labour unions, the unemployed, ethnocultural groups and constituents from his riding of Ontario filled his daily agenda. Starr had to deal with these and other issues and also to promote and defend his policies at every opportunity across the country, in his own riding and, especially, in the House of Commons.

Starr's first month after the election began with his attempts to deal with the growing labour problems. His efforts to find practical solutions to the national labour problems were based on his own experiences in municipal politics, his personal political philosophy and his understanding of Progressive Conservative policies regarding these issues. Preventing national strikes was directly related to the problem of reducing unemployment.

In April 1958, the unemployed numbered 522,000 and constituted 10.6 per cent of the national labour force. That same month, Starr addressed the Canadian Labour Congress convention in Winnipeg about rising levels of unemployment. Starr told delegates he planned as soon as possible to bring together representatives of labour, industry, commerce and government to obtain their advice and suggestions regarding seasonal unemployment in Canada. He wanted to reach agreements through the mutual co-operation of labour and capital. Starr said:

> To give you some idea of my approach in these matters I would refer you to the words of a great American president, Abraham Lincoln, "Labour is prior to and independent of capital. Capital is only the fruit of labour and could never have existed if labour had not first existed. Labour is the superior of capital and deserves much the greater consideration. Capital has its rights which are as worthy of protection as any other rights. Nor is it denied that there is and probably will always will be a relation between Labour and Capital producing mutual benefits." My own view is that Labour of course cannot function without capital and capital cannot function without Labour. . . . In Canada we have managed to maintain a balance between Labour and Management that has greatly contributed to our steadily increasing standard of living. . . . In the interests of both Capital and Labour, it is essential that the balance continue to be maintained. It is essential that both Labour and Management, in their mutual concerns, take a large view of problems and endeavour thereby to arrive at solutions consistent with the greatest good of the greatest number.[1]

Starr also stressed his own personal commitment to his portfolio, telling delegates

---
1. *Canadian Labour*, May 1958.

> When I accepted this job of Minister of Labour for Canada it was my hope that I might be able to do a good job. In fact, I wanted to be as good a Minister of Labour as we have ever had. I am not prepared to say, after ten months that I have carried out that wish—but I will say that I can only do so with your help and cooperation. I hope that I can count on this and assure you that you can count on mine at all times.[2]

However, the CLC decided to seek other solutions to Canadian social and political problems. Perhaps the most important motion adopted by the convention was a resolution to form a new political party. The delegates voted for

> a fundamental realignment of political forces in Canada in . . . a broadly based people's political movement which embraces the CCF, the labour movement, farmer organizations, professional people and other liberally minded persons interested in basic social reform and reconstruction through our parliamentary system of government.[3]

The 1958 election had reduced the CCF to eight seats in the House of Commons, so they readily accepted this proposal. A National Committee for the New Party was formed, sponsored by the CLC and the CCF. Stanley Knowles was appointed to the position of executive vice-president of the CLC. As a leading CCF member, his main task was the implementation of the CLC resolution on the formation of the new party. This new political party based on social-democratic principles eventually became an alliance of organized labour, the old CCF and new party clubs. The organization of this new political party stimulated the growing political involvement of Canadian unions during the years 1958–1961 independent of some of the traditional connections to the Communist Party of Canada. These developments further complicated the national political and economic situation and had a definite impact on Starr's attempts to find permanent solutions to national labour problems and the unemployment crisis.

Among his early duties, Prime Minister Diefenbaker gave Starr responsibility to settle the deadlock between the Canadian Pacific Railway (CP) and the Brotherhood of Locomotive Firemen and Enginemen, a dispute involving 3,000 men. This strike reflected the fundamental technical changes transforming the economy during these years. In the attempt to make the railway more efficient, CP began to convert their engines from steam to diesel. Firemen were redundant on the new diesel engines but railway unions fought these changes to save their jobs. This dispute had been earlier referred to the Labour Department in April 1956.[4] A royal commission was appointed on January 17, 1957, to inquire into the continuing dispute between the union and CP. CP representatives alleged the union repudiated previous agreements, while the union delegates described the breakdown as a suspension of negotiations. The commission published its report in February 1958. After discussions were broken off on February 14, 1958, the CPR announced the issues was being referred to the Labour Minister "for appropriate action."

---

2. *The Labour Gazette*, June 15, 1958, p. 596; see also, *Canadian Labour*, May 1958.
3. Desmond Morton, *Social Democracy in Canada*, Toronto, 1977, p. 20.
4. *Department of Labour, Annual Report for the Fiscal Year Ended March 31, 1958*, Ottawa, 1958, p. 7.

During the evening of May 13, 1958, Starr was in his Parliament Hill office talking on the phone to Norris R. Crump, president of CP, and Jack Graham, chairman of the Brotherhood of Locomotive Firemen and Enginemen. Starr had little difficulty talking directly with either man; Crump had started his career as a sixteen-year-old labourer at CP yard in Revelstoke, British Columbia. As the conciliator, Starr made seventeen long-distance phone calls to the two men that evening. By phoning back and forth, Starr was able to personally settle this strike just after midnight.[5] The railway strike was finally over. Starr had a personal interest in settling this dispute because General Motors in Oshawa shipped the new automobiles by train and any strike would have interfered with the economy in his riding. The last CP steam locomotive finally went out of regular service in November 1960.

Some of industrial disputes were settled relatively quickly through Starr's efforts at conciliation. However, others deteriorated to the point where Starr was obliged to find a radical solution. The first session of the twenty-fourth Parliament opened on May 12, 1958. On May 16, the only ferry service between Vancouver Island and the British Columbia mainland was interrupted by a strike by the Seafarers International Union. The federal government became involved because the ferry service was part of the Canadian Pacific system. After two months, it became obvious that there could be no negotiated settlement. Starr attempted to arrange a settlement by inviting CPR President Norris R. Crump and Hal Banks, the Seafarers International Union leader, to his office. They negotiated all day and late into the night. However, neither would budge from their respective positions. In exasperation, Starr said that he would run the ferry himself.[6]

On July 23, Starr announced that the government would introduce the necessary legislation. The British Columbia Coast Steamship Service Act was passed on July 25, 1958 and would be effective no later than the thirtieth sitting day of the next session of Parliament. According to this act, an administration was required to carry on the business of the ferry company. Starr asked his cabinet colleagues who that administrator might be, and George Nowland jokingly proposed his sixty-five year old messenger. Starr understood that Nowland was joking, however he asked to interview this messenger. After speaking with him, Starr gave the man travel authority, made reservations at the Vancouver hotel from where he could see the ferry, and gave him a cheque for expenses. Starr also gave him a copy of the act in case anyone questioned his authority. The messenger then left for the west coast and began his term of ferry administration.

After several months, it became necessary to find a permanent solution. Starr contacted Norris Crump and had lunch with him at the Club Universitaire in Ottawa. Crump suggested that another lunch should be arranged between his vice-president and Hal Banks to discuss settling this dispute. This invitation, according to Starr, gave Banks some of the recognition that he always sought and eventually the labour dispute ended through Banks' intervention.[7] An agreement was eventually reached and contracts were signed effective February 1, 1959.[8]

---

5. Fraser Kelly, "Labour Minister Starr: Service at the Cleaner's Shop," *Saturday Night*, June 21, 1958.
6. LAC, MG 31, D 78, Vol. 16, Interview with Mike Starr, 19 October 1973, pp. 30-32.
7. Ibid.
8. H. L. Cadieux and G. Griffiths, *Dogwood Fleet, The Story of the British Columbia Ferry Authority From 1958*, p. 111.

As soon as cabinet ministers returned to Ottawa following the landslide election victory, Starr had to deal with the national unemployment problem. This economic, social and political problem was essentially a double one—to find work for the unemployed and to provide adequate benefits while they were unemployed. In May 1958, Bill C-9 was passed in the House to provide a temporary six-week extension of seasonal benefits under the Unemployment Insurance Act. During the parliamentary debates on this bill, Liberal MP Jack Pickersgill criticized Diefenbaker about statements made during the election campaign: Pickersgill quoted from a *Montreal Star* article of March 5, 1958, reporting on a speech in which Diefenbaker said that "As long as I am Prime Minister, this government will not rest while one Canadian remains out of work. No one will be allowed to suffer."[9] In reply, Starr said ". . . this government did not intend to bring in this measure as one putting an end to unemployment. It was brought in to help in a situation which has been serious and which we admit had been serious. It was brought in to help those who find themselves affected by this situation to tide over the period of time before employment in Canada is at its highest peak . . . ."[10] Louis-Joseph Pigeon, a Conservative Member of Parliament from Quebec, congratulated Starr for introducing this measure. He added, "The difference between this government and the administration led by honourable friends from the opposition is that the Minister of Labour is more readily able to cope with an emergency or to recognize when an amendment to the Unemployment Insurance Act is in order."[11]

Early in his tenure as minister, Starr developed a practical and methodical approach to his work. Since he had worked in a factory office for over twenty years, he quickly became familiar with office procedures in the public-service environment. Among his staff, he constantly emphasized teamwork. Starr was particularly fortunate to have Thomas Van Dusen work for him as an executive assistant. Van Dusen had been born in Ottawa, grew up in Gracefield, Quebec, and graduated from the University of Ottawa. He wrote for the *Ottawa Journal* from the Parliamentary Press Gallery from 1946 to 1951 before becoming an information officer with the National Film Board from 1951 to 1956. He joined Starr's office in 1957. Van Dusen knew his way around Parliament Hill and had extensive contacts with politicians, public servants and reporters.[12]

Starr's average day was often up to fourteen hours long. He rose at 8:00 a.m. and walked from his room at the Lord Elgin Hotel to Parliament Hill, where he ate breakfast in the parliamentary cafeteria.[13] He then stopped at his office to read the mail and meet with visitors prior to entering the House at approximately 11:00 a.m. During the typical day, he met officials, attended cabinet and Treasury Board meetings, and studied numerous reports. On any given day he could also be meeting with the unemployed, businessmen seeking aid for factories in economically depressed areas, new immigrants, representatives of ethnocultural groups, and members of Parliament who were dealing with labour problems in their constituencies. After a long day, Starr returned to his room at the Lord Elgin Hotel and usually went to bed reading a newspaper or a departmental report.

---

9. *House of Commons Debates*, May 15, 1958, p. 106.
10. Ibid., p. 107.
11. Ibid., pp. 109-110.
12. The Thomas Van Dusen fonds is preserved at the Library and Archives Canada.
13. *Sudbury Star*, September 13, 1961.

In his daily work as Minister of Labour, Starr felt that on a more personal level, common sense and a thorough knowledge of labour conditions were more relevant than an academic background with years of theoretical study of economic problems. Starr did not feel he was at a disadvantage because he was the only member of Diefenbaker's cabinet who did not hold a university degree. Whenever this question was raised, Starr replied, "As a matter of fact, in a way it's an advantage. It helps me to understand the average person and how he thinks." Starr, however, did not neglect his own "academic studies" and spent all of his spare time reading reports and studying documents related to his responsibilities.[14]

Diefenbaker gloried in his position as prime minister and called cabinet meetings to suit his own schedule on Saturdays, Sundays and weekday evenings. During summer weekends, Diefenbaker called cabinet meetings at Harrington Lake (Lac Mousseau), the Prime Minister's summer residence in the Gatineau Hills, north of Ottawa. Starr, however, felt his duty as a minister and MP was also to maintain contact with his constituents; he left for Oshawa on weekends and typically did not stay in Ottawa. Also, Anne Starr liked Oshawa and did not want to move the family to Ottawa.[15] On Friday evenings, Starr would board the 11:40 p.m. train from Ottawa and arrive in Oshawa at 7:00 a.m. He would have breakfast and then visit his wife's dry-cleaning business on Simcoe Street South. On most Saturday mornings, Starr could be found at the dry-cleaning business, where he discussed local and national politics with visitors and customers. Constituents who wished to discuss their particular problems knew that Starr could be reached either at home or at the business. Anne would make appointments during the week for constituents who wished to see Mike during the weekend. He would do his best to make them feel relaxed and comfortable when they met with him.[16]

The Starrs gradually established an effective system to receive the constituents. On some days, there were over forty people waiting to discuss problems ranging from job requests to settling marriage disputes. Anne scheduled appointments during a one- or two-hour period on Saturday mornings, a system that proved effective for several reasons. The large numbers that gathered and waited outside his house impressed both the visitors and the passers-by. Individuals were obliged to briefly state their case to allow others the opportunity to meet Starr. Attempts were made to control the number of visitors with never-ending stories and those who came for a social visit. Also, Starr was able to meet with many constituents in the morning and this gave him more time with his family in the afternoon.

Starr was also visited in Oshawa by the Soviet defector Igor Gouzenko. He sought Starr's assistance in receiving increased financial support from the Canadian government. Gouzenko had defected from the Soviet Embassy in late 1945 and lived in continual fear of Soviet agents. Thus he concealed his travel arrangements: when Gouzenko requested to meet Starr, he phoned Starr to meet him at the Oshawa bus station at a certain time. Starr waited, but at the appointed time there was no sign of Gouzenko. After another phone call, Gouzenko said that the conditions were not right for a visit. Then, on a Sunday, there

---

14. Fraser Kelly, "Labour Minister Starr: Service at the Cleaner's Shop," *Saturday Night*, June 21, 1958, p. 39.
15. Thomas Van Dusen, *The Chief*, McGraw Hill Company of Canada Limited, 1968, p. 28.
16. Kelly, "Labour Minister Starr," p. 39.

was a knock at the door and Gouzenko introduced himself as "Mr. Brown." Gouzenko was not allowed to work for security reasons and he had made some unfortunate financial investments. With a growing family, he requested additional financial assistance. With Diefenbaker's approval, Starr was able to arrange a pension for Gouzenko. They became good friends and Gouzenko would make several visits to Starr in Oshawa.[17] Gouzenko held some strong opinions regarding the alleged spread of communist ideology in Canada. He would share his political opinions with Starr and they would discuss the recent events of the Cold War.

At home, Starr would relax by reading a novel or by watching a western on television. He attended Rotary Club meetings to meet "the boys" and talk with his friends and acquaintances. The Starrs were usually invited to most social functions, particularly Ukrainian weddings and anniversaries, in the Oshawa area during the weekends. They enjoyed attending these events to meet with old friends and acquaintances in general. At home, Starr dressed casually when he relaxed in his backyard, much like his neighbours. For recreation, Starr would play a few rounds of golf. On the golf course, he had the opportunity to meet with managers and executives from General Motors and other Oshawa factories and discuss current social and political issues. He also took advantage of these encounters to inquire about employment opportunities for some of his constituents. After a weekend in Oshawa, Starr would leave by the Sunday night train that arrived in Ottawa on Monday morning for another full week of work on Parliament Hill.[18] This schedule continued for most of Starr's political career.

During the first week of July 1958, Starr attended the 42nd Session of the International Labour Conference in Geneva, Switzerland. He spoke to delegates about Canada's legislation regarding collective bargaining. He said that this legislation established a procedure for employers to recognize the union representing the majority of their workers and for bargaining in good faith between parties. He explained that Canada's high average standard of living enabled the federal government to pay more attention to groups below the average—older workers, handicapped workers and minority groups. Starr also explained that the federal government normally provided information and statistics on various economic trends that the bargaining parties could take into consideration during their own deliberations. According to Starr, this approach provided a generally favourable economic climate.[19]

On his trip to Europe, Starr was accompanied by Anne and their daughter, Joan. They left for Geneva on June 7, 1958, and also visited London, Paris and Brussels. In Rome, Starr and his wife had an audience with Pope Pius XII. Starr was introduced to the pope as the Minister of Labour from Quebec and had to clarify that he was actually the Minister of Labour for all of Canada. A photograph of their meeting with the pope was printed in several Canadian newspapers. When questions were raised in the House about Starr's trip to Europe, the Hon. Howard C. Green, the acting Prime Minister, replied that "The

---

17. Len Scher, *The Un-Canadians, True Stories of the Blacklist Era*, Lester Publishing Limited, 1992, p. 8; *Oshawa/Whitby This Week*, October 28, 1987.
18. Kelly, "Labour Minister Starr," p. 40; see also, *Sudbury Star*, September 13, 1961.
19. *Labour Gazette*, July 15, 1958.

Minister of Labour has various duties and I think most fair-minded members of this House will agree that since his appointment he has done an excellent job as Minister."[20]

Starr's main problem throughout his tenure as Minister of Labour continued to be the unemployment situation and, more particularly, seasonal unemployment. Canadian economic dependence on resource-based industries had established a tradition of seasonal work that had become a serious economic obstacle in a modern industrial country. Although some Conservative Party strategists advised that the seasonal unemployment issue should be ignored, Starr acknowledged the seriousness of the situation and deliberately tackled the issue, proposing fundamental solutions in the Department of Labour. A major requirement towards a permanent solution was the need for a national consensus and unity of purpose regarding the definition and also the solution of the seasonal unemployment problem. In pursuit of this objective, the National Winter Employment Conference was held in Ottawa on July 14 and 15, 1958. Over one hundred representatives of provincial and municipal governments, national organizations, national labour unions, chambers of commerce and manufacturers associations participated in this conference.

Starr, who was chairman of this conference, emphasized the gravity of the situation and acknowledged he had been aware of this problem since the beginning of his municipal career. He said, "it was brought home to me more forcibly; not just in terms of economic slogans; but in terms of men and women out of work; of families suffering; of a deterioration in the standard of living; even of actual want."[21] Starr was not interested in economic theories because "in the end, all the theories resolve themselves in terms of people."[22] He hoped that this conference would produce "suggestions for practical and positive measures" to deal with the seasonal unemployment problem.[23] Prime Minister Diefenbaker attended this conference and made some opening remarks. Delegates agreed the federal government alone could not solve the seasonal unemployment problem but declared government should lead in providing financial incentives to create winter work. The result of this two-day conference was a report that recommended a municipal incentive program.[24]

Starr continued accepting invitations to speak to various ethnocultural groups. He was invited to speak at the thirty-seventh annual conference of the Macedonian Patriotic Organization of America and Canada, scheduled for August 17–18, 1958, in Toronto, home to the largest Macedonian community in North America.[25] The fact that one of his brothers-in-law was of Macedonian origin was another reason why Starr agreed to make this speech. Prior to the conference, Starr drafted a speech in English emphasizing his support for the oppressed nations of Central and Eastern Europe. He then sent a copy of this draft to the parish priest of the Saints Cyril and Methodius Church in Toronto for translation into Macedonian. Starr studied the translated speech carefully until he felt comfortable with the Macedonian pronunciation. At the conference, his speech in Macedonian was followed by

---

20. *House of Commons Debates*, July 1, 1958, p. 1797.
21. *National Winter Employment Conference, Ottawa, July 14 and 15, 1958, Summary of Proceedings*, Department of Labour, p. 6.
22. Ibid.
23. *House of Commons Debates*, February 13, 1959, p. 1018.
24. Ibid.
25. *Press Digest*, Vol. 14, No. 10, October 1958, p. 10.

stunned silence, then cheers and applause erupted from the more than 1,200 delegates.[26] The reaction to Starr's speech was immediate: the Embassy of Greece in Ottawa protested and a diplomatic representative visited Starr at his office attempting to persuade him to withdraw the speech, or at least a part of it. Starr refused and informed the Greek representative in Canada he could express his opinion on any matter of political interest to him. When Diefenbaker was informed of Starr's speech and the reaction of the Greek Embassy, the prime minister supported Starr in his opinions and positions in regards to the oppressed nations of Eastern Europe.

Some of Starr's legislative actions in Ottawa also had results in Oshawa. On April 24, 1958, Starr announced that a $500,000 housing project consisting of fifty units would be built in Oshawa. When Starr and about fifty guests were invited to the opening of the low-rental housing project on August 22, the hotel where they were supposed to dine was picketed by the hotel staff. Starr and the other guests, including Ontario Transport Minister Matthew Dymond and T. D. Thomas, the local CCF member of the provincial legislature, refused to cross the picket lines and the mayor of Oshawa, Lyman Gifford, took the guests to luncheon at a local drive-in restaurant.[27]

Starr spoke about the unemployment situation at the 1958 Labour Day luncheon at the Canadian National Exhibition in Toronto. He suggested the largest single reason for unemployment was the large increase in the Canadian labour force. A major solution was "more and more jobs," which meant developing and promoting Canadian manufacturing industries because that was where the wages were the highest. He emphasized that the aim of all economic expansion activities should be raising the standard of living. Starr repeated his belief that "[l]abour is not a commodity. It is men and women and their families."[28]

The first session of Parliament began on May 12, 1958 and ended on September 6, 1958. Starr also reached a notable landmark in his own personal life: on September 6, 1958, Mike and Anne celebrated their silver wedding anniversary with a dinner and dance at St. Gregory's Auditorium, one of the largest halls in Oshawa.

With the coming of winter, Starr began to seriously develop the program of encouraging winter work as a crucial part of the permanent solution to winter unemployment. Starr officially opened National Home Week on September 8, 1958, and brought his message personally to the Home Builders Association of Ottawa. He stressed the need to continue homebuilding activities into the winter months. He claimed that this program could provide employment directly and indirectly for 375,000 workers. He added that a new house would provide six months of work for two men on-site and three off-site. In addition, the family would purchase furnishings and equipment providing even more work.[29]

In September 1958, the unemployed numbered 271,000, approximately 5.4 per cent of the national labour force. In October 1958, federal government officials held a conference with representatives of the Canadian Federation of Mayors and Municipalities. At this conference, agreement was reached that some of the municipal incentive projects could be accomplished during the winter months providing the additional cost was offset by a

---

26. *Toronto Telegram*, August 18, 1958.
27. *Oshaworker*, September 4, 1958; *The Globe and Mail*, August 23, 1958.
28. *The Labour Gazette*, September 15, 1958.
29. *The Labour Gazette*, October 15, 1958.

contribution from the federal government. Starr prepared and pushed the Municipal Winter Works Incentive Program through cabinet and it was passed on October 27, 1958. Under the provisions of this program, the federal government reimbursed one half of the direct payroll cost of the municipality for projects that would normally not have been undertaken during the winter months. Although some of Starr's cabinet colleagues did not approve of the idea of spending federal funds to create employment, Starr persisted in implementing his programs. During this same period, Starr also proposed a National Development Act to coordinate the federal government's national policy but his proposal was not accepted. Instead, a committee was established to coordinate departmental initiatives.[30]

The year 1958 ended with many of the major labour and unemployment problems still largely unresolved. In December, the unemployed numbered 440,000, which constituted 8.7 per cent of the labour force. However, Canada was in a relatively better situation compared to the United States. The United States was also undergoing a major economic recession during this period and Canada, as the United States' major trading partner, was directly affected. In its January 5, 1959 issue, *Time* magazine included an article comparing the rates of the Canadian and United States economic recovery. *Time* reported that Canada had survived a difficult year largely through natural resilience and sensible hard work. In Canada, unemployment affected a smaller proportion of the working forces, except during winter months, than in the United States. Compared to the United States, the Canadian government had placed "more spending money in wage earners pockets with tax cuts, it increased social welfare payments and provided $43 million for the grain growers. In the biggest boom in history, 160,000 new homes were started, providing jobs directly for some 250,000 workers and touching off subsidiary booms in a dozen home-supply industries." During this period, house building benefitted from the arrival of immigrants from Italy who were talented tradesmen, especially in the field of concrete work. However, the growing introduction of power tools reduced the time and number of carpenters required to build a house.

The plans and procedures for the winter works program were prepared by the staff of the Department of Labour. One of the prominent architects of this program was George V. Haythorne, who began his career in the public service during the Second World War. After the war, he was involved in plans to recruit Polish veterans and other displaced persons from Europe to meet the labour shortages of those years. He was the director of the Economics and Research Branch of the Department of Labour, later assistant deputy minister and deputy minister under Starr. As director, Haythorne fell under suspicion of the RCMP regarding his political "reliability" because of his circle of friends and acquaintances in the 1930s when young intellectuals debated solutions to the Depression. His name and that of his wife continued to appear on RCMP lists for several years, but his friendship with Norman Robertson, then chairman of the Security Panel of the federal government, saved his career.[31]

---

30. Margaret Conrad, *George Nowlan, Maritime Conservative in National Politics*, University of Toronto Press, Toronto, pp. 986, 247.
31. Obituary, *Ottawa Citizen*, November 23, 2002; Emanuella Grinberg, "George Vickers Haythorne (1909-2002) Deputy Minister of Labour 'believed in social justice;'" *The Globe and Mail*, November 23, 2002; Reg Whitaker and Gary Marcuse, *Cold War Canada: The Making of a National Insecurity State, 1945–1957*, University of Toronto Press, Toronto, 1994, pp. 177–178.

Chapter 8
Minister of Labour, 1959

In the midst of these developments and other problems, especially in the battle against unemployment, Starr was confronted with a new and special problem. On December 29, 1958, the production of the regular programs at Radio-Canada, the Canadian Broadcasting Corporation's (CBC) French network, was halted. The French-language producers went on strike against the CBC, demanding recognition of their right to organize and recognition of their association as the producers' bargaining agent with the CBC. In effect, the CBC French-language producers in Montreal had gone on an illegal strike to establish the first executive union. The CBC management resisted this demand because it would have created an uncomfortable precedent. The Toronto English-language producers went on a sympathy strike for a brief time but then returned to work. The CBC French-language producers' strike committee appealed for public support.

On January 7, 1959, the producers made their first direct appeal to John Diefenbaker as Prime Minister and to Mike Starr as Minister of Labour. The first of a series of telegrams were sent to Starr requesting that the federal government intervene[1] because negotiations were deadlocked; he declined. The second session of Parliament opened on January 15, 1959, and the next day Starr explained his reasoning to the House. He said, ". . . it has not been customary nor is it contemplated by the Act that the Minister of Labour should intervene in representational disputes in view of the provisions of the Act."[2] Starr added that the producers' association had resorted to strike action to resolve a dispute on employee status and bargaining rights in place of taking action to resolve these issues in the manner provided for in the Industrial Relations and Disputes Investigations Act, namely by application and reference to the Canadian Labour Relations Board. In other words, Starr felt the producers were seeking to bypass existing procedures and were ignoring provisions in the existing legislation designed to settle disputes dealing with representation. Also, Starr felt that it was not the role of a minister to interfere in the affairs of the CBC, a Crown corporation. However, there was some dissention in cabinet because the Solicitor General Leon Balcer, supported the producers, as did many prominent religious, intellectual and cultural leaders from Quebec. Among the well-known authors, actors, journalists, university professors who came out to the picket lines in the dead of a Montreal winter to support the strikers were René Lévesque and Pierre Trudeau.[3]

---

1. Barbara J. Fairbairn, "The Gentlemen's Strike: The Radio-Canada Television Producers' Dispute, December 29, 1958 - March 9, 1959," MA thesis, Carleton University, 1982, p. 46; see also, Dale C. Thomson, *Jean Lesage and The Quiet Revolution*, Macmillan, Toronto, 1984, p. 86.
2. *House of Commons Debates*, January 16, 1959, p. 781.
3. Knowlton Nash, *The Microphone Wars, A History of Triumph and Betrayal at the CBC,* McClelland and Stewart, Toronto, 1994, p. 281.

To the producers, it was an urgent matter since the French-language population was left without any television programs—there were no French-language private television networks at this time—and it was felt that they would turn more and more to the English-language stations. If this situation continued, some of the more nationalist producers feared that they would lose an important battle in the centuries-old struggle to preserve French language and culture in Quebec.

A large demonstration was organized in Ottawa on January 27, 1959, to support the producers in their strike. A delegation from the demonstrators, including René Lévesque, met with Starr and other cabinet ministers. Starr felt that there was little he could do by intervening directly in the strike. He was generally in favour of the government appointing a mediator if both sides requested one. Although Starr sympathized with producers, he could not commit himself entirely to their cause. He felt that he had to deal with more important issues. He was more concerned with getting unemployed people back to work and helping ordinary Canadians with "bread and butter" issues. The producers, most of whom were middle-class and well-educated, did not particularly strike Starr as being in a desperate personal situation and requiring his direct and immediate intervention.

On February 6, 1959, Liberal MP Lionel Chevrier formally asked the Minister of Labour to intervene in the dispute. Chevrier told the House ". . . the Minister of Labour has a great responsibility too but he will do nothing. He sits there on the fence like a mugwump, with his mug on one side and his wump on the other."[4] As the debate became more heated, Starr left the chamber. René Lévesque in particular was annoyed at the lack of federal government action. He felt the strike would have been immediately settled had the English-language network gone on strike. He was instrumental in turning the labour conflict into a "language and culture" struggle with the French Canadians on one side and the CBC management and the Diefenbaker government on the other side. Lévesque felt Diefenbaker, Starr and the other members of the Conservative government did not understand the special situation in Quebec. Lévesque said, "What really burnt me up was that Starr not only did not understand one word of French but did not know what the French network represented."[5]

In Montreal, a picket line confrontation between 1,000 picketers and 200 police officers in front of the CBC Montreal building on Dorchester Boulevard resulted in a riot; twenty-nine people were arrested, including René Lévesque and Jean Marchand, a trade unionist and future MP.[6] The incident convinced the federal government that a politically expedient resolution to this strike had to be arranged as soon as possible. On March 9, 1959, a compromise back-to-work agreement was signed and the strike ended; producers returned to work but the conflict continued. In late 1959, an arbitrator was appointed to settle the dispute. In the end, producers won their demands and Lévesque emerged as a high-profile nationalist and activist intellectual, contributing to his entry into politics, first with the Liberal Party of Quebec, and then with the Parti Quebecois. René Lévesque viewed this

---

4. *House of Commons Debates*, February 6, 1959.
5. Gerard Pelletier, *Les Années d'Impatience, 1950-1960*, Editions Internationales, Alain Stanké, 1983, pp. 304, 309; see also, "Comment René Lévesque est devenu independantiste," *Le Magazine Maclean*, Fevrier, 1969.
6. Nash, *The Microphone Wars,*, p. 286.

strike as a national issue for French Canadians and interpreted this struggle as a question of national survival, a fundamental theme in Quebecois history and politics. Starr, on the other hand, tended to view this dispute between the French producers and the CBC as a regional and provincial issue, not significantly different from many other labour actions.

With the opening of the second session of Parliament on January 15, Starr had to face another series of reports about high unemployment by the Bureau of Statistics and the inevitable barrage of opposition questions in the House. The intensity of the debates increased with reports of higher rates of unemployment. The opposition insisted on comparing current employment rates with those of the previous Liberal administration. The Liberals were always probing to find weaknesses in the Diefenbaker government and focused on the unemployment problem in the hope that this debate would be followed by interested voters and, hopefully, influence future elections. Starr became frustrated at the Liberals' persistent calls for remedial action against the chronic unemployment situation in the country. Not only did Starr defend his record in the House, he also went on the offensive and criticized his parliamentary opponents, Paul Martin in particular. Starr asked why Martin did not do anything to help the unemployment in his own city of Windsor, where the unemployed numbered over 12,000 people.[7] Paul Martin regularly used statistics from the Dominion Bureau of Statistics to question the government's actions or apparent lack of action. Starr replied that much of these claims were from "Martin's Bureau of Statistics."[8] These confrontations between Starr and Martin resulted in long and complex debates in the House on labour and unemployment that became a regular feature of Starr's years as Minister of Labour. Starr defended the federal government policies of direct involvement to promote employment. Starr said, ". . . this is a field in which the federal government has never before participated. Its participation is an indication that the government is concerned about unemployment and that we are trying to do something."[9]

Letters of complaint to Starr brought immediate action. He personally phoned local offices and instructed unemployment insurance officials to involve themselves directly in particular cases. In his view, the processing of unemployment benefits should be the secondary priority. Starr toured unemployment offices across Canada to obtain a personal experience of their operations. Some offices in dingy, dirty and rundown locations were replaced within several months by bright new offices.[10] In Oshawa, the unemployment office was on Simcoe Street, a short walking distance from his home on Olive Avenue. In February 1959, a lone picketer was marching up and down on Parliament Hill parading a signboard "Wanted—a job, any job." Starr saw this picketer from his office window and phoned the Ottawa offices of the National Employment Service, which sent a car to Parliament Hill to pick up the picketer. The car took him back to the employment office and had him placed in a job as a handyman within thirty minutes.[11]

---

7. *House of Commons Debates*, Session 1959, Vol. I, January 22, 1959, pp. 186–191.
8. Ibid., January 27, 1959, p. 385; *Ottawa Journal*, January 22, 1959; see also, Paul Martin, *A Very Public Life, So Many Worlds*, Deneau, Toronto, 1985, pp. 336–337.
9. *House of Commons Debates*, Session 1959, Vol. I, February 13, 1959, p. 1019.
10. Thomas Van Dusen, *The Chief*, McGraw-Hill, 1968, p. 34.
11. *Ottawa Journal*, February 28, 1959.

Figure 8.1 John Diefenbaker with Frank Hall, Stanley Knowles (standing), Claude Jodoin (seated left) and Minister of Labour Mike Starr (seated right) in the prime minister's office. Image: University of Saskatchewan, University Archival Special Collection.

In the House of Commons, Starr's efforts to cope with the unemployment problem was met with mixed reaction by some members of his own party and especially by the opposition parties. During one of the debates on the unemployment problem in the House, Frank Howard, a CCF Member of Parliament, representing the riding of Skeena in British Columbia, said on February 17, 1959:

> The Minister also made reference to the planning which is necessary . . . I know that the Minister basically, deep down inside himself is a sort of socialist, if I may put it that way. He is a socialist-minded person, but there are too many arch-Tories in the Cabinet and he cannot get his point of view across.[12]

During his tenure as Minister of Labour, Starr was regularly the target of political attacks, including some that originated from his home riding. During this period, small European and American cars were being imported to Canada and these cars quickly became popular with the consumers. The trend toward smaller cars was seen by the automotive unions as a threat to jobs. Clifford Pilkey, president of the UAW Local 222 in Oshawa, said that any crisis which may arise in the Canadian auto industry due to the importation of small cars

---
12. *House of Commons Debates*, Session 1959, Vol. 8, p. 1098.

would be blamed on the Conservative government. Pilkey further criticized Starr for turning down an invitation to attend two mass union-membership meetings to discuss the impact of small cars on the Canadian market. Starr had replied in a telegram that he would appreciate a report on the outcome of these meetings. Pilkey added, "We feel it was Mr. Starr's duty to attend our meetings so he could meet the situation first hand. Surely nothing is more important than looking after his own constituents in Ontario Riding."[13]

The cancellation of the Avro Arrow project on February 20, 1959, was another political decision by the Diefenbaker government that resulted in political repercussions for decades. The decision to cancel this project had been debated by the previous Liberal government from the early 1950s and the debate continued with the election of the Conservative government. This aircraft contained the most modern electronics and weapons systems, and some of the equipment was still being developed as the plane was being built and assembled. The jet interceptor was considered one of the most advanced fighter aircraft in the world at that time. However, the cost to build this plane increased enormously and claimed a larger portion of the budget of the Department of National Defence and the larger federal government budget. Plans to sell the Avro Arrow to the United States and Britain were initially optimistic but, due to domestic politics, faded away. There was a strong reluctance by the United States to acquire military weapons from foreign countries and there was a suspicion that they did not want competition in the area of high-performance aircraft.[14] Starr visited the factories where the Avro Arrow was being built but left with some doubts about the project. He noticed that some highly paid experts and specialists had to be flown in from England to work on the project, and their work consisted mostly of wandering about the plant with clipboards. With the national unemployment situation as a high priority, Starr realized that a difficult decision had to be made regarding the financial priorities of the cabinet. The Avro Arrow project was cancelled.

The Avro Canada Ltd. laid off 14,000 workers from its factories in Toronto in one day and they flooded into the local unemployment offices. This caused a strong and negative reaction in the Canadian press especially in the Toronto area and the Diefenbaker government was severely criticized. Starr suggested the Avro company "was adopting a vindictive attitude and that in their layoffs, they were going far beyond what was necessary."[15] As a result, many skilled engineers and scientists left Canada and went to work for the space program in the United States. When the cancellation of the Avro Arrow program unleashed a storm of protest, the Ukrainian newspaper *Vilne Slovo* claimed editorially that the overwhelming majority of Ukrainians supported the government's decision to terminate the Avro Arrow program. It was perceived as a minor problem "which could undoubtedly be solved by Prime Minister Diefenbaker and the Federal Minister of Labour."[16] The Avro

---

13. LAC, Michael Starr Papers, MG 32, B 15, Vol. 7, File 2, Scrapbook, March 3, 1959.
14. Thirty years later, it was rumoured that the production of an Israeli jet fighter suffered the same fate for the same reasons. Hugh Schofield, "Israel scraps production of high-tech fighter plane," *The Globe and Mail*, August 31, 1987; Gregory Ip, "Pressure from U.S. suggested in memo on fate of Arrow," *The Globe and Mail*, November 21, 1988.
15. Quoted in Denis Smith, *Rogue Tory, The Life and Legend of John G. Diefenbaker*, Macfarlane Walter and Ross, Toronto, 1995, p. 308.
16. LAC, Michael Starr Papers, MG 32, B 15, Vol. 7, File 2, Scrapbook, April 1959, Vol. 15, No. 4.

Arrow story grew to reach mythical proportions and the aircraft acquired a core of supporters that perpetuated its memory for many more decades.[17]

The Newfoundland loggers' strike began on December 31, 1958. The strike was called because the Newfoundland Loggers' Association (NLA) was perceived by some of its members as ineffective in obtaining higher wages and better working conditions for the loggers. The International Woodworkers of America (IWA) was invited to represent the loggers and began to enrol loggers despite opposition from the NLA. According to Premier Joey Smallwood, this rivalry was actually a "war."[18] A strike was called by the IWA and continued for six weeks. Premier Smallwood intervened in this strike because he felt that it was damaging the Newfoundland economy and blamed the IWA. There was also suspicion that the leadership of the IWA was pro-Communist. The IWA appealed to the International Labour Organization, in Geneva, Switzerland, which then referred the matter to the Minister of Labour who then requested a statement from Premier Smallwood.[19] Smallwood had asked Diefenbaker for a royal commission to find out the facts regarding the strike, but Diefenbaker refused to appoint one. The Newfoundland legislature passed a resolution to decertify the IWA and this was passed unanimously. On March 9, 1959, a new union, the Newfoundland Brotherhood of Wood Workers, began contract talks with the Grand Falls Paper Company. In a confrontation with picketers on March 10, a policeman was struck and killed. Smallwood also had asked the federal government to provide additional RCMP reinforcements. This request was discussed in cabinet, but Diefenbaker refused to send additional police in the fear that this would aggravate the situation.[20] Eventually the strike was ended almost on the same terms originally proposed by the IWA.[21] Starr later wrote that the federal government did not disallow this legislation because this issue came under provincial jurisdiction and it was felt that the federal government should not interfere in that jurisdiction.[22]

On May 1, 1959, the federal government announced the appointment of A. F. MacArthur of Toronto as a member of the three-person Unemployment Insurance Commission, and the Canadian Labour Congress (CLC) immediately declared that it was withdrawing its commission advisors in protest. This action was widely publicized in the national press and frequent questions were asked by the opposition in the House. MacArthur was international representative for Canada of the Office Employees International Union, an affiliate of the CLC and a former president of the Ontario Federation of Labour. Claude Jodoin, president of the million-member CLC accused in a letter to Starr that the appointment was political. MacArthur had not been nominated by the congress. According to MacArthur, the opposition to his appointment by Claude Jodoin and the CLC was due to his disagreement with the new policy of the national labour union to support the emergence of a new political

---

17. Jeff Gray, "Replica of legendary fighter jet draws a crowd," *The Globe and Mail*, October 9, 2006; Philip Stamp, "The rousing lessons of the Avro Arrow," *The Globe and Mail*, July 15, 2017.
18. Joseph R. Smallwood, *I Chose Canada, The Memoirs of the Honourable Joseph R. Smallwood*, Macmillan of Canada, Toronto, 1973, p. 401.
19. Frederick W. Rowe, *The Smallwood Era*, McGraw-Hill Ryerson Ltd., Toronto, 1985, p. 188.
20. House of Commons Debates, March 16, 1959, p. 1959.
21. Smallwood, *I Chose Canada*, p. 410.
22. LAC, Canadian Labour Congress fonds, MG28 I103, Volume 323, File F-20, Newfoundland Loggers' Strike, 1959–60, 1968, n.d.; Letter January 25, 1968, M. Starr to Dr. Kwavnick.

party (the future New Democratic Party). Starr denied the charges of political patronage. He added that it was quite obvious that political considerations motivated the resignation of the three trade union representatives.[23] Starr, however, did not question or wish to limit unions despite criticism from some elements in the Conservative Party. Starr told the House of Commons that anyone who does not feel that unions are required in the twentieth century ". . . has got an 18th century mentality."[24]

Charles Lynch, a perceptive political observer and veteran journalist in Ottawa, summarized the dispute in a newspaper article in the *Ottawa Citizen* of May 2, 1959, entitled "Bitter Row Has Roots in Politics." He wrote, "Reliable informants say it indicates the government's intention to treat CLC leaders as officials of an opposition political party. The technique will be to bypass the CLC hierarchy and shoot directly for the support of the union members, tens of thousands of whom voted Conservative in last year's election . . . But as the new political party, to be formed by a marriage between the CCF and the CLC emerges in the coming months, Mr. Jodoin can expect the government's attitude to be that he is turning into a political leader, and will be treated accordingly."

Starr confirmed that the partisan political activities of the CLC leadership had an influence on their relations with the federal government. Starr said, "The labour leaders are losing their strength in their dealings with government because of that dual capacity of being labour leaders and politicians for the NDP."[25] The appointment of A. F. MacArthur became one among many other issues raised in the House by the opposition. Lester B. Pearson, the leader of the Liberal Party, said in the House, "If I criticize as I propose to do the policies of the Minister and of the Government, the Honourable Gentleman (Starr) will know that I have a high regard for the sincerity, the industry and the goodwill with which he approaches this subject . . . that is quite apart from the criticisms I may feel called upon to make." Hazen Argue, an NDP member agreed that Starr was ". . . a most genial, a most disarming person." He commended the Labour Minister's example to other government ministers. With these compliments, both proceed to criticize the government's labour policies. Starr's actions received notice not only in Canada but also in the United States. In Boston, the International Association of Personnel in Employment Security gave its highest award—the Citation of Merit—to Starr for his contribution to Canada's National Employment Service.[26]

The appointment of A. F. MacArthur resulted in a break of diplomatic relations between the CLC and the Conservative government. On May 15, Starr sent a letter to CLC president Claude Jodoin, asking for nominees to the Unemployment Insurance Advisory Committee. The two names proposed by the CLC were those of Andy Andras, CLC director of legislation and CLC Executive Vice-President Stanley H. Knowles. Andy Andras was appointed to the advisory committee but Knowles was not. Starr said, "Knowles was a politician. He wasn't acceptable because he was a political appointment for the NDP."[27] It was obvious

---

23. *Toronto Telegram*, May 1, 1959.
24. *Vancouver Sun*, May 20, 1959.
25. David Kwavnick, *Organized Labour and Pressure Politics: The Canadian Labour Congress, 1956–1968*, McGill-Queen's University Press, Montreal, 1972, p. 116.
26. *Toronto Star*, June 31, 1959.
27. Kwavnick, *Organized Labour and Pressure Politics*, p. 121.

to Starr and the other government leaders that the CLC was attempting to act as a partisan political group and at the same time claim the privileges of a non-partisan interest group. On July 3, a meeting was held between Diefenbaker and Starr and representatives of the CLC. An attempt was made to resume direct contact between the CLC and the federal government.

Unemployment-insurance benefits paid during the winter of 1958–59 drained the Unemployment Insurance Fund to the point that the commission was obliged to sell heavily from its portfolio of Canada bonds. During the first two years, the Unemployment Insurance Fund was depleted by $382 million. Starr guided the bill in the Commons that included extensive amendments to the Unemployment Insurance Act to increase the length of seasonal benefit periods and increase the number of benefit periods for which claimants could apply. The opposition immediately charged Starr with mismanagement of the Unemployment Insurance Fund and violation of the Unemployment Insurance Act. The Liberal speakers pressed this case for four days in the House; Donald Fleming and Starr defended their actions. Their defence was followed by a vote of 133 to 34 in favour of a second reading of the Unemployment Insurance Act amendments. During the debate the Liberals pointed to the rapid decline of the Unemployment Insurance Fund from $926,777,100 in 1956 to $496,251,000 on March 31, 1959. The Liberals accused the government of mismanagement, arguing that special seasonal benefits should have been paid out of the treasury rather than the fund.

The Conservatives introduced amendments increasing contributions by employers and employees by as much as thirty per cent in some cases, adding about 80,000 new wage earners to the insurance plan and lengthening the period for paying benefits from thirty-six to fifty-two weeks. Starr said that the fund was always intended to reduce hardships resulting from unemployment and it was used for exactly that purpose. Starr said, "Canadians will not suffer merely to keep actuarial tables intact."[28]

Paul Martin led the Liberal attacks on this legislation, questioning Starr's claims that the bill improved benefits. The long and acrimonious debates obliged Starr to cancel plans to attend a meeting of the International Labour Conference in Geneva. When the bill was examined by the Industrial Relations Committee of the House of Commons, those debates were equally unpleasant.

When the debating finally ended, Martin crossed the floor to tell Starr that his sarcastic comments were in no manner intended to be of a personal nature.[29] However, Starr commented on more than one occasion about the lack of cooperation from the opposition parties in reducing unemployment. Starr said,

> If we had from the members of the opposition the same cooperation and constructive and reasonable suggestions as we get from the provinces, municipalities, organizations, and individuals across this country who are endeavouring to cooperate with us to overcome and alleviate the situation, we would put thousands of people to work. But

---

28. Michael Starr Papers, MG 32, B 15, *The Mike Starr Story*, Vol. II.
29. Paul Martin, *A Very Public Life, So Many Worlds*, Vol. II, Deneau, Toronto, 1985, pp. 337–339. See also, *The Globe and Mail*, May 27, 1959, and *The Ottawa Journal*, May 30, 1959.

we are not getting that cooperation from the opposition. All we are getting is destructive criticism.[30]

He added that the actions taken had been effective within the existing government limits. He felt that the problem of unemployment was above politics.

During the summer of 1959, plans were made for the Municipal Incentives Program for the following winter. Learning from the lessons of 1958, the federal government did not wait until the coming of cold weather to announce an extension of the Municipal Winter Works Incentive Program. The municipalities now had enough time to prepare their plans and do their "homework." During the previous year, there was a degree of misunderstanding among some of the municipalities and those who could have benefitted from the program. Starr announced there would be another program in operation for the coming winter and he hoped that it would be an even bigger program. Within the Department of Labour, there was a strong belief that winters in Canada were a main cause of high unemployment in an economy so dependent upon the exploitation of natural resources. They believed the winter works program should become a permanent program of the Canadian federal government to break the tradition of seasonal work that dated back to Canada's colonial past.

When the Municipal Incentives Program was first announced in the fall of 1958, the Duplessis government in Quebec hesitated to implement the federal plan. As in the case of the federal educational grants, Quebec subscribed to the principle that the federal government should levy taxes and raise revenue only for purposes constitutionally within the federal areas of responsibility. However, Quebec municipal politicians who saw the effects of unemployment first hand were able to lobby their provincial government, and during the fall of 1959, the municipalities in Quebec were active participants in the federal program.[31]

Soon after the first session of Parliament ended in September 1958, Prime Minister Diefenbaker began to implement his policy regarding "unhyphenated Canadianism," which directly affected ethnocultural groups. A major achievement was Diefenbaker's introduction in the House of Commons of the Canadian Bill of Rights in October 1958 that sought to ensure that all Canadians were equal before the law. This was an enduring part of Diefenbaker's policy to eliminate the category of "second class citizenship." This bill of rights was the first step in the political evolution that led towards the eventual repatriation of the Canadian constitution.

As Minister of Labour, Starr authorized the publication of a reprint from the *Labour Gazette* for November 1958, one prepared for the tenth anniversary of the Universal Declaration of Human Rights. The booklet, entitled *Human Rights in Canada*, signified Starr's personal interest in the question of human rights not only in Canada but also in countries where the lack of human rights was a fundamental and permanent problem.

During this period, the Conservative Party sought to consolidate its support in the Ukrainian community through the establishment of a Ukrainian Conservative Club of

---
30. *House of Commons Debates*, Session 1959, Vol. I, p. 188.
31. LAC, Michael Starr Papers, MG 32, B 15, Vol. 8, File: Municipal Incentives Program, 1958-60, Press Clippings, p. 3.

Canada. The first would be based in Winnipeg but plans were made to establish similar clubs in Ukrainian communities across Canada. The aim was to discuss current Canadian and international problems and encourage active participation of Ukrainian Canadians in politics. The president of the Winnipeg club was Paul Yuzyk, a professor from the Slavic Studies Department at the University of Manitoba.[32] In March 1959, the appointment of John Hnatyshyn to the Senate was a personal triumph for the well-known Saskatchewan lawyer as well as recognition of the work and growing political influence of the Ukrainian Canadian community.[33]

Support for the Diefenbaker government was not unanimous in the Ukrainian community. The traditionally Liberal-supporting Ukrainian newspapers continued to raise questions on a number of issues. When the National Housing Act was discussed in Parliament, *Ukrainski Visti* (Ukrainian News) claimed that the Minister of Public Works had held that "we are living in a free enterprise economy and therefore we do not wish to set wages and control prices." This statement was viewed as a contradiction between the government's house-building program and the theory of a free enterprise economy "which does not provide state aid."[34] The Ukrainian pro-Communist organizations continued to raise the unemployment issue in their press.[35]

When Diefenbaker's campaign against hyphenated Canadianism proposed deleting the question dealing with a person's ethnic origins from the 1961 census questionnaires, the reaction from the Ukrainian press was negative. The Ukrainian-language newspaper *Kanadiiskyi Farmer* (Canadian Farmer) claimed that this proposal "greatly disturbed" Ukrainian Canadians. A delegation of the Ukrainian Canadian Committee met with Diefenbaker and members of cabinet, including Starr. The delegation stated that the UCC stood for the principle of integration of the various ethnocultural groups into the Canadian mosaic rather than the "melting pot" approach. The delegation was in favour of maintaining the question of a person's ethnic origins on the census forms as this information provided an excellent source of information on the composition of the Canadian population.[36] The delegation noted that one-third of Canada's population were other than English or French in origin and that this group of Canadians could receive substantial assistance from the Canada Council in maintaining and developing their cultural heritage. This request was submitted in the belief that Diefenbaker's policy against second-class citizenship extended to the Canada Council, which awarded grants to English and French Canadians to preserve and promote their cultural heritages.

This question was discussed by cabinet on January 5, 1959. Diefenbaker stated he personally preferred to have the question of ethnic origin omitted from the 1961 census. He said he found it difficult to see how the "bonds of unity and the development of the concept of one nation" can be promoted by perpetuating a census that emphasized the racial origins of groups. During the discussions, it was pointed out that the Ukrainian Canadian Committee and the French-Canadian groups among others preferred to retain

---

32. *Press Digest*, November 1958, Vol. 14, No. 11.
33. Ibid, March 1959, Vol. 15, No. 3.
34. Ibid, March 16–April 30, 1959, Vol. 15, No. 5.
35. *Ukrainske Zhyttia* (Ukrainian Life), January 28, 1959.
36. *Press Digest*, July 1–31, 1959, Vol. 15, No. 8.

Figure 8.2 Starr was always a supporter of the monarchy and in 1953 he recommended in the House of Commons that the federal government issue a coronation medallion to all school children to commemorate the coronation of Queen Elizabeth that year. This photograph of Starr and his wife greeting Queen Elizabeth upon her visit to Canada in 1959 was prominently displayed in Starr's home in Oshawa for all visitors to see.

the ethnic-origins question. The cabinet then agreed that the question regarding ethnic origin be retained for the 1961 census.[37]

East European ethnocultural groups were primarily and exclusively interested in one topic—Canada's relations with the Soviet Union. In May 1959, a delegation representing various ethnocultural groups from Eastern Europe visited Prime Minister Diefenbaker and Minister of Labour Michael Starr, to whom they presented a brief requesting, among other items, that the Canadian government not recognize the Communist East European regimes. In reply, the Prime Minister stated the West should strive for the freedom of all people and that he personally supported the struggle for the freedom of the "enslaved nations."[38] The national executive of the Ukrainian Canadian Committee sent an appeal to Diefenbaker requesting him to raise the question of Ukraine at the Commonwealth Conference of Prime Ministers. The appeal stated that if Commonwealth nations were so strongly opposed to all forms of discrimination they should collectively raise the problem of Ukraine, a member of the United Nations being exploited by "Moscow Tyrants."

The appointment of Howard Green as Secretary of State for External Affairs generated some criticism among ethnocultural communities. He was perceived as having little interest

---

37. LAC, RG2 A5a Volume LXVI, January 6, 1959.
38. *Press Digest*, May 1-31, 1959, Vol. 15, No. 6.

Figure 8.3 During the summer of 1959, Queen Elizabeth and Prince Philip toured Canada and Starr, as Minister of Labour, accompanied them for part of this tour. This photograph was also one of Starr's prized possessions and was prominently displayed in Starr's home in Oshawa. Image courtesy of Walter Kish.

in foreign affairs and would follow rather than lead in the making of Canadian foreign policy regarding the Soviet Union. The ethnocultural groups placed their faith in Diefenbaker and he did not disappoint them. Diefenbaker spoke at the Sixth Congress of the Ukrainian Canadian Committee, held in Winnipeg. Lester Pearson, leader of the Liberal opposition, also spoke to the delegates. In his speech, Diefenbaker stated that the "enslaved Ukraine has the sympathy of Canada in her struggle for liberation." This statement was described in the Ukrainian press as being of historic importance since it was the first time that the leader of a democratic country had officially taken such a stand.[39] Among the resolutions passed at the congress was a motion for the newly elected executive of the UCC to take the necessary steps in cooperation with the Ukrainian Congress Committee of America to call a world congress of free Ukrainians.[40]

During the summer of 1959, Queen Elizabeth and Prince Philip toured Canada. For Diefenbaker, a dedicated supporter of the monarchy, the royal tour was a proud and emotional event. Starr was appointed minister in waiting for the Queen for one week during this tour.

He flew to Sault Ste. Marie and he travelled on board the *HMS Britannia* with the Queen to Thunder Bay. His duty was to introduce local mayors and other local officials to the Queen. During this trip, Starr had the opportunity to discuss their families during a dinner party. A photograph taken with the Queen during this trip became one of Starr's treasured mementos.[41]

The ethnocultural groups, however, complained about the lack of their representatives from the guest list for a banquet given in Toronto in honour of the Queen.[42] Although Diefenbaker sought to eliminate second-class citizenship through legislation, one particular incident during the royal tour emphasized that, in practice, this would be a long and incomplete process. The ethnocultural newspapers accused royal tour organizers of practicing

---

39. Ibid. July 1-31, 1959, Vol. 15, No. 8.
40. Ibid.
41. *Oshawa News*, February 3, 1999.
42. *Press Digest*, June 1–30, 1959, Vol. 15, No. 7.

Figure 8.4 Michael Starr with Diefenbaker's cabinet and Queen Elizabeth and Prince Philip (1959). Image courtesy of Library and Archives Canada, Mikan 4314032.

discrimination. In Edmonton, a flower girl named Terry Bytskal was introduced to the Queen as Terry O'Brien, thereby perpetuating the image of Ukrainians as second-class citizens.[43]

During the summer Starr continued to attend various ethnocultural events to emphasize the interest of the Progressive Conservative Party in their participation in Canadian political life. The tenth meeting of Ukrainians from Canada and the United States was held in July in Toronto. This gathering was held in the Canadian National Exhibition grounds and was sponsored by the Canadian League for the Liberation of Ukraine. The gathering was attended by Mike Starr, Dr. J. Kucherepa, Arthur Maloney, Paul Hellyer, John Yaremko and Andrew Thompson.[44]

---

43. Ibid. August 1–31, 1959, Vol. 13, No. 9.
44. Ibid, July 1–31, 1959, Vol. 15, No. 8.

Chapter 9
Minister of Labour, 1960

When the House resumed sitting on January 14, 1960, it was soon obvious that the continuing unemployment problem had become the dominant issue in the political debates between the Conservatives and the opposition parties. In December 1959, there were 370,000 unemployed, constituting 7.2 per cent of the national labour force. The political parties sought to dominate the debates by arguing the accuracy of the monthly unemployment statistics. On one occasion, Starr, pointing at Paul Martin, claimed that the figures he cited on unemployment had been exaggerated and manipulated "by that man over there." Martin objected to the use of the term "manipulated" and stood by his privilege. The Speaker tried to diffuse the charged situation by reading from his dictionary that "manipulation" could also be interpreted as "to handle with skill."[1]

Despite the relatively large numbers of unemployed across Canada, Oshawa was experiencing an unprecedented period of prosperity. On January 29, 1960, Starr spoke in the House about the conditions in his riding since his appointment as Minister of Labour. Starr said:

> The people in my riding are earning more, spending more and saving more. Business generally is very good. Our population is increasing, particularly in our industrial areas of Oshawa, Whitby and Ajax. The population of the City of Oshawa has more than doubled in the past ten years. One thing of which we are especially proud in the city of Oshawa is that home ownership in that community where I have lived for 39 years is approximately 85 percent. . . . Because of the location of General Motors of Canada in Oshawa—which is known as the motor city of Canada—people from all over the Dominion flock to the area in order to secure jobs. The automobile industry in the past number of years has experienced its best years of productivity.[2]

Starr said that since becoming Minister of Labour, he had done his best to improve the lives and conditions of Canadian workers and he would continue to do so. The wishes and the desires of Canadian workers would always receive his consideration and his personal attention.[3]

In a radio broadcast on February 4, 1960, Starr optimistically declared the recession over and that the federal government's policies were boosting employment. He promised that further measures were planned to continue the growth in employment. Later Starr was

---

1. *House of Commons Debates*, January 19, 1960, p. 86.
2. Ibid., *Session 1960*, Vol. I, p. 511.
3. Ibid. pp. 517–518.

frequently reminded of his optimistic employment forecasts in the House by the Liberal opposition.[4]

During his trips across Canada, Starr continued condemning obstacles to employment such as racial and religious discrimination. He spoke in Sudbury during the annual Brotherhood Week to emphasize discrimination in the workplace was forbidden by law. Starr told the crowd that action would be taken when cases of discrimination were reported and, he added,

> Canada is a welding of many nations and creeds. Let us not forget that in this great country we are all minorities. We are a nation of minorities. But we are minorities learning to work together. There is no place in such a nation for intolerance. . . . No one is being asked to conform. No one is required to conform. Each makes his contribution in his own way, but they are not any the less Canadians for all that.

Starr claimed that Canada would achieve world recognition by establishing a moral leadership, by guaranteeing those customs and national differences that would enable all Canadians to contribute most richly from their own store of national cultures to the common heritage of all.[5] In this speech, Starr outlined his philosophy of multiculturalism; it was among the first recorded expressions of such a policy by a federal cabinet minister. Multiculturalism eventually was proclaimed as an official federal government policy by Prime Minister Pierre Trudeau in October 1971, and the Ukrainian community continues to be among the strongest supporters of this policy and its implementation.

Through his example, Starr encouraged other Ukrainian Canadians to enter politics. Mike Wladyka, who was a member of the Oshawa Ukrainian Professional and Businessmen's Club, was elected as alderman in Port Hope in December 1954. In January 1960, he was acclaimed as mayor of Port Hope and the club sent a telegram of congratulations.[6]

As Minister of Labour, Starr's proposals and projects to increase employment continued to meet with strong opposition from the Liberal Party in the House of Commons. On March 2, 1960, the opposition was criticizing the government's $15 million Municipal Winter Works Program. With the debate entering its sixth sitting day, Starr lost his patience. He charged opposition members with deliberately holding up the House business while not making any concrete alternative proposals to solve the unemployment problem.

Despite the general prosperity in Canada and the annual increases in the number of employed since 1956, there were also substantial yearly increases in unemployment as well. After February 1960, the increases in unemployment were even larger. In 1960, there were 446,000 unemployed, or 7.0 per cent of the workforce.[7] It became very obvious that unemployment, instead of fluctuating with the seasons, high in winter and low in summer, was now remaining relatively in the high figures. During 1960–61, the Liberals concentrated

---

4. J.W. Pickersgill, *The Road Back, By a Liberal in Opposition*, University of Toronto Press, Toronto, 1986, p. 91.
5. *Sudbury Star*, February 23, 1960.
6. Archives of Ontario, Ukrainian Professional and Business Club, Oshawa.
7. Statistics Canada, Labour Division, *Facts About the Unemployed 1960–1971*, Catalogue 71-520 Occasional, September 1971.

their efforts in the House to portray the Conservative Party in a definite negative role, hopefully reviving the party's image of the 1930s and the Depression. Every month there was the spectacle of Paul Martin rising in the House and asking Starr as Minister of Labour how many unemployed workers were seeking work. Martin asked this question on the same day as the Dominion Bureau of Statistics announced the unemployment statistics of the preceding month. Starr was obliged to announce in the House figures on the number of unemployed that were already known to the press and the public.

Within the Conservative Party, Starr would regularly encounter opposition from Donald Fleming, the Minister of Finance, in his attempts to aid the unemployed. In May 1960 Diefenbaker raised in cabinet the question of aid to Nova Scotia coal miners. Starr argued that unemployment was rising and something had to be done to reduce it. At this time, the number of unemployed across the country was over 580,000. Starr repeated that according to most Canadians, unemployment was the most serious national problem. Despite his appeals, Fleming delayed Diefenbaker's proposal to aid the Nova Scotia coal miners. Finally, on June 3, cabinet approved the renewal of an agreement with Nova Scotia and the coal mines.[8]

In the Ontario riding, Starr's popularity had reached the highest level of his political career. A journalist, Anthony Wright, wrote in *The Globe Magazine* "Today Starr probably could carry the riding if he campaigned from a hearse."[9] There were several improvements resulting from Starr's actions in Ottawa that were directly beneficial to Oshawa and the region. On June 9, 1960, for example, the federal government enacted the Oshawa Harbour Commission Act and administration of the Oshawa harbour by the Federal Department of Transport was transferred to the local governing body. By the end of 1963 extensive improvements had been made to the harbour and its facilities.

Starr's national prominence and his efforts on behalf of the Ukrainian community in Canada were appreciated by the community leaders and by most Canadians of Ukrainian descent. Starr earned the special appreciation of Michael Luchkovich, the first federal Member of Parliament of Ukrainian descent. In response to the article by Anthony Wright in *The Globe Magazine* of July 4, 1960, Luchkovich wrote ". . . the life history of Michael Starr in some respects reads like a fairy tale, so unbelievable are the real facts in his 'rags-to-riches' story, with truth being stranger than fiction." Luchkovich, who was fully aware of the difficulties and pressures of parliamentary life, accurately described Starr's historical role. He wrote,

> As for we Ukrainians we are justly proud of our Michael Starr. He is a real star in the Canadian political galaxy. We honour him as we in turn are honoured by him cognizant as we are to the fact that we are now the equal of any other ethnic group as we walk with dignity and are accepted with equality. As so it might be said that the saga of Ukrainian immigration has culminated in Michael Starr's high advancement. But this saga has by no means come to an end.[10]

---

8. Donald Fleming, *So Very Near: The Summit Years*, Vol. 2, pp. 222–225.
9. LAC, Progressive Conservative Party Collection, Vol. 79, Starr 1960-63, *The Globe Magazine*, June 4, 1960.
10. LAC, The Michael Starr Papers, MG 32, B 15, *The Mike Starr Story*, Vol. III, 1958-62, June 25, 1960; see also *Novyi Shliakh*, August 1, 1960.

In his attempts to cope with the nation's unemployment problems, Starr was concerned with increasing the efficiency of the services provided by the Department of Labour. Starr announced in the House,

> The administration of this department caused me some concern when I first took over my present responsibilities. Over the past two and a half to three years, I have endeavoured to help in any way I could to obtain the maximum possible service from this department and to see that the maximum possible service was rendered to all Canadians. To this end I have continuously emphasized the need of courtesy on the part of commission staffs.

Starr attempted to make every possible effort to provide better accommodation, to secure more qualified people and to enlist the cooperation of labour and industry in the general departmental administration.[11]

Throughout 1960 the unemployment situation in the country continued to be the most serious national problem and some economists were predicting a recession before the end of the year. Starr began to seek approval not only for a renewal but also an extension of the winter works program as early as June 10, 1960. Fleming, the Minister of Finance, was opposed to any announcements at that time because he felt that they might forecast a pessimistic prediction of the employment situation for the coming winter.

During the summer of 1960, the Department of Labour began planning an even more elaborate Municipal Winter Works Incentive Program for the winter of 1960–61. On July 12, 1960, cabinet approved an expansion of loan guidelines under the National Housing Act to boost winter housing construction. On July 23 the Prime Minister announced a new and expanded program for the winter of 1960–61. On the same day, Starr announced an increase from 50 per cent to 75 per cent in the federal government's contribution to the cost of training unemployed workers.

Prime Minister Diefenbaker was particularly concerned about the unemployment statistics that represented about 7 per cent of the labour force. On September 7, 1960, Diefenbaker appointed a cabinet committee headed by George Nowlan to study various proposals to stimulate the economy and expand employment opportunities. The members included George Hees, Alvin Hamilton, I. Waldo Montieth, David Walker and Starr. Fleming, as Minister of Finance, was not included on this committee and he threatened to resign from cabinet if he could not maintain responsibility of the federal government's fiscal policy.[12] On September 21, 1960, the federal government announced that the winter works program would begin on October 15, 1960, and, therefore, extend the effective period of the plan from six and a half months by advancing the opening date by six weeks.

Diefenbaker sincerely believed in promoting the political cause of the ethnocultural groups from Eastern Europe and rarely hesitated to denounce the Soviet Union and communism in general. In the minds of many Canadians from Eastern Europe, the Conservatives appeared more strongly anti-Communist than any of the other Canadian political parties. Diefenbaker fulfilled the wishes of the leadership of the ethnocultural groups by speaking

---

11. *House of Commons Debates*, July 28, 1960, p. 7147.
12. Fleming, *So Very Near: The Summit Years*, pp. 222–225.

before the United Nations on September 26, 1960 on the subject of the dismantling of the Soviet colonial empire. He said,

> I turn now to a subject dealt with at great length by the Chairman of the Council of Ministers of the USSR [Nikita Khrushchev], the subject of colonialism. He asked for and advocated a declaration at this session for "the complete and final elimination of colonial regimes." I think it would be generally agreed that, whatever the experience of the past, there can no longer be a relationship of master and servant anywhere in the world. He has spoken of colonial bondage, of exploitation and of foreign yokes. Those views uttered by the master of the major colonial power in the world today, followed the admission of fourteen new member nations to the United Nations—all of them former colonies . . . I pause to ask this question: How many human beings have been liberated by the USSR? Do we forget how one of the postwar colonies of the USSR sought to liberate itself four years ago, and with what results? I say that because these facts of history in the Commonwealth and other countries invite comparison with the domination over peoples and territories sometimes gained under the guise of liberation but always accompanied by the loss of political freedom. . . . What of Lithuania, Estonia, and Latvia? What of the freedom-loving Ukrainians and many other Eastern European peoples which I shall not name for fear of omitting some of them? . . . There can be no double standard in international affairs. I ask the Chairman of the Council of Ministers of the USSR to give to those nations under his domination the right of free elections—to give them the opportunity to determine the kind of government they want under genuinely free conditions. If those conclusions were what his words meant, for they must apply universally, then indeed there will be new action to carry out the obligations of the United Nations Charter; then indeed will there be new hope for all mankind. My hope is that those words of his will be universally acceptable and that he will give the lead towards their implementation here and now.[13]

In the "reference notes" file in the Diefenbaker fonds, there is the document "Russian Imperialism and Colonialism, Memorandum to the United Nations General Assembly XV Session, Submitted by Ukrainian Canadian Committee, September, 1960, Msgr. B. Kushnir, President and W. J. Sarchuk, General Secretary." Diefenbaker's speech had an immediate international impact and raised strong objections from the Soviet Union and, in Canada, from pro-Communist organizations and newspapers.[14] However, his speech produced a great wave of support and gratitude from the Canadian ethnocultural groups who traced their origins to Central and Eastern Europe. Reports about this speech were heard as far

---

13. LAC, The Hon. John G. Diefenbaker Fonds, (Microfilm Reel 9394), MG 01XII/B/372, United Nations, n.d., 1960–1962, p. 028860-028890, Address by the Right Honourable John G. Diefenbaker Q.C., Prime Minister of Canada to the General Assembly of the United Nations, New York City, September 26, 1960; see also, p. 028790-028785; B.T. Richardson, *Canada and Mr. Diefenbaker*, McClelland and Stewart, Limited, pp. 83–85; and H. Basil Robinson, *Diefenbaker's World, A Populist in Foreign Affairs*, University of Toronto Press, Toronto, pp. 151–156.
14. Ibid., p. 028899; see also, *Canadian Tribune*, October 10, November 28, 1960.

Figure 9.1 John Diefenbaker with Ellen Fairclough, William Hamilton, Gordon Churchill, Michael Starr and others in the Centre Block office. Seated: Ellen Fairclough (left) and John Diefenbaker (right). Standing, from left to right: Professor Paul Yuzyk, the Honourable William Hamilton, the Honourable Gordon Churchill, the Honourable Michael Starr, the Very Reverend S. W. Sawchuk, Monsignor Basil Kushnir, John Hnat Syrnick, and Wladimir Kossar. Image courtesy of the University of Saskatchewan, University Archival Special Collection.

away as the Siberian gulags and boosted the morale of the political prisoners.[15] Letters and telegrams of support flooded Diefenbaker's office.[16] The ethnocultural press, especially the Ukrainian-language press, praised Diefenbaker for this courageous act at the United Nations. This political gesture solidified the support of the ethnocultural groups, in particular the Ukrainian Canadians, for the Conservative Party for many more years.

His speech became a standard for the East European ethnocultural groups to evaluate other Canadian politicians in their commitment to denounce the Soviet Union. On October 30, 1960, Starr spoke at the Ukrainian National Federation Hall in Toronto where he said that he was proud that in Canada "... we can speak in defence of our brothers in Ukraine." He assured his audience, all Canadian citizens of Ukrainian descent, that he and other

---

15. When Cardinal Joseph Slipyj, a former Soviet gulag prisoner, met with Diefenbaker in October 1976 in Ottawa, he told Diefenbaker that his speech at the United Nations was the "... greatest moral support ever received by political prisoners in Soviet Russia," *The Globe and Mail*, October 29, 1976.
16. H. Basil Robinson, *Diefenbaker's World, A Populist in Foreign Affairs*, University of Toronto Press, Toronto, 1989, p. 154.

Figure 9.2 An editorial cartoon from September 9, 1960, entitled "Getting to the Bottom of the Matter," and depicting Mike Starr launching a boat christened "Winter Works Program." Library and Archives Canada, Mikan 28617262.

members of parliament did not miss any opportunity to raise the Ukrainian question. According to Starr, the freedom of Ukraine and the other nations under Soviet domination was the only path towards real peace in the world, one which would free people from the threat of nuclear war and catastrophe. He reminded the audience about Diefenbaker's speech at the United Nations and added that Diefenbaker voiced his sincere beliefs and Canadian government policy.[17]

Although Diefenbaker scored a remarkable political accomplishment on the international level, problems at home remained, and directly affected a larger proportion of Canada's population. On October 1, 1960, unemployment in Canada reached 7.6 per cent, the highest percentage to date in the postwar period. On October 6, 1960, the federal government announced a $100 million winter works program. Starr made a strong plea for increased cooperation and action from provincial and municipal governments and from industry and labour. He knew the serious unemployment problem could not be solved at any one level of government. Every accusation that Starr was not doing enough brought back memories of the Depression of the 1930s and its consequences.

---

17. *Homin Ukrainy* (Ukrainian Echo), November 5, 1960.

To initiate the implementation of this policy, a conference on unemployment was held on October 24–25, 1960, in Ottawa. Diefenbaker opened this conference with representatives of twenty-one national organizations offering solutions to the unemployment problems. At this conference were represented the Canadian Labour Congress, Canadian Bankers Association, Canadian Federation of Agriculture, Canadian Fisheries Council, Confederation of National Trade Unions (formerly the CTCC), Canadian Manufacturers Association and the Canadian Chamber of Commerce. The proposals ranged from long-range planning and public investment advocated by labour to conflicting suggestions from businessmen on tariffs and taxes.[18] The recommendations of this Conference eventually resulted in the proposal to establish the National Productivity Council modelled on the British Productivity Council formed in 1952. It was proposed that this Canadian National Productivity Council would have a $1 billion fund sufficient to stimulate primary and secondary industries. The twenty-five members of this council, appointed from business, labour, agriculture, education and civil services, were to coordinate the resources, manpower and manufacturing facilities of the country.[19]

Diefenbaker also made cabinet changes to deal with various problems: George Nowlan had already replaced Quebec Member of Parliament Pierre Sevigny as head of the cabinet committee on unemployment. Four new ministers were appointed, six were given new portfolios and two were retired. Starr was generally considered to be among the few "demonstrably capable ministers" and remained Minister of Labour.[20]

---

18. John T. Saywell, ed., *Canadian Annual Review for 1960*, University of Toronto Press, 1961, p. 61.
19. Productivity Committees were discussed and implemented in Canada since the 1930s and had some success in various industries during the Second World War and later. See P.S. McInnis, "Teamwork for Harmony: Labour-Management Production Committees and Postwar Settlement in Canada," *Canadian Historical Review*, September, 1996.
20. Denis Smith, *Rogue Tory, The Life and Legend of John G. Diefenbaker*, Macfarlane Walter and Ross, Toronto, 1995, p. 368.

Chapter 10
Minister of Labour, 1961

The fourth session of the twenty-fourth Parliament opened on November 17, 1960. The Diefenbaker government immediately became involved in a diplomatic controversy that was, no doubt, influenced by Diefenbaker's strident anti-Communist speech at the United Nations. Dr. John Kucherepa, Member of Parliament for High Park in Toronto, had been appointed head of the Canadian parliamentary delegation to the North Atlantic Treaty Organization (NATO) Parliamentarians Conference that met in Paris, November 19–26.[1] At this conference, Kucherepa introduced a resolution to ban the Communist Party in all NATO countries. He was supported by Arthur Maloney, Member of Parliament for Toronto Parkdale and Starr's parliamentary assistant since August 7, 1957. This proposal was met with opposition from some delegates from the United States and England and was eventually defeated.[2] The Ukrainian newspaper *Kanadiiskyi Farmer* (Canadian Farmer) reported that a representative of the Department of External Affairs said the two Progressive Conservative members had expressed their own personal views and not those of the Canadian federal government. This resolution was debated in the Ukrainian Canadian press, with some newspapers supporting the resolution while other newspapers, both pro- and anti-Communist, condemned it.[3] The debate influenced the almost total support of the East European ethnocultural groups for Diefenbaker's position at the United Nations and obliged some Ukrainian community leaders to question the sincerity of Diefenbaker's own policies on opposition to Soviet occupation of Central and Eastern Europe.

In Oshawa, the rivalry between the anti-Communist and pro-Communist groups continued, resulting in a confrontation later in the year when William Kashtan, executive secretary of the Communist Party of Canada, was invited to speak at the Ukrainian Labor Temple on Bloor Street. This meeting was organized by the Oshawa chapter of the Communist Party of Canada on October 15, 1961, and was open to the public but was disrupted by an anti-Communist group shouting down the speaker; the meeting ended in name-calling. A resolution was quickly drafted by a member of the anti-Communist group and read to cheers, calling for a condemnation of Russia, freedom for the subjugated nations and the prohibition of the Communist Party of Canada.[4]

A week after the opening of the parliamentary session, Starr launched a new campaign against unemployment. On November 25, he introduced the Technical and Vocational Training Assistance Act. He said in the House, "It is designed to undergird the government's programme

---

1. *Canadian Farmer*, November 14, 1960.
2. Ibid., November 28, 1960.
3. *Press Digest*, November 1960, Vol. 16, No. 12, p. 12, and January 1961, Vol. 17, No. 1, pp. 12–13, 18.
4. *The Globe and Mail*, October 16, 1961, "Reds shouted down at Oshawa Meeting."

Figure 10.1 In a 1961 cartoon entitled "Au Canada, le chômage à son plus haut niveau depuis 15 ans," a fire-breathing dragon, labeled after the title, attacks John Diefenbaker who pulls along Labour Minister Michael Starr. Image Library and Archives Canada, Mikan 2878448.

to increase employment and foster national development . . . the need for more training facilities . . . is further substantiated by the facts of the present unemployment situation."[5]

In the quest for a permanent solution to the unemployment problem, several groups and categories of unemployed were identified. In additional to seasonal workers and older workers, there were also the structurally unemployed who were poorly educated and unskilled labourers who lacked the necessary skills required in a modern industrial economy. This group could not be rapidly absorbed in a growing technical society without the necessary training and skills. Starr introduced the new legislation to deal with the problem on a permanent basis and also to improve vocational education.

The Technical and Vocational Training Assistance Act raised the federal contribution to provincial retraining programs from 50 per cent to 75 per cent of their cost for expenditures made before March 31, 1963. The act authorized a federal subsidy of 75 per cent of the capital costs incurred by a province in building facilities for technical and vocational training. In summary, the act was intended to assist the structurally unemployed through vocational and technical education and at the same time, the act provided a stimulus to the construction industry.

In November 1960, the government was again faced with national labour problems and was obliged to introduce back-to-work legislation. The national railway unions were threatening a general rail strike. The railways and the unions were unable to arrive at an agreement

---

5. *House of Commons Debates*, November 25, 1960, pp. 231–2.

Figure 10.2 "Don't Call Us, We'll Call You." An editorial cartoon dated May 11, 1961, depicting Labour Minister Michael Starr pushing away a group of men who demonstrate against their unemployment as Diefenbaker consults a crystal ball. Library and Archives Canada, Mikan 2861789.

and a strike was called for December 3, 1960. Attempts were made to postpone the strike until the Royal Commission on Transportation submitted its report on May 15, 1961. These attempts also failed and Starr was obliged to introduce a bill, the "Act to Provide for the Continuation of the Operation of Railways," which prohibited strikes before May 15, 1961. On November 30, 1960, the House debated the emergency legislation designed to prevent the strike. Starr stated during the debate that "The first effect of a strike at this time would be to throw out of work some 170,000 railway employees. This figure could be doubled by the resulting unemployment of those who depend upon the railways as a means of economic subsistence.... There is, first of all the primary consideration of public interest. This must rank first and foremost in the thinking of any responsible administration." Ten days before the deadline of May 15, 1961, the railways and the unions reached an agreement.[6] Again,

---

6. J. W. Pickersgill, *The Road Back, By a Liberal in Opposition*, University of Toronto Press, Toronto, 1986, pp. 40–42.

the functioning of the railways was crucial to the economy of Oshawa and the automobile industry.

On January 5, 1961, Starr extended special greetings to all Canadians, especially those of Eastern European descent celebrating Christmas on January 7, Starr said,

> I extend my very best wishes to all who will be observing the Festival of the Nativity according to the Julian Calendar whose age-old traditions are so closely linked to their religious and national heritage. As they enjoy the right to perpetuate the faith of their fathers, many Canadians on this festive occasion will find themselves thinking of friends and relatives in other countries of the world in which the rights of freedom of conscience and religious observance are discouraged or denied. I ask all Canadians to join the prayers of those who observe Christmas tomorrow for the speedy deliverance of millions of God-fearing men and women who find themselves on yet another Christmas Day under the yoke of alien rule and ideologies.[7]

During this period, Starr was continually busy in Ottawa and also across Canada. His schedule during the month of January 1961, for example, illustrates the extent of his travels and the range of his engagements. On January 11 he spoke at the opening of the new technical institute in Moose Jaw; on January 12 to a Ukrainian gathering in Hamilton, Ontario; on January 13 to magazine editors in Ottawa; on January 21 he addressed the Ukrainian Canadian Committee in Montreal; on January 23 the Winnipeg Chamber of Commerce; on January 27 the Vancouver Board of Trade; and on January 30 he opened the new UIC building in Edmonton.[8] At the local level, Starr was elected honourary president of the Ukrainian Professional and Businessmen's Club of Oshawa on April 10 that he helped establish in 1952.[9]

The Technical and Vocational Training Assistance Act had an important impact on Ontario, and especially on the political career of John Robarts. On March 28, 1961, Ontario agreed to accept the federal plan in principle. Robarts, as Minister of Education, phoned Starr in Ottawa on May 18 to inquire if his proposal for a high school with two vocational streams rather than one would qualify effectively as a vocational school. Starr replied positively that such vocational schools would fall within the terms of the act.[10] The Ontario Department of Education developed the so-called Robarts Plan of curriculum reform based on three separate streams within the high-school system: arts and science; science, technology and trades; business and commerce. The second and third streams were defined as vocational. The Robarts Plan was announced in August 1961 and received widespread support. With this federal financial support, 196 projects were initiated in the next fiscal year for new trades institutes, teacher's colleges and vocational schools. The Robarts Plan became very popular and the new education minister received most of the credit. His

---

7. LAC, Progressive Conservative Party, MG 28, IV 2, Vol. 317, General Correspondence, M. Starr, Labour, 1959–60, 1957–58.
8. LAC, Michael Starr Papers, MG 32, B 15, Vol. 4.
9. Archives of Ontario, Ukrainian Professional and Businessmen's Club, Oshawa.
10. A. K. McDougall, *John P. Robarts: His Life and Government*, University of Toronto Press, Toronto, pp. 55–57.

personal success was well timed because the announcement of the Robarts Plan coincided with the leadership race to succeed Leslie Frost as leader of the Progressive Conservative Party and Premier of Ontario.[11]

After the passage of the act, the Department of Labour approved projects with a total estimated cost of $332,829,844 during the first fiscal year of 1961–62. The new act had enabled the federal government to support the construction, expansion and equipping of 375 schools and institutions. The Department of Labour had to submit supplementary estimates twice during 1961 to meet the obligations for that year. Ontario received almost 70 per cent of the total.[12] The other provinces were also interested in benefitting from the new act. The Province of Quebec, however, lacked a department of education—and this would come only in 1964—a fact that greatly limited its ability to mobilize its planning resources. Also the province was waiting for the report of the Parent Royal Commission on Education and was uncertain of the future directions of their educational policy.[13] Quebec received only a small percentage of the grants received by Ontario and this difference gave rise to claims from Quebec for special arrangements due to the particular conditions in Quebec. On the whole, this program was instrumental in preparing the national groundwork for the establishment of the system of community colleges that during the 1960s added another career path to youth and workers.

In February 1961, unemployment reached 719,000 and this was 7.9 per cent of the national labour force on a seasonally adjusted basis and another postwar record. During the presentation of the Canadian Labour Congress memorandum to the government of February 1961, Starr appealed for the co-operation of the congress. Starr said, "We are doing everything we possibly can to remedy that situation [high unemployment]. We are not running away from it. We are not hiding. We are open to suggestions that may be made and your suggestions will be given careful study. But no single government is able to bring about an alleviation or solution of the problem of unemployment. It needs the cooperation of all three levels of government, industry and labour."[14] During March 9–10, 1961, the House discussed the economic recession. Starr defended the policies and programs of the federal government as a massive attack on unemployment that was more comprehensive than any comparable program in the United States.

Starr was also engaged in a verbal battle with the Liberal Member of Parliament Jack Pickersgill over the CBC television program "Close-Up" of March 7, 1961, regarding the case of Glen Exelby. This incident received national media attention and encouraged numerous questions and attacks against Starr by the Liberal opposition in the House.[15] Mr. Exelby, an unemployed salesman from Hamilton, Ontario, was interviewed on this CBC television program as an example of the unemployment situation among individuals in Canada. Starr,

---

11. Ibid., p. 55–57.
12. *Annual Report of the Department of Labour, 1961-62*, Ottawa, Queen's printer, 1963.
13. J. Stefan Dupré et al., *Federalism and Policy Development: The Case of Adult Occupation Training in Ontario*, University of Toronto Press, Toronto, 1973, pp. 18–19.
14. *Unemployment in Canada, Tables and Charts*, Dominion Bureau of Statistics, April, 1962, p. 7; David Kwavnick, *Organized Labour and Pressure Politics: The Canadian Labour Congress 1952–68*, McGill-Queen's University Press, Montreal, 1972, pp. 167–168.
15. *House of Commons Debates*, March 10, 1961, pp. 2854–2856.

anticipating questions from the Liberal opposition, arranged in cooperation with the House Speaker that a Conservative Member of Parliament from British Columbia raise the question of Mr. Exelby's case in the House. Starr was prepared and replied that Mr. Exelby was offered by the UIC in Hamilton a position as a foreman at a factory that he had turned down. When Starr took his seat in the House, the Conservative members pounded their desks with approval. This revelation by Starr caused a sensation in Parliament. According to the information presented, Mr. Exelby had postponed accepting this job in the hope that, as a result of the publicity on television, he would receive much better offers of employment. In reply, Pickersgill accused Starr of violating the confidentiality provisions of the Unemployment Insurance Act regarding Exelby and implied that the reputation of the CBC was damaged.[16] After Starr made his statement in the House, the job offers made earlier to Exelby were withdrawn but he did eventually find employment within two months as a salesman, which was his previous line of work. Pickersgill later wrote that "the Liberals might have pursued this question further if they believed that Starr had knowingly abused the UIC information . . . or if he had not been so well-liked on both sides of the House."[17] The lesson from this experience encouraged the CBC television producers to ensure that their researchers provided factual information and not to take the word of Starr or anyone for granted. This experience also increased Starr's suspicions of the news media's motives in reporting political news.

On March 25, 1961, Starr was in Oshawa where he addressed the Junior Chamber of Commerce annual spring conference at the Hotel Genosha. In his speech, Starr reviewed the history of the recent economic recession and attributed its origins to international events that were beyond Canada's control. He attributed the prosperity of the early 1950s to "the Korean War, the Marshall Plan and American defence stockpiling." He spoke on economic growth in Canada and the measures taken by the Conservative government to stimulate manufacturing. In the public sector, he remarked that the educational facilities were not up to standards required by a modern industrial economy. He added that the increased federal government expenditures were intended to help "take up the slack" until the private sector of the economy renewed its capacity for production and thereby creating more jobs.[18]

At this conference, Starr was jeered by about 100 unemployed and UAW Local 222 union members who picketed the hotel. Starr went out to meet the demonstrators, greeting many of the union men by their first names, and asked what he could do for them. When the demonstrators replied they wanted jobs, Starr approached one demonstrator and asked, "How long have you been unemployed?" The man answered, "I am not unemployed—I work at General Motors but . . ." Starr interrupted him, "Just as I thought—I understood this was a delegation of the unemployed." Starr quickly realized that the demonstration was a "media event" organized by union men for the so-called New Party.[19] According to Starr, the New Party ". . . is the same old half-baked socialism. There is the difference that the

---

16. Pickersgill, *The Road Back*, pp. 135–137.
17. Ibid., p. 137.
18. *The Oshawa Times*, March 27, 1961.
19. *The Globe and Mail*, March 27, 1961. The New Party was a precursor to the New Democratic Party.

old Socialists came right out and wanted to take over everything. The New Party seems intent on taking over funds in the organized labour movement."[20] This incident was an example of the growing and determined effort by local New Party members to gain public attention and support. New Party strategists across Canada knew that Oshawa, with its large union membership, had potential for New Party support. Advice and assistance were directed into the riding to assist the local political organization.

In reply to municipal representations, Starr announced on March 23, 1961, that the closing date for the Municipal Winter Works Incentive Program would be extended from April 30 to May 31. The government reported that federal payments under the 1960–61 program amounted to $36 million and 121,197 direct on-site jobs had been provided.

In Toronto, the National Unemployment Lobby Committee organized a "March to Ottawa" and approximately 1,000 protesters travelled by train to Ottawa on April 24, 1961. Their box lunches were provided by the pro-Communist Canadian Congress of Women and supporters. In Ottawa, they were joined by protesters from other centres and a delegation met with Starr as Minister of Labour and also with several other cabinet ministers. The delegates requested an extension of seasonal unemployment-insurance benefits and of the winter works program. They did not want a return to the Dirty Thirties.[21]

The Unemployment Insurance Fund had declined by May 31, 1961, to $110,051,922 from a total of $926,726,930 on December 31, 1956. During this period the government had increased the maximum benefit and extended the benefit period from thirty-six to fifty-two weeks. Also, premiums had been increased but coverage was extended to fishermen and married women. The inclusion of married women and fishermen seriously reduced the fund because the employment among these two groups was in many ways temporary, and in the case of the fishermen obviously seasonal.

The Liberal opposition introduced a non-confidence motion accusing the government of mismanaging the fund and the motion was debated May 8–9, 1961. When the suggestion was made to withdraw fishermen and seasonal workers from the scheme and establish an alternative form of compensation, Liberal Members of Parliament Jack Pickersgill and Louis Robichaud[22] (from New Brunswick), for example, strongly opposed any such proposal. Despite their repeated and vocal criticism, the Liberal opposition was hesitant to make specific suggestions for dealing with this problem. Countering accusations of mismanagement, Starr argued that the Unemployment Insurance Fund had been properly managed and based on "humanitarian instincts" when the federal government extended the coverage of the fund and suggested there would be further amendments.[23]

The Senate Committee on Manpower and Employment submitted its report on June 14, 1961. The committee was established on November 22, 1960, to review Canada's manpower requirements and the unemployment situation. Various groups and organizations made submissions and a number of economic studies were commissioned. The report concluded that a combination of short-term and long-term developments had resulted in the high average rate of unemployment. The 1960–61 economic recession, the general

---

20. *Toronto Daily Star*, April 15, 1961.
21. *The Globe and Mail*, April 24, 1961, "500 Jobless go to Ottawa for talks with Starr."
22. Pickersgill, *The Road Back*, p. 47.
23. *Canadian Annual Review for 1961*, pp. 190–191.

decline in the rates of economic expansion, capital investment and growth of exports and the increased competition in the domestic markets all had a negative effect on Canadian manufacturing industries and on economic growth. Also, technological developments and rapid changes to innovations in consumer demand required significant adjustments in monetary and fiscal policies to improve Canadian economic prospects. The report recommended an increased level of private and government investment in social capital, with the necessary federal-provincial cooperation, financing and planning in this area. The report concluded that unemployment was in part a regional problem, especially in the Atlantic provinces and in Quebec. It recommended these provinces should benefit from increased economic opportunities rather than encourage the unemployed to move to economically more prosperous regions. This was a constant problem in promoting employment in Canada because many unemployed refused to move to other parts of Canada in search of employment and the federal government could not oblige them to move. The committee also recommended more investment in education and training and supported the federal government initiatives in this area. Starr replied that the federal government had generally accepted the recommendations of this report, and many of the proposals had been and were later implemented in whole or in part by the government.[24]

Diefenbaker and Starr attended the ceremonies in Winnipeg at the Ukrainian Canadian Committee Congress relating to the unveiling, on July 9, 1961, of the huge bronze monument of Taras Shevchenko, the national poet of Ukraine. Starr's wife and daughter also attended the ceremonies. The celebrations marked a double anniversary since it was also the seventieth anniversary of Ukrainian settlement in Canada. This event was heavily publicized in the Ukrainian Canadian press and was attended by representatives from across Canada. The unveiling of the Shevchenko monument on the grounds of the Manitoba Legislative Building in Winnipeg came to symbolize the peak of Ukrainian Canadian political participation in Canadian life up to that time. National, provincial and local Ukrainian political and community leaders were assembled to honour Taras Shevchenko as well as celebrate their own political success.

At a Ukrainian Youth Festival held on July 8, 1961, Starr said, "... in Canada, freedom is ours.... There is freedom for our institutions, freedom for our folkways and for culture. There is freedom for our language and there is freedom to participate in the democratic way of life. This is the freedom Shevchenko did not live to see."[25]

On July 9, 1961, Diefenbaker spoke of his concept of Canada and Canadianism. He described Canada as "a garden of Canadianism" rather than a mosaic of peoples or a melting pot. He described a mosaic as a static thing with each element separate and divided from the others. Also, the melting pot destroyed the individuality of each element to produce a new and totally different element. Diefenbaker said:

> It is rather a garden into which have been transplanted the hardiest and brightest flowers from many lands, each retaining in its new environment the best of the qualities for which it was loved and prized in its native land. Yet each adapts itself to the new soil

---

24. Ibid., pp. 183–186.
25. *Ukrainskyi Holos* (Ukrainian Voice), August 23, 1961.

and climate, meanwhile blending its beauty with that of its new neighbours to create a new and different garden.[26]

This description of Canadian society attracted the attention of Paul Yuzyk, who later wrote to Diefenbaker and asked if he could use this quote in the future.[27]

Premier Duff Roblin announced at the ceremonies that the Ukrainian language would be taught as an optional subject in selected Manitoba high schools starting in 1962. Saskatchewan had earlier introduced Ukrainian as an optional subject in 1949 and Alberta in 1954.[28]

The 1962–63 budget had targeted unemployment as its main enemy. The heavy drain on the Unemployment Insurance Fund was repeatedly drawn to the attention of the House by the opposition. On July 15, 1961, cabinet approved the reintroduction of the winter works program from October 15, 1961, to April 30, 1962.

On July 17, 1961, Prime Minister Diefenbaker announced the appointment of a special committee to study the Unemployment Insurance Act and related social-security programs. The committee was also responsible for investigating the seasonal unemployment problem and the unemployment-insurance system. The committee held public hearings and received representations and briefs from various organizations and individuals. Many presentations were critical that unemployment benefits were used to pay seasonal workers. The Chamber of Commerce, for example, suggested that after a specified period the unemployed should be required to accept alternative employment. The committee continued its investigations into 1962 and submitted the Report of the Committee of Inquiry into the Unemployment Insurance Act in November 1962. However, the unemployment problems remained.[29]

During this period, new political developments in Ottawa and across Canada had the potential to influence the political career of Starr and of the Conservative Party. Between July 31 and August 4, over 2,000 delegates met in Ottawa and founded the New Democratic Party.[30] The founding of the NDP completed the implementation of the Canadian Labour Congress resolution of April 1958 to form a new political party. Tommy Douglas was elected leader of this new political party based on social democratic principles and determined to appeal to a broader electorate than did the old CCF. With a new political party, a new revised program and a new leader, the New Democrats renewed their strength and determination to campaign more vigorously during future election campaigns. The New Democrats organized from New Party supporters, union activists and former CCF members, targeted certain ridings that demographically gave them some hope of success. Oshawa, with its large union membership, was an ideal target.

---

26. *The Winnipeg Tribune*, July 10, 1961.
27. LAC, The Hon. Paul Yuzyk fonds, MG32 C67, Volume 5, file: Rt. Hon. John Diefenbaker, Correspondence, 1959–64 (August 31, 1963). Paul Yuzyk was later popularly known as the "Father of Multiculturalism."
28. *The Winnipeg Tribune*, July 10, 1961.
29. Report of the Committee of Inquiry into the Unemployment Insurance Act, November, 1962 (Ottawa).
30. *Canadian Annual Review for 1961*, pp. 81–83; *The Globe and Mail*, August 4, 1961.

Figure 10.3 An editorial cartoon depicting Michael Starr building a "1962 winter works program" snowman under a blazing summer sun and talking to a "summer unemployed" man who stands in a "61 winter works program" puddle. Library and Archives Canada, Mikan 2861802.

One of the main themes constantly stressed by Starr in the battle against unemployment was increased cooperation among management, labour and government. For example, on February 2, 1961, Starr had repeated this theme in his speech to 600 Canada Labour Congress delegates in Ottawa, where he claimed the solution to Canada's unemployment problems required the cooperation of all levels of government, labour and industry. Although he emphasized the government did not wish to interfere with the affairs of management and labour in their respective spheres, he added that they also had a responsibility with respect to the affairs of the country.[31]

On February 28, 1961, Diefenbaker announced the full membership of the National Productivity Council. This council was received with mixed reactions and representatives of labour and business were not very enthusiastic.[32] The Department of Finance also had

---
31. *House of Commons Debates*, February 13, 1961, p. 970.
32. *Canadian Annual Review for 1961*, pp. 188–190.

some doubts about it and questions were raised about the council's financial authority, political influence and bureaucratic powers that could severely dislocate the national economy.[33] The government had established the National Productivity Council to assist in developing new industry, a larger skilled labour force, and to coordinate activities aimed at increasing production. The council was also intended to serve as a "clearing house" for information and ideas through regional and industrial committees. The membership of the council was composed of prominent Canadians representing every sector of the national economy however, the government claimed not to exercise any control over their activities.[34]

Under the auspices of the council, thirty business and labour leaders met in Ottawa on March 15, 1961 to discuss labour-management cooperation and the improvement of the competitive position of Canadian products. A steering committee was appointed to prepare plans for future meetings. The productivity council met on March 20, 1961, and spent six months trying to cope with the various issues relating to economic growth and employment. In September, the council announced its programme but it was not substantially different from its original terms of reference. In its recommendations the council stressed the theme of labour-management cooperation to achieve "national objectives" and the need to work as a "national team." Another meeting was held on November 28, 1961.[35] Those political observers who had expected immediate results from the council were disappointed. The more realistic observers realised that the council's primary purpose was educational and it was only with time that any progress could be evaluated.

In addition to on-going programs to reduce unemployment, the federal government had introduced a program to aid chronic-unemployment areas in the supplementary budget of December 1960. According to this new program, firms could benefit financially and claim double depreciation on their facilities in the first year if they located them in a chronic unemployment area or if they manufactured a new product. When Starr announced the selection criteria on March 2, 1961,[36] for chronic unemployment regions, both opposition parties questioned the effectiveness of the program and criticized the criteria as inadequate and restrictive. Over March 20–21, 1961, during long debates, the opposition expressed its non-confidence in this plan.[37] Although only a few municipalities had inquired in March, Starr argued that by September 21, 1961, the program was working well and had already produced some results. In total over thirty areas had qualified under this program.[38] On September 21, 1961, Starr said to the House

> ...that unemployment has taken a dramatic downturn in recent months. My opinion that the figures were considerably improved was confirmed when hon. members opposite failed to ask me any questions when the Dominion Bureau of Statistics release was

---

33. Margaret Conrad, *George Nowlan, Maritime Conservative in National Politics*, University of Toronto Press, Toronto, 1986, pp. 207–209.
34. *House of Commons Debates*, September 21, 1961, p. 8652.
35. *Canadian Annual Review for 1961*, pp. 188–190.
36. *House of Commons Debates*, March 2, 1961. p. 2569.
37. Ibid., March 20, 1961, pp. 3177–3215.
38. *Canadian Annual Review for 1961*, pp. 187–188.

Figure 10.4 As Minister of Labour, Starr enjoyed an international reputation in dealing with the seasonal unemployment problem and shared his knowledge and experience with Arthur Goldberg, the Secretary of Labor in the Kennedy administration, during Goldberg's visit to Ottawa.

>   made the other day. This situation is quite understandable but how different the attitude is when the figures show an increase in unemployment in this country.

Starr continued, "I believe that full employment is the objective of all of us, or as close to full employment as we possibly can get. For those of us who have the responsibility of government it is always a matter of concern to see to it that people who are seeking work are provided with the opportunity of finding work."[39]

Information regarding the various programs instituted by the Department of Labour to reduce the number of seasonally unemployed became well known throughout Canada and also came to the attention of government officials in Washington, DC. Starr received a phone call from Arthur Goldberg, the Secretary of Labor, to visit Washington because President John Kennedy wanted to meet him.

Starr visited Washington and took part in conversations with Secretary Goldberg on October 5–7, 1961. He was invited to the White House and met with President Kennedy in the Oval Office where they discussed the winter works program because the northern

---

39. *House of Commons Debates*, September 21, 1961, pp. 8649–8650.

Figure 10.5 This photograph of Mike Starr with President John Kennedy was prominently displayed in Starr's home in Oshawa and one of his prized possessions. Starr was invited to Washington to meet with President Kennedy and Secretary of Labor Arthur Goldberg to discuss the Canadian approach to reduce seasonal unemployment that also plagued the northern United States. Image courtesy of Walter Kish.

states were experiencing the same seasonal problems as in Canada.[40] A photograph taken on this occasion with the president, and signed with a dedication to Starr, became one of Starr's proudest possessions.[41] As a result of this meeting with Secretary Goldberg and President Kennedy, a series of recommendations was prepared to promote joint consultations regarding employments measures, labour-management relations and international affairs.[42]

40. *Courtice Bowmanville News*, May 27, 1998.
41. *Oshawa News*, February 3, 1999.
42. LAC, MG31 E23, Volume 1, File 6, Conversations Between Secretary Goldberg and Labour Minister Starr, October 5–7, 1961.

Chapter 11
Minister of Labour, 1962

During his official visits across the country, Starr was frequently invited to meet with the local Ukrainian communities. In November 1961, while visiting St. Thomas, Ontario, Starr was a guest at a "New Canadian Night." When he was in Cornwall, Ontario, attending a "Do It Now" meeting, part of the campaign to develop winter works, he met with representatives of the local Ukrainian community and attended an impromptu Ukrainian concert. The Toronto Ukrainian newspaper *Homin Ukrainy* (Ukrainian Echo) noted approvingly that Starr was proud of his Ukrainian origins and that such contacts were beneficial for the Ukrainian Canadian community.[1]

A conference of ethnic-press editors was held in Ottawa on December 4 and 5, 1961, and it received national coverage in the ethnocultural press. While most editors were pleased with the conference and the opportunity to meet senior government representatives, there was some criticism that this event was essentially a public-relations exercise organized for the benefit of the Conservative Party. A Ukrainian editor speculated whether this ethnic-press conference, like Diefenbaker's words at the foot of Taras Shevchenko's monument in Winnipeg, were merely "courteous official words made by a politician who stands on the threshold of an election?"[2] The Ukrainian press reported Diefenbaker had promised to raise the matter of the independence of Ukraine at the next General Assembly of the United Nations. While this would be a "great achievement" according to some newspapers, it was realized that not all Canadian politicians supported Diefenbaker's views of a free world and that some politicians had even interpreted such a move "as impudent and even foolish."[3] The Edmonton Ukrainian newspaper *Ukrainski Visti* (Ukrainian News) stated on December 11, 1961, that there was an apparent discrepancy between Diefenbaker's position on the Ukrainian independence issue and the position of Howard Green, Secretary of State for External Affairs, and his department. The newspaper suggested the Diefenbaker government could prove its support of Ukrainian independence by recognizing Soviet Ukraine as a sovereign state, which, under the constitution of the Soviet Union, it claimed to be.

The position of the Department of External Affairs on the Ukrainian question was outlined in a confidential memorandum to the minister from Norman Robertson, Under Secretary of State for External Affairs, dated January 15, 1962. In this memorandum, Robertson explained that recognizing Soviet Ukraine would legitimize the Soviet Constitution on the world political scene. He also dismissed Ukrainian nationalism as a significant historical movement and informed Howard Green that "spoken Ukrainian is a

---
1. *Homin Ukrainy*, December 9, 1961. *Ethnic Press Digest*, January 1962, Vol. 18, No. I, p. 8.
2. *Ethnic Press Digest*, January 1962, Vol. 18, No. I, p. 5.
3. Ibid., p. 18.

dialect of Russian."[4] In public and private meetings with leaders and members of the Ukrainian Canadian community, Howard Green generally supported the views and positions of his departmental officials on the "Ukrainian question."

The newspaper *Vilne Slovo* (Free Word) suggested Diefenbaker was not receiving the political support he required to pursue his anti-Communist policies from some members of his cabinet and from the larger Canadian public. Howard Green, in particular, was perceived as a "pacifist" following a "capitulating policy" in relations with the Communist world.[5] This newspaper suggested Green should be transferred to another portfolio, such as labour, where he could pursue his "pacifist" policies and ". . . that the Hon. Michael Starr should have been made Secretary of State for External Affairs."[6]

Diefenbaker's captive-nations statement was a "dangerous and war-like line," criticized the Communist Party of Canada.[7] The Ukrainian left-wing organizations and their press were also dissatisfied with Canadian government policy. They interpreted Canadian government policies as promoting the Cold War. These organizations mounted a campaign against the federal government by raising the specific question of the alleged denial of Canadian citizenship. The national executive of the Association of United Ukrainian Canadians claimed the federal government had denied Canadian citizenship to many Ukrainians and other East Europeans who had lived in Canada for many decades because they were known to have been members in left-wing organizations.[8]

However, both *Ukrainski Visti* (Ukrainian News), an anti-Communist newspaper, and *Ukrainian Canadian*, a pro-Soviet periodical from Toronto, agreed Starr should visit Kyiv, the capital of Ukraine, to see how the Ukrainian people were living. The *Ukrainian Canadian* suggested that such a visit was preferable to continuing the Cold War policies that the Diefenbaker government was pursuing against the Soviet Union.[9] The continuing political debates in the press about relations with the Soviet Union fuelled speculation in the Ukrainian community whether Canadian politicians were genuinely interested in promoting the independence of Ukraine or simply preparing for another election campaign.

In Ottawa, all the programs promoting employment were continued during 1962. The large and growing costs of the various government programs prompted the writing of a few articles in business newspapers on the dangers of inflation in Canada. In response to an article in *The Northern Miner* on inflation dangers, Starr wrote to Diefenbaker on January 16,

---

4. Department of External Affairs (Canada), History Section, File 6126-40, quoted in Bohdan S. Kordan, Lubomyr Y. Luciuk, *A Delicate and Difficult Question, Documents in the History of Ukrainians in Canada 1899-1962*, The Limestone Press, Kingston, Ontario, 1986, pp. 171–173.
5. *Ethnic Press Digest*, February 1962, Vol. 18, No. 2, pp. 14–15.
6. Ibid., p. 15.
7. W. Kashtan, "Diagnosing Anti-Communism," *The Marxist Quarterly*, Autumn, 1962, p. 76.
8. *Ethnic Press Digest,* February 1962, Vol. 18, No. 2, p. 3. The Canadian Slav Committee, a left-wing organization, published a booklet by John Weir entitled *The Case of Canada`s Stepchildren, Foreign-born Canadians Discriminated Against by the Department of Citizenship and Immigration*, Canadian Slav Committee, Toronto (1961).
9. *Ethnic Press Digest*, February 1962, Vol. 18, No. 2, p. 16.

... what about the morality of a system where persons who have devoted a third or a quarter of a lifetime to a particular industry can be all at once turned out into the street? I cannot believe that the preservation of free enterprise is geared to this type of human waste. The difference between a State of communism and a State of free enterprise is that in a State of free enterprise the human element is of prime consideration, whereas communism sacrifices the human element for the building up of the State. The element of public welfare must be the determining factor. Thus a move by labour to shift objectives in favour of greater security, better pension plans and so on, might well be advantageous, both from the social and economic points of view.[10]

The fourth session of Parliament ended on September 29, 1961, and the fifth session of the twenty-fourth Parliament began on January 18, 1962. On February 26, 1962, the deadline for the Municipal Winter Works Incentive Program was extended from April 30 to May 31, 1962.[11] The 1961–62 Municipal Winter Works Incentive Program was the most successful since its introduction in 1958. More than 8,000 applications for federal contributions to municipal projects were processed. The winter employment campaign was again expanded and had now operated since the winter of 1955–56. The Do It Now campaign continued through the winter months. Under the Technical and Vocational Training Assistance Act passed in 1961, financial and other support for provincial training programs continued. In 1961–62, the act enabled the federal government to support the construction, expansion and equipping of 375 schools and institutions.[12]

The unemployment statistics during 1962 indicated a significant improvement in the employment situation. The number of unemployed in 1962 remained below comparable levels in 1961. In February 1961, unemployment was 11.3 per cent of the labour force, but in February 1962 it was 9.1 per cent in terms of a seasonally adjusted basis. However, the patterns of unemployment from previous years persisted. Memories of the Depression of the 1930s continued to haunt Starr. The Atlantic provinces, Quebec and areas of seasonal employment continued to maintain a higher-than-average unemployment rate. The ranks of the unemployed continued to be filled primarily by males, young people and those with little or no education.[13]

On March 14, 1962, attacks on Starr in the House by opposition parties during a heated debate on unemployment—particularly those of Paul Martin—left Starr angry and shaking his fists while arguing a point of privilege concerning one of Martin's allegations. Martin and Jack Pickersgill suggested figures prepared by the Dominion Bureau of Statistics on the employment and unemployment situation were being withheld. Starr responded emphatically, "You have too much to say. You had better sit down. I have the floor now. You can push somebody else around but you are not pushing me around. I know you would like

---

10. LAC, The Hon. John G. Diefenbaker Papers, MG26 M, Series VI, File 210, Labour - General - Confidential (1962).
11. *Canadian Annual Review for 1962*, p. 161.
12. Department of Labour, *Annual Report for the Fiscal Year Ended March 31, 1963*, Ottawa 1963, pp. 2–4.
13. *Unemployment in Canada, Tables and Charts, Dominion Bureau of Statistics, April, 1962*, pp. 7–8; *Canadian Annual Review for 1962*, p. 161.

to very much ... I am not going to be bulldozed by anyone who does not observe the rules of the house."[14] The debate was punctuated by points of privilege, points of order, charges and counter charges. One such exchange lasted ten minutes before Deputy Speaker Paul Martineau was able to restore order.[15] Despite their rivalry in the House, Paul Martin and Mike Starr remained on cordial terms.

Starr was requested on numerous occasions by various national unions and major companies to arrange for conciliation boards to deal with national industrial disputes during 1961-62. Some of these were not resolved to the satisfaction of all concerned and dragged into 1963. The opposition within the national labour movement to Starr's policies did not decrease. On April 10, 1962, Starr was received at the Canadian Labour Convention in Vancouver with only a few seconds of polite applause and a few boos when he rose to speak.[16]

On April 18, Diefenbaker rose in the House and announced that he would seek the dissolution of Parliament on the following day. The Conservative members threw their papers in the air confident that they would be returned to power. With this announcement the fifth session of Parliament ended. The next federal election was scheduled for June 18, 1962.

---

14. *House of Commons Debates*, March 14, 1962, p. 1790.
15. Greg Donaghy, *Grit, The Life and Politics of Paul Martin Sr.*, UBC Press, Vancouver, 2015, p. 179; *The Ottawa Citizen*, March 15, 1962.
16. *The Vancouver Sun*, April 11, 1962.

Chapter 12
Politics in Ontario Riding, 1962

On May 1, 1962, Norman Cafik, a Pickering Township businessman, was nominated as the Liberal Party candidate in the Ontario riding. Cafik won the nomination over John Lay, the Liberal candidate in the two previous federal elections. The main issue revolved around the question of whether the Liberals would be successful with a new candidate. In their speeches to the nominating convention, both candidates stated that they held no personal antagonism toward Starr. In fact, both admitted that Starr was quite a likeable person. Lay said that the Liberal candidate would find a good target in this election if he sought to unseat a cabinet minister. He added:

> He [Starr] is a very nice person and I don't think there is anyone who knows him who does not like him. But as a Minister in the Diefenbaker government, he has to share in the responsibility of that government and if we want to defeat the Diefenbaker government—it may be too bad, but we will have to defeat the sitting member.[1]

According to Cafik, Starr should not be underestimated because he was well-liked, well-respected and "no-man's fool." Norman Cafik's father was a Canadian of Ukrainian descent and his mother was of Scottish origin. By profession, Cafik was a former tool designer and tool-and-die maker who had become a financial consultant and executive.[2] Liberal Party headquarters no doubt considered his ethnocultural and working-class background to be positive assets in the election against Starr. On May 4, 1962, Allan Alexander Alton of Uxbridge was nominated as the candidate for the Social Credit Party.

Early in the election campaign, union leadership began to criticize Starr as Minister of Labour. On May 11, 1962, M. J. Fenwick of Toronto, assistant director of United Steelworkers of America, CLC (Canadian Region), accused Starr of "playing politics with vengeance" instead of doing anything for labour. He alleged Starr had appointed "Party hats" to positions that should have been filled by labour representatives. He argued Starr had become one of the most politically minded labour ministers in Canadian political history. Fenwick added that Starr had gone too far "in playing politics when there is a job to be done. It is time he should be put to pasture."[3] Fenwick, a former member of the Communist Party of Canada, had known Starr when he was organizing a union in Starr's factory during the Second World War. On May 16, the Ontario riding New Democrats nominated Miss Aileen Hall, a teacher in English and mathematics at

---

1. *Oshawa Times*, May 2, 1962.
2. *Toronto Daily Star*, June 11, 1962; Kieran Simpson (ed.), *Canadian Who's Who, 1989*, Volume XXIV, University of Toronto Press, p. 39.
3. *Oshawa Times*, May 12, 1962.

the Oshawa Collegiate and Vocational Institute in Oshawa, as the New Democratic Party candidate.[4]

During the election campaign, Arthur Maloney spoke in support of Starr and claimed he rivalled Prime Minister Diefenbaker in popularity as a public speaker. Maloney suggested the secret of Starr's popularity was that he kept in touch with his constituents.[5] Starr, however, displayed a strong reluctance, as did Diefenbaker, to become involved in debates with political opponents despite challenges from Norman Cafik, the Liberal candidate.[6] Starr's electoral plan was to decline invitations for public debates in order to avoid raising controversial issues that could negatively affect him politically, both at the local and national political levels. According to Cafik, Starr was not anxious to debate with him because he was afraid that Cafik would "show him up."

After surviving several federal elections, Starr had become a shrewd and experienced campaigner with a strong organization throughout the riding. But he had a demanding campaign schedule. He had not only his own campaign to look after but was among the most requested cabinet ministers to speak in other ridings and among ethnocultural groups.[7] Closer to home, Starr gave a talk to the Whitby Rotary Club on May 22, reviewing the economic progress of the Oshawa-Whitby area. He reported in some detail that, as a member of the legislative committee, he had to critically review all laws passed by Parliament during his term in office. There were two with which he was closely associated. In the fall of 1958, Parliament had passed the first municipal winter works bill. When the winter works program first began in the winter of 1958, over 700 municipalities took part, employing 35,000 people for an average of forty-five days. The second winter saw an increase in both municipalities using the program and the number of people employed. In 1961, winter employment for 140,000 people was provided under the program.

Another plan Starr strongly supported was labour training and education. The government had entered into an agreement with the provinces whereby facilities for workers' technical training and education were organized. As part of this program, all employers in Canada were contacted and asked to change any policies that may have discriminated against the hiring of older men. Also an appeal to young people was made not to leave school at an early age to find jobs in high paying industry. In December 1960, the Technical Training Assistance Act was passed for training institutions built before March 1963. Starr also mentioned the federal government's support of schools and public works in the Ontario riding. Starr emphasized that federal government support of school building had reduced the financial burden on the taxpayer. He pointed out that in 1956 the average wage in Oshawa was $69.00 a week and had recently increased to $107.00. Starr claimed that this trend was the result of federal government policies and that he would do all in his power to continue this upward trend if he was returned in the June 18, 1962, federal election.

On May 23, Starr was the guest speaker at the annual Civic Night held by the Oshawa Builders Association at the Genosha Hotel. In his speech, Starr emphasized that the Conservative government was interested in housing and the prosperity of the building

---

4. Ibid., May 4, 1962.
5. Ibid., May 16, 1962.
6. *Toronto Daily Star*, May 24, 1962.
7. *Oshawa Times*, May 18, 1962

industry. He reminded the audience that the federal government made financing available for housing research and community planning, for university students' housing projects, for municipal sewage-treatment projects and for home-improvement loans.

According to Starr, the two main causes of seasonal unemployment were the cold winters and the belief that outside work should stop in winter. It was up to builders to prove this attitude wrong and that winter work was possible. The Conservative government made efforts to provide winter employment through the federal-provincial public-works program and the Do It Now campaign. The past president of the Oshawa Builders Association concluded the meeting by stating that the secret of Starr's success as a politician was that he kept close contact with his friends.[8]

On May 25, 1962, Starr registered early as the official Progressive Conservative candidate because he had to campaign for about a week in western Canada.[9] During his tour of western Canada, Starr criticized the New Democratic Party approach to the unemployment problem. On June 1, 1962, Starr said at Vernon, British Columbia, that the type of full employment the NDP advocated was the same practiced in the Soviet Union. He told an audience of 150 voters of Ukrainian descent that New Democratic Party leader Tommy Douglas had proposed a program which would mean workers would be forced by the government to take certain jobs and would need a permit to quit.[10] This policy was generally followed in the Soviet Union where everyone, in theory, was guaranteed a job. Although Starr placed a high priority on jobs, he placed an even higher priority on individual freedom of choice and movement.

The Ukrainian press generally supported the Conservative Party and Ukrainian political candidates. The *Novy Shliakh* (New Pathway) declared its support for Dr. John Kucherepa and Mike Starr and praised the Diefenbaker government's achievements. The newspaper noted that during Diefenbaker's tenure, Ukrainian Canadians enjoyed "a golden era in Canadian politics." There were five Ukrainian members in the House of Commons, one of whom was a cabinet minister.[11]

Starr evidently considered the farming vote in the Ontario riding to be extremely important because, after a political meeting in Penticton, British Columbia, on Friday night, June 1, 1962, he was present and campaigning north of Oshawa at the Brooklin Spring Fair early Saturday morning. His return to the Ontario riding added some excitement to the campaign that was otherwise conducted in a conventional manner and did not make for stimulating newspaper headlines.

While Starr was campaigning out west, his NDP and Liberal opponents attended receptions, tea parties, carnivals, dances and canvassed workers outside the General Motors plant gates. Their campaigns gathered momentum as the election date approached but the campaign was a relatively quiet one.[12] However, there were hints that there was growing pessimism in both the NDP and Liberal campaign headquarters. Their biggest problem was to get their candidates heard by the largest number of voters in a comparatively short time.

---

8. *Ibid.*, May 24, 1962.
9. *Ibid.*, May 25, 1962.
10. *Ibid.*, June 2, 1962.
11. *Ethnic Press Digest*, May 1962, Vol. 18, No. 5, Supplement, p. 2.
12. *Oshawa Times*, June 2, 1962.

This was difficult because many local voluntary and service associations refused to become involved in the political campaign, even on a non-partisan basis.[13]

Aileen Hall, the NDP candidate, began her campaign by inviting Tommy Douglas to the riding. The NDP leader was optimistic that the 12,000-member United Auto Workers Union Local 222 would provide significant support for the NDP.[14] Hall made attempts to gain some support from the ethnocultural community in Oshawa by speaking a few words of introduction in their languages. On June 2, 1962, she opened her speech to a meeting of the Friends of Polish Youth by saying a few words in Polish. She also spoke a few words in German at the opening of the Loreley Club.[15] She averaged little more than four or five hours sleep during the campaign and had conducted an intensive door-to-door campaign not only in Oshawa but also in the rural areas. The NDP were well organized and felt that Starr could eventually be defeated. Cliff Pilkey, president of the Oshawa and District Labour Council, was confident that the NDP were the only political party in the Ontario riding that had a chance of defeating Starr. There were soon four candidates officially contesting the riding. Allan Alexander Alton paid his $200.00 deposit as the Social Credit candidate.

On June 9, 1962, Starr was present at the opening of the two-lane bridge at Ajax. A day earlier, approximately 300 people gathered in the Pickering Village Community Hall to hear Starr.[16] He stressed the accomplishments of the Conservative government, claiming that no government in history had undertaken or done as many things for the country as the Conservatives during their four and a half years in office. He added that the Conservatives had cut income taxes in 1957 and had not raised them since; grants to the provinces had doubled; the government financed the building of new trade and technical schools; the winter works program had saved the taxpayers many dollars. Speaking about his "open-book" record of twenty-four years of public service to the district, Starr said, "That record is being looked over by a novice and a stranger a few blocks away just now." Starr was referring to his political opponents, Norman Cafik and Aileen Hall.

The problem of unemployment continued to haunt Starr. The Social Credit candidate, Allan Alton, commented that Starr should be called "Minister of Unemployment" rather than Minister of Labour.[17] Starr defended the Conservative Party's record on the unemployment question and claimed that the promises of full employment by other political parties meant nothing more than regimentation of the workers. According to Starr, the contemporary employment situation in Canada represented full employment in a free-enterprise economy. He promised the Conservatives would take measures to ensure that every Canadian who was willing to work could find a job. Starr added that the Conservatives' great mistake was their failure to tell the Canadian people what they were doing.

In his speeches, Starr repeatedly stated the Liberals wanted to regain power at any price. He emphasized they had not been able to produce any new issues and were criticizing the Conservatives because it was always possible to criticize people who were doing something. He said that unemployment in Canada dropped by half and the Ontario riding was enjoying

---

13. Ibid.
14. *The Globe and Mail*, May 25, 1962.
15. *Oshawa Times*, June 6, 1962.
16. Ibid., June 9, 1962.
17. *Toronto Daily Star*, June 11, 1962.

the highest rate of prosperity; General Motors was showing a 22 per cent increase in sales. According to the Dominion Bureau of Statistics, Oshawa had the highest earnings of any region in Canada: the average weekly earnings in Oshawa were $107.00, compared to the national weekly earning rate of $79.00. General Motors, Starr claimed, was not able to produce all the automobiles it had orders for before the 1963 models came out.

On June 14, 1962, Aileen Hall summarized the main points of the NDP campaign before the Oshawa Builders. She stressed the NDP was a party of workers and suggested a consumer bill of rights would be passed. Her program included the expansion of the Industrial Development Bank, a medica-health plan, free education, and an increase in old age pensions. Her solution to the unemployment problem was a planned economy. To carry out these proposals, Hall said the NDP did not intend to increase or cut taxes. In conclusion, she stated the NDP was against nuclear weapons but she also admitted that the party was idealistic.[18]

At the national level, the Conservative election campaign stressed that Diefenbaker had put heart back into federal government policies in keeping with his lifelong concern for the average Canadian. Also, Diefenbaker's great new national development policy had opened the northern frontier further than ever before in history. The Conservatives claimed their policy had greatly expanded the international sales of manufactures, wheat, minerals and other products, and special incentives had brought about business expansion. The Conservatives were proud of their record and did not hesitate to point out that they appointed the first woman cabinet minister, First Nations senator, Ukrainian cabinet minister, gave Canada the first Member of Parliament of Chinese origin and appointed the first African-Canadian on the Sports Council. The Conservatives were proud that they had increased the representation of labour and ethnocultural groups in political positions. They also claimed they had given the franchise to members of Canadian First Nations, humanized the immigration laws and appointed more Canadian women to high political office.

Starr's election campaign again centred primarily on his past record of service to Oshawa, including his tenure as alderman and mayor. Starr kept emphasizing that, as Minister of Labour, he successfully had the government eliminate the excise tax on automobiles, introduced the Municipal Winter Works Incentive Program, brought in the Technical Training Assistance Act, Vacations with Pay Act, and had amended the Unemployment Insurance Act to provide greater benefits for longer periods. However, at various election rallies and in the press, questions about unemployment dogged Starr. Olive Diefenbaker, the Prime Minister's wife, visited the area and a tea reception was organized at the Ajax Community Centre where she, Mike, and Anne Starr greeted over 1,000 guests.[19]

In the Ontario riding, the Starr electoral organization had offices in Oshawa, Whitby, Ajax, Port Perry, Uxbridge, Brooklin and South Pickering.[20] Aileen Hall continued her election campaign by making personal appearances until the last minute of the campaign. She visited senior citizens in Whitby, campaigned in downtown Oshawa, and attended various teas and coffee parties in the Bay Ridges area.[21] As a cabinet minister, Starr had to be away

---

18. *Oshawa Times,* June 14, 1962.
19. *Toronto Daily Star,* June 15, 1962.
20. *Oshawa Times,* June 14, 1962.
21. Ibid., June 16, 1962.

from Oshawa during a large part of the election campaign. At various all-candidates election rallies, when Starr's absence was noted the news was met with jeers, mostly from the younger members of the audience.[22] According to the local press, the election campaign was often animated and interesting but did not involve unethical tactics by any political party.

On election day, June 18, 1962, Starr again won the riding for the Conservative Party. Across Canada the Conservatives were reduced to 116 seats, the Liberals had 100 seats, the New Democrats 19 seats, and the Social Credit Party took 30 seats, mainly in the province of Quebec. The Conservatives won the election but as a minority government. In the Ontario riding the vote was distributed as follows:[23]

Candidate	Party	Votes	Votes (%)
Michael Starr	PC	23,158	42.75%
Norman Cafik	Lib.	16,051	29.64%
Aileen Hall	NDP	14,461	26.70%
Allan Alton	SC	488	0.90%

In his victory speech, Starr said:

> I was away much of the time during this campaign, I helped to campaign in 46 ridings because that is the national responsibility of a cabinet minister—as a member of cabinet you have to share such a big responsibility. In accepting his heavy responsibility, I want to say that I am only human. I too make mistakes but I will do my best to serve you.[24]

After his victory speech, Starr started off for his traditional victory parade across the riding in a fourteen-car cavalcade headed by a sound truck. The procession stopped first at Whitby to visit Harry Jermyn, the election returning officer. The victory procession then continued through the rural areas of the riding.[25]

Starr again won the city of Oshawa by a comfortable majority. The votes in the city were distributed as follows:[26]

Candidate	Party	Votes	Votes (%)
Michael Starr	PC	11,458	41.37%
Aileen Hall	NDP	8,495	30.67%
Norman Cafik	Lib.	7,559	27.29%
Allan Alton	SC	185	0.66%

Starr won all thirteen municipalities in the riding. In the local press, it was generally agreed that Starr won this election because he was personable, capable, had a large personal

---

22. *Toronto Daily Star*, June 11, June 15, 1962.
23. *Twenty-Fifth General Election 1962, Report of the Chief Electoral Officer*, Queen's Printer, Ottawa, 1963, p. 155.
24. *Oshawa Times*, June 2, 1962.
25. Ibid.
26. Ibid.

following and a strong organization. Starr claimed that from 2,500 to 3,500 people had worked on his campaign. The fact that the NDP candidate was a woman had no doubt influenced some voters; Hall was also relatively unknown to most of the voters in the riding and the campaign was short. On top of that, the NDP riding association was handicapped by their small budget compared to those of the Conservatives and Liberals. However, in the City of Oshawa, the NDP candidate had placed second after Starr, an accomplishment the party noted and included in its future plans.

At the national level, the election was a serious personal setback for Diefenbaker. Five cabinet ministers were defeated and among them were some of Diefenbaker's closest friends and supporters. In the Ukrainian community, the press noted positively that five Ukrainians were elected. The press regretted however that Dr. John Kucherepa had been defeated and that Stanley Frolick, Progressive Conservative candidate in Toronto, also failed to win a seat.[27] Arthur Maloney was defeated by Dr Stanley Haidasz, a Liberal candidate, and Richard Thrasher, Parliamentary Secretary to the Minister of Labour since November 19, 1959, was also defeated in Essex South by another Liberal candidate, Eugene Whelan.

The *Oshawa Times* commented that, compared to the election record of many of Starr's Conservative colleagues, his victory guaranteed him a relatively stronger voice in cabinet. With the decline in Conservative Party fortunes after this election, Starr's political prominence increased and he could now be regarded as one of the most influential and popular members of Diefenbaker's reshuffled inner cabinet. Starr's Ontario riding success and his perceived stature within the Progressive Conservative Party increased speculation among some of his friends and supporters. Rumours began to circulate that Starr might—if and when Diefenbaker's tenure as leader came to an end—be a candidate for Prime Minister or party leader. Although Starr's qualifications for high political office were, at that time, questioned by some political observers, there was no doubt he assisted in negotiating the Conservative Party through some difficult sessions in the House of Commons and that he was popular both inside and outside the Conservative Party.[28]

---

27. *Ethnic Press Digest*, Supplement, Vol. 18, No. 6, June 1962, p. 3.
28. *Oshawa Times*, June 23, 1962.

Chapter 13
Minister of Labour in a Minority Government, 1962–1963

Like other Canadian newspapers, the ethnocultural press commented on the results of the federal election and the Conservative minority government: most expressed concern that "a strong government" had not been formed at a time when Canada was faced with serious economic problems—and a strong government was considered as necessary to legislate appropriate measures and solve the country's economic problems. The speculation was that a new federal election would soon be held.[1]

Prime Minister Diefenbaker spoke at the seventh congress of the Ukrainian Canadian Committee held in Winnipeg on July 5–7, 1962. Diefenbaker said he had instructed the Department of External Affairs to prepare a resolution regarding Russian colonialism to be presented to the United Nations General Assembly.[2] Earlier, on June 14, at the end of the federal election campaign, Diefenbaker spoke to a deportation commemoration meeting in Massey Hall in Toronto. At this gathering, Diefenbaker promised that Canada would grant diplomatic recognition to the representatives of the Baltic nations in Canada. Soon after the election, a letter was sent to Estonian, Latvian and Lithuanian consuls in Canada stating that their names would appear in the Department of External Affairs booklet listing diplomatic representatives in Canada.[3]

The death of Senator William Wall on July 7, 1962, was widely reported in the Ukrainian press. He was the first senator of Ukrainian origin and had been appointed to the Senate by then-Prime Minister Louis St. Laurent on July 28, 1955. His death raised speculation whether another Ukrainian would be appointed. At the time of Wall's death, there was one other Ukrainian Canadian in the Senate: John Hnatyshyn had been appointed on January 15, 1959, by the Conservative government. Since Wall was a Ukrainian Catholic and Hnatyshyn was a Ukrainian Orthodox, it seemed that another Ukrainian Catholic should be appointed. Starr was consulted during the selection process and he suggested that the national executive of the Ukrainian Canadian Committee be consulted. Diefenbaker then postponed any decision regarding the appointment of another Ukrainian Canadian to the Senate.

Although it was in the middle of the summer, Starr and his departmental staff were already planning the winter works program for the following winter. The Liberals had continued to criticize the annual winter works program as ineffective. Despite this criticism,

---

1. *Ethnic Press Digest*, Vol. 18, No. 6, June 1962, Supplement, p. 1.
2. Ibid., Vol. 18, No. 8, August 1962, p. 13.
3. Ibid., Vol. 18, No. 9, September 1962, p. 11.

Starr announced on July 12, 1962, that this program would be continued for the 1962–63 winter from October 15, 1962, to April 30, 1963.[4]

On July 23, 1962, Diefenbaker announced Michael Starr would be the principal Canadian representative attending the Jamaican independence celebrations that were to take place in Kingston, Jamaica, from August 4 to 8, 1962. Her Royal Highness the Princess Margaret represented the Queen and Lyndon B. Johnson—the Vice-President of the United States—represented the American President.[5] Starr's participation in the Jamaican independence celebrations reinforced his faith and admiration in Canadian parliamentary democracy that had its origins in the British parliamentary tradition. He was profoundly impressed by the civilized manner in which the people of Jamaica—this former British colony—obtained their independence: peacefully and orderly, with formal ceremonies and general celebrations; a tribute to British democracy. Canadians, including Ukrainian Canadians, owed their political and democratic freedoms to these same British traditions, and Starr was sincerely and profoundly grateful.

On August 9, 1962, Diefenbaker shuffled his cabinet: Donald Fleming was appointed Minister of Justice and George Nowlan became the new Minister of Finance. Davie Fulton was appointed Minister of Public Works and Ellen Fairclough became Postmaster General, R. A. Bell became Minister of Citizenship and Immigration and Paul Martineau was appointed Minister of Mines. Wallace McCutcheon was appointed to the Senate and became a minister without portfolio. Mike Starr remained as Minister of Labour. He was one of just three retaining their original appointments.

Dean Rusk, the United States Secretary of State, visited Canada on August 24, 1962, and met with Diefenbaker and Howard Green, Secretary of State for External Affairs, to discuss the Berlin crisis of 1961.[6] The Ukrainian Canadian press speculated that Rusk came to Ottawa in order to dissuade Diefenbaker and the Canadian government from proceeding with the proposed resolution at the United Nations condemning Soviet colonialism. The *Vilne Slovo* (Free World) was suspicious of Rusk's motives because, a few months earlier, he had allegedly described Ukraine as a traditional province of Russia.[7]

The continuing and growing labour problems on the Great Lakes between the Seafarers International Union of Canada (SIU) and Upper Lakes Shipping Limited and associated companies seriously interrupted shipping and threatened to halt transportation on the St. Lawrence Seaway. In February 1962, Starr appointed a three-man conciliation board to settle the disputes. The main dispute centred on the rivalry for members from the Canadian Maritime Union (CMU), a recently formed seamen's union affiliated with the Canadian Labour Congress.[8] The conciliation attempts were unsuccessful and the spring and early summer of 1962 were a difficult period on the Great Lakes. The newspapers were full of

---

4. J.T. Saywell, ed. *Canadian Annual Review for 1962*, Toronto, p. 161.
5. LAC, The Michael Starr Papers, MG 32, B 15, Vol. 5, File 2, Information Booklet for Use at Jamaican Independence Celebrations, August, 1962.
6. *The New York Times*, August 25, 1962.
7. *Ethnic Press Digest*, Vol. 18, No. 10, October 1962, p. 10.
8. William Kaplan, *Everything That Floats, Pat Sullivan, Hal Banks and the Seaman's Union of Canada*, University of Toronto Press, Toronto, 1987, pp. 109–112. Also, Peter Edwards, *Waterfront Warlord, The Life and Violent Times of Hal C. Banks*, Key Porter Books, Toronto, 1987, pp. 122–123.

reports of violent incidents related to picketing and boycotting of vessels operated by Upper Lakes Shipping Limited and operated by members of the CMU. These incidents took place in American as well as in Canadian ports.

The Canadian Labour Congress was lobbying the Canadian government for a detailed inquiry into SIU activities. Starr was hesitant to become directly involved in investigating a Canadian union because of the potential negative political consequences in investigating a Canadian voluntary association. The CLC threatened a boycott of the St. Lawrence Seaway if no action was taken and, on July 5, 1962, the boycott began. On July 17, Starr appointed the Hon. Justice Thomas G. Norris to head an industrial commission of inquiry to investigate and report on the circumstances leading to the disruption of shipping in the Great Lakes area. As soon as the commission began its hearings in mid-August 1962, its proceedings and the revelations of union gangsterism became front-page news across Canada.[9]

The first session of the Twenty-Fifth Parliament began on September 27, 1962. During this session the Liberal opposition immediately went on the offensive, attacking the Prime Minister and attempting to encourage and exploit growing divisions within the cabinet and Conservative Party. Parliamentary members of the recently established New Democratic Party joined in this offensive against the Conservative government. Starr was concerned about the attacks on Diefenbaker by the Liberals, whose main objectives according to Starr were

> to destroy the image of this great man who has done more in the space of time he had been Prime Minister than any other Prime Minister in the history of this country. These attacks have not diminished. Regardless of the state of the economy and the damage that might be done to the economy and to the Prime Minister himself, as long as they can get back into office they will employ every tactic that can possibly be employed.[10]

The opposition questions in the House continued and were now raised by newly elected members. On October 4, 1962, David Lewis, the new NDP Member of Parliament representing York South, in his maiden speech in the House of Commons strongly emphasized the need for planning in government as an important part of the solution to unemployment. Lewis said,

> "planning" used to be regarded as a disreputable word, a disreputable idea, but now it has become a popular one. In fact, it has become so popular that the government and the official opposition vie with each other as to which one of them made a planning proposal first, forgetting to look at history and see where the planning ideas really came from. However, that consideration is unimportant. What is important is that all over the world and in every part of the world, economic and social planning has become an idea which people grasp as essential to our modern complex and interdependent society.

---

9. For a popular description, see the article by Peter Gzowski, "The Fight to Break Canada's Waterfront Warlord," *Maclean's,* May 18, 1963.
10. *House of Commons Debates*, October 4, 1962, p. 191.

Mike Starr rose in the House and replied that the planning referred to by David Lewis was "planning in the socialistic sense of the word, an entirely different planning from what a free democracy believes in. Planning in a socialistic sense . . . means regimentation and nothing else." In reviewing his term as Minister of Labour, Starr told the House that "we have been listening to forecasts of doom and gloom for five years. Owing to the measures taken by this government, the forecasts have not been realized." He acknowledged that it was the opposition's role to criticize the government's actions because "after all, they are the opposition. . . . Let us then declare a moratorium on disaster and for the rest of the parliament address ourselves to the people's business in a positive and constructive way."[11]

The Cuban Missile Crisis began on October 15, 1962, when a United States U-2 aircraft took photographs that provided evidence that the Soviet Union was building missile bases in Cuba. On October 22, President John F. Kennedy made a televised speech announcing a naval blockade of Cuba. The crisis ended on October 28 when the Soviet leader, Nikita Khrushchev, agreed to withdraw the Soviet missiles from Cuba in exchange for an American pledge not to attempt an invasion of Cuba and to withdraw United States nuclear weapons from Turkey. Perhaps no event since the Second World War as greatly concerned the United States government because the world seemed to be heading towards a nuclear war. In Canada, Diefenbaker was hesitant during this crisis in providing immediate and total support for the United States plans and actions against the Soviet Union and Cuba.[12] This support was expected by the United States under the terms of NORAD and NATO agreements. Diefenbaker was annoyed that President Kennedy did not inform him prior to his announcements regarding actions against Cuba and the Soviet Union. Kennedy had become aware of Diefenbaker's hesitant position and this indecisive stand further contributed to the deterioration in personal relations between both men. Diefenbaker's actions or lack of action during the Cuban Missile Crisis contributed to the disillusionment of the more militant anti-Communists in Canada, including those in the Ukrainian community who praised President Kennedy for his decisive action in face of the Soviet threat in Cuba.[13]

When Diefenbaker cancelled the Avro Arrow program in 1959, he had claimed that new Bomarc missiles would largely defend Canada from hostile Soviet bomber threats. However, the Bomarcs required nuclear warheads to become totally effective. During the Cuban Missile Crisis, Canada did not have nuclear warheads and the crisis showed clearly the weakness of Canada's defenses. The crisis practically obliged the Canadian government to arrive at a definite decision in regards to the acquisition of nuclear weapons for the Canadian Armed Forces both in Canada and with NATO forces in Europe.

Although Diefenbaker was an ardent anti-Communist, and convinced that Canada should actively contribute to defending the "Free World" from the Soviet Union, he was determined to ensure Canada would not be "pushed around" by the United States. Diefenbaker anticipated a federal election in the near future and hesitated in making a decision on the acquisition of nuclear weapons until after the election. He was certainly influenced by the large number of letters and telegrams from anti-nuclear and peace groups throughout Canada. This issue split the cabinet, with Howard Green, Secretary of State for

---
11. *House of Commons Debates*, October 4, 1962, p. 195.
12. "Ottawans remain calm in face of Cuban crisis," *Ottawa Citizen*, October 26, 1962.
13. *Ethnic Press Digest*, Vol. 18, No. 12, December 1962, p. 12.

External Affairs, and Douglas Harkness, Minister of Defence, at opposite ends of the issue. Douglas Harkness strongly supported the need for the nuclear weapons and believed in providing full support to the United States at this crucial time.[14] Green, with the support of the Department of External Affairs, campaigned against the acquisition of nuclear weapons and for a policy of nuclear disarmament. After many long cabinet debates, Diefenbaker was still personally indecisive, which further divided the cabinet and prolonged the crisis therein.[15]

Regarding the ongoing national debate, militant anti-Communists in the Ukrainian-Canadian community supported the acquisition of nuclear weapons. At their national convention, the Ukrainian Association of Victims of Russian Communist Terror reported that "[W]e, Canadian patriots, believe that our army must be armed not only with guns but also with modern atomic weapons, which naturally, will not be used by our country to attach another."[16] In the Ukrainian press and community, Diefenbaker's proposed resolution condemning Soviet colonialism at the United Nations continued to be a dominant theme. A few Ukrainian newspapers stated that if Diefenbaker failed to obtain the necessary support for his resolution then it should not be introduced. If such a resolution was introduced and it failed to obtain the necessary support, the Communists would claim a significant victory.[17] The Department of External Affairs made an intensive effort to promote the resolution among friendly countries at the United Nations but with little favourable response. On September 6, 1962, the cabinet decided not to pursue this campaign at the United Nations.[18] The Canadian delegation at the United Nations had failed to gain the support of the emerging Afro-Asian countries that interpreted colonialism in terms of the European presence on their continents and not as a European problem, and, therefore, they had no sympathy for the Ukrainian cause.

Diefenbaker condemned Soviet imperialism in Eastern Europe and contemplated raising the question about the independence of Ukraine in the United Nations. In particular, he also thought it might be a good idea to declare the Ukrainian and Byelorussian Soviet Republics as "purely fictitious countries" and have the seats allotted to them removed from the United Nations. Once the Soviets became aware of this suggestion, they made it clear to Canadian diplomats that they, in turn, would raise the question of the independence of Quebec. As a result, no further action was contemplated.[19]

Howard Green, Secretary of State for External Affairs, addressed the United Nations, where he raised the question of Soviet colonialism and pointed out that there were millions of Soviet citizens who were denied the rights of self-determination. He appealed to the United Nations to examine the plight of the nations within the Soviet bloc. But Green's

---

14. Peter Stursberg, *Diefenbaker: Leadership Lost 1962-67*, University of Toronto Press, 1976, pp. 14–15.
15. John F. Hilliker, "Diefenbaker and Canadian External Relations," in J. L. Granatstein (ed.), *Canadian Foreign Policy, Historical Readings*, Copp Clark Pitman Ltd., Toronto, pp. 193–194.
16. LAC, The Hon. John G. Diefenbaker Papers, MG26 M Series VI, File: 045 - Ukrainian Language and Ethnic Groups, July 1962-1963.
17. *Ethnic Press Digest*, Vol. 18, No. 10, October 1962, p. 10.
18. Hilliker, "Diefenbaker," p. 189.
19. Robert A. D. Ford, *Our Man in Moscow, A Diplomat's Reflections on the Soviet Union*, University of Toronto Press, Toronto, 1989, p. 104.

speech was interpreted in the Ukrainian press as "extremely restrained and cautious."[20] Green's parliamentary secretary, Heath Macquarrie, gave a speech that was described by the Canadian mission at the United Nations as "the harshest and most direct attack ever levelled against Soviet colonialism in the UN."[21] On November 23, Macquarrie, Member of Parliament and Canadian delegate to the seventeenth session of the General Assembly of the United Nations, delivered a statement on the granting of independence to colonial countries and the problem of Soviet imperialism and domination. At the United Nations and among the Canadian ethnocultural groups the speaker was as important as the contents of his speech and, in this case, only Diefenbaker as Prime Minister of Canada could have had the required impact on world opinion.

In November 1962, unemployment in Canada was 5.2 per cent of the labour force and this number was not significantly different from the previous year, when unemployment was 5.4 per cent of the labour force. However, these figures were lower than the figure of 7.1 per cent average for 1961.[22] By November 1, 1962, 474 projects had been approved under the Technical and Vocational Training and Assistance Act. According to Starr, this was part of a "massive national effort to increase training facilities and programs." Among these projects were 222 new schools, 156 major additions and 76 minor additions or equipment purchases. The federal government provided $284 million of the total cost of the $442 million program.[23] The statistics regarding unemployment and plans to increase employment were questioned and disputed in the House of Commons, especially by Paul Martin, and these debates were described in the press.[24]

On November 22, 1962, Starr introduced legislation in the House of Commons for the Provision for Organization and Maintenance of Manpower Consultation Service, including the establishment of an advisory council on industrial change and manpower adjustment. The problem of automation was viewed as "the supreme challenge to our industrial and social development." According to Starr, the solution continued to lay in cooperation among government, labour and management on the social and economic fronts. Starr reviewed the Conservative government's attempts to study and deal with the problem of chronic unemployment. In November 1957, the federal government had established an advisory committee on technological change, whose members were experts from management, labour, government and universities, to guide a research program on the manpower effects of technological change in Canada. This committee revealed the contemporary average worker had to make many adjustments during his working life, shifting to new occupations often at new and higher levels of skill and knowledge. It also determined that new patterns of labour-management-government consultation and co-operation would have to be developed.

The proposed legislation was based on certain fundamental principles: the required cooperative actions had to be undertaken voluntarily by all concerned, and procedures had to be established well in advance of worker displacement to ensure that full services were

---

20. *Ethnic Press Digest*, Vol. 18, No. 11, November 1962, p. 11.
21. Hilliker, "Diefenbaker," p. 189.
22. *Canadian Annual Review for 1962*, pp. 160–161.
23. Ibid., p. 162.
24. *Toronto Star*, November 16, 1962.

provided to the worker in seeking new employment. An essential requirement was co-ordination of government efforts at both the federal and provincial levels to deal with the effects of manpower displacement resulting from industrial change. Provision had to be made for financial assistance for the movement of workers to new employment. Implementation of the legislation was based on the provision of financial incentives, primarily to employers in cooperation with unions. The responsibility and initiative rested with management and with labour.

Starr was fully aware that this legislation would not solve all problems created by technological change. Starr added, "There are no firm guidelines for this type of legislation as it is the first of its kind anywhere in the world."[25] The Canadian Labour Congress and the Confederation of National Trade Unions were informed by Starr on December 11, 1962, that the federal government was planning to hold a national management-labour conference in January 1963. Starr had plans for legislation on automation and manpower resources and this conference would study problems of technical change and automation.[26] Starr now had several years of experience in dealing with the unemployment problem. He understood very well that this problem was integral to the Canadian economy at that time and could not be separated from other serious problems such as inflation. Debates and policy recommendations based on research and analysis of the unemployment situation reflected differences of opinion among the university, labour and government experts. Starr's reliance on the recommendations of economists and other specialists often produced as many different opinions as there were experts.[27]

During the winter of 1962–63, the Municipal Winter Works Incentive Program provided an estimated 6,170,000 man-days of on-site work for an estimated 145,000 men. In the previous winter of 1961-62, the program had provided 5,870,000 man-days of work for 147,200 men. By the end of March 1963, the number of projects approved under the Technical and Vocational Training Assistance Act had risen to 513 and, for a time during the year, there was one completed project per day.[28] The Department of Labour mandate to find work for the unemployed resulted in raising the level of stress and conflict among department staff. One manager was accused of threatening his branch managers with dismissal if regional employment statistics were not improved. As a result, there were cases of fictitious placement figures.[29]

Although the unemployment situation remained a concern among politicians, the nuclear issue gained rapid prominence in the press and across Canada. During this period, the Liberal Party under the leadership of Lester Pearson was also divided on the issue of acquisition of nuclear weapons. Partly in response to the growing divisions within the Conservative Party, Pearson began modifying his position. In a speech made in Toronto on January 12, 1963, Pearson committed the Liberal Party to a policy of accepting nuclear

---

25. *House of Commons Debates*, November 22, 1962, p. 1896–1897.p
26. *Canadian Annual Review for 1962*, p. 163.
27. Robert Malcolm Campbell, *Grand Illusions: The Politics of The Keynesian Experience in Canada, 1945–1975*, Broadview Press, Peterborough, 1987, pp. 129, 200.
28. Department of Labour, *Annual Report for the Fiscal Year ended March 31, 1963*, Ottawa, 1963, p. 1.
29. LAC, George Vickers Haythorne Papers, MG31 E23, Vol.1, File 1–2, Departmental Correspondence memoranda - general (July 15, 1963).

weapons "to discharge fully commitments undertaken for Canada by its predecessor." When Parliament returned from Christmas recess on January 21, 1963, the cabinet remained undecided about nuclear weapons. Douglas Harkness, the Minister of Defence, threatened to resign from cabinet if no definite position was taken on this question.[30]

Starr was seen to be a "devoted friend of the Prime Minister" by other cabinet ministers who were growing disappointed with Diefenbaker's leadership; they began planning his removal from the party leadership and Starr was not invited to join in these deliberations. Starr made it known that his basic political principle was loyalty regardless of who was the leader. During this period of turmoil within the cabinet, Starr would meet from time to time with Walter Dinsdale, Gordon Churchill, Angus MacLean, Eric Winkler and others in their offices to consider how to avoid the political pitfalls that appeared daily.[31] Starr felt it was impossible to counteract the various schemes to remove Diefenbaker because the dissident cabinet ministers seemed to be very determined in pursuing their goal.

In reviewing his own role during this period, Starr claimed he was mainly "one of the onlookers." He was never attracted by the excitement of the political intrigues and never felt the urge to investigate the deeper motives and actions of the main actors. He judged these intrigues to have an essentially negative rather than positive influence on the Progressive Conservative Party and on Canadian politics in general and, therefore, he tried to avoid any direct involvement. In this and other political disputes within cabinet and the Conservative Party, Starr suggested he was "a lone wolf."[32]

During the February 3 cabinet meeting, Douglas Harkness bluntly told Diefenbaker the Canadian people no longer had confidence in him and that Diefenbaker should consider submitting his resignation. In the resulting confusion, Diefenbaker left the room and was followed by Green, Churchill, Hamilton and Starr. However, the ministers, followed by Diefenbaker, soon returned.[33] The meeting resumed and debated other issues Diefenbaker considered important but he did not make a decision on the question of acquisition of nuclear weapons. On February 4, 1963, the cabinet debated issues related to bilingualism and biculturalism. The Liberals had raised these issues to national prominence by proposing a royal commission on bilingualism and biculturalism. The cabinet resolved these issues were an appropriate subject for a federal-provincial conference since any action by the federal government would directly affect the provinces in their areas of responsibility. Diefenbaker asked Fleming to draft a statement to be reviewed by Mike Starr and Pierre Sevigny. The Prime Minister then announced a federal-provincial conference would be called "to examine biculturalism and bilingualism in a comprehensive manner."[34] Another decision made by Diefenbaker on the same day was the appointment of Prof. Paul Yuzyk to the Senate. This appointment was well publicized in the Ukrainian Canadian press. Yuzyk was a

---

30. *Canadian Annual Review, 1963,* p. 287.
31. LAC, Hon. G. Churchill Papers, MG 32, B 9, Vol. 104, Memoirs, p. 211.
32. Ukrainian Canadian Research and Documentation Centre, "Memoirs of the Honourable Michael Starr" (1998). See also Denis Smith, *Rogue Tory, The Life and Legend of John D. Diefenbaker,* Macfarlane Walter and Ross, Toronto, 1995, pp. 478-785.
33. Donald M. Fleming, *So Very Near: The Political Memoirs of the Honourable Donald M. Fleming,* Volume 2, *The Summit Years,* pp. 599–600.
34. Ibid., p. 602

dedicated worker for the Progressive Conservative Party among the Ukrainian Canadian community in all parts of Canada and also served as Diefenbaker's personal adviser on Soviet and East European politics.

On February 4, Harkness announced his resignation from the cabinet. On the same day, Pearson moved a motion in the House that "this government because of lack of leadership, the breakdown of unity in the cabinet, and confusion and indecision in dealing with national and international problems, does not have the confidence of the Canadian people."[35] When the House voted on this motion of no confidence, on February 5, the Diefenbaker government was defeated. Ninety-eight Liberals, twenty-eight Social Credit members, and sixteen New Democrats voted to defeat 109 Conservatives and two New Democrats. A federal election was called for April 8, 1963.

George Hees entered Diefenbaker's office that same day and asked him to resign as Prime Minister and leader of the Progressive Conservative Party. Reporters were alerted and gathered in front of Hees's office. Starr was leaving his office when he saw this large crowd of reporters and politicians. He was surprised by the large gathering and asked, "What's going on?" When Starr heard the rumour that Diefenbaker had resigned, he exclaimed, "What's that, what's going on. Nobody has said anything to me about it." Diefenbaker, however, did not resign. When Gordon Churchill called Diefenbaker's loyal supporters to tell them about Hees's visit to Diefenbaker's office and his request that Diefenbaker resign, Starr was among the few called to rally around their leader.[36]

---

35. *House of Commons Debates*, February 4, 1963, p. 3409.
36. Patrick Nicholson, *Vision and Indecision: Diefenbaker and Pearson*, Longmans Canada Limited, Don Mills, 1968, pp. 247–249.

Chapter 14
The 1963 Federal Election

No longer willing to support Diefenbaker's leadership, George Hees and Pierre Sévigny resigned from cabinet on February 8. Starr could neither believe nor understand this news and refused to join in any opposition to Diefenbaker in the Progressive Conservative Party.[1] In Oshawa, he called a two-hour closed-door meeting of senior Progressive Conservative riding organizers "to explain the government's position" in the coming federal elections. The meeting was actually called to address various rumours of discontent with Diefenbaker's policies. The attendees at the Hotel Genosha meeting, numbering over seventy-five, were considered to be "members of Starr's inner court circle from all parts of Ontario Riding—the top policy-makers and confidants." At the meeting Starr openly declared his complete support for Diefenbaker and he received a standing ovation at the conclusion of his speech and the question-and-answer period.

On February 10, 1963, the Ontario Riding Progressive Conservative Association officially supported Mike Starr and John Diefenbaker in the coming federal election. According to some party officials, there were no "rebel groups" but only a number of "confused groups" in the Ontario riding association. The sudden political changes in Ottawa created some confusion among the ranks of Progressive Conservatives in Oshawa but Starr's speech re-established solidarity within the association. The meeting was considered highly successful and the membership now had a more informed perspective on the association's official position.

On February 18, Starr told his supporters, "We didn't have the same feeling of fight at the last elections, we held 208 seats and the only way we could go is down." This time however, Starr predicted a heavy Liberal loss, because "They can't sell Pearson. The trend is toward the Conservative Party." Starr told the riding association that he was not going out of Ontario in the coming federal election and planned to spend much of his time in the riding. Starr concluded, "I hope we get a majority government so we can have a stable government and not the same stable the Liberals will be in."

James Walker, a former Liberal Member of Parliament, said at a political meeting on February 20 in West Rouge, "I'm pleased to see Mr. Starr in the House. He's a courteous and nice fellow but he's only got one problem, he's in the wrong party and has the wrong leader. I'm convinced he's a Liberal by persuasion but a Tory by desperation." He added, "The government had given him the task of solving the unemployment problem. This problem is tied up with the economic situation of the country, a responsibility of the whole government."[2]

The Ontario riding NDP once again nominated Aileen Hall as its candidate, on February 26. The organization was encouraged by the fact that Hall had finished third the

---
1. *Toronto Telegram*, February 9, 1963.
2. *Oshawa Times*, February 21, 1963.

previous June, with 14,457 votes, which were "more votes than any CCF candidate has ever received in this riding."[3] On March 1, 1963, Norman Cafik was again chosen as the Liberal candidate for the riding.

Earlier, on February 26, Starr said in a speech:

> I am of course happy that Oshawa and the district are enjoying a period of expanding prosperity due to the continuing upward movement in automobile production brought about to some extent by the improved business climate and by measures which the Federal Government has taken to assist that industry. The automobile industry is the cornerstone of our progress in this area and it is a source of great satisfaction that progress has been so marked this year.
>
> [...]
>
> It is interesting to note that in 1962 payrolls in the industry increased by more that $11,000,000 and that employment in the industry has now increased to a monthly average of 33,750, and increase of about 2,000 over last year. A great deal of this increase has been in Oshawa ... temporary surcharges on imported motor vehicles and the devaluation of the Canadian dollar has been instrumental in stimulating production and employment in Canada. This, of course, was the objective in bringing forward these measures.[4]

On February 27, 1963, Starr was again officially nominated as the Progressive Conservative candidate at a nomination meeting attended by approximately 400 supporters. He said, "The greatest progress in Canada's history has been brought about with the Conservative Government in the last five and a half years. Tory times are good times. Right here in Oshawa it is evident that ours is not the 'sick stagnant' economy so often referred to by other parties."

Starr remarked that in 1957, employees at General Motors in Oshawa totalled 12,267 but had now increased to 14,275 employees. In the same period, car production had almost doubled and Canadians were buying these cars because they were enjoying an "era of prosperity." Starr credited "prosperity and expansion in this industry" to the actions of the Progressive Conservative government. He quoted the President of General Motors that the demand for automobiles was at an unprecedented level and the outlook for 1963 was even better than the record year 1962. Starr also referenced the comment of Malcolm Smith, president of UAW Local 222, that 1962 was the most prosperous year the workers in General Motors and other affiliated plants had ever had and that prosperous times would continue.

Speaking on behalf of Starr in the Ontario riding, Progressive Conservative Senator Gratton O'Leary said that in more than half a century in journalism and politics he had never seen a Minister of Labour who did as much for labour-industry relations than Mike Starr. The seventy-four-year-old Senator said, "No man in public life today has been of more loyal heart and no man commands the respect and affection of the House of Commons more than your Minister of Labour."

---

3. Ibid., February 26, 1963.
4. Ibid.

On March 1, 1963, Judy LaMarsh, Liberal Member of Parliament for Niagara, attacked the labour policy of the Conservative Government in general and Starr in particular. Speaking on behalf of Liberal candidate Norman Cafik, LaMarsh called Starr

> a nice boy, the world is full of them, but a nice boy is the last thing this riding needs. I like Mike Starr as you like him but do not vote for him for if you do then you support John Diefenbaker. You will support a man who will bring this party and his country down, a man whose overriding ambition is to be Prime Minister in 1967. If Mr. Starr was to have said that unemployment was deplorable and he wished to do something about it, I would not be talking like this tonight. In my three years in the House of Commons, I have heard him do nothing but deny that there is unemployment.

LaMarsh added that Starr had failed in his department, since "unemployment is the greatest problem in Canada and has been the weakest spot in the government from the day it took power." LaMarsh continued, "I like Mike Starr as a man but not as a Minister of Labour. Mike is a nice boy, but the woods are full of them. What we need are more members who have the know-how and ability to get things done. Nice people won't make decisions because they don't want to offend. Mike has been so busy being nice he hasn't paid enough attention to his own department."[5] Norman Cafik refrained from criticizing Starr.

At the national level, Starr and the Department of Labour were criticized by Jean Marchand, President of the Confederation of National Trade Unions, for showing "a complete lack of decency towards French Canada" because there were no senior officials who were bilingual or of French-Canadian origin. More specifically, he had suggested to Starr during one of their meetings that there should be a French-Canadian assistant to one of the deputy ministers in the Department of Labour. This remark appeared in the *Montreal Gazette* in an interview with Jean Marchand. George Haythorne, Deputy Minister in the Department of Labour, replied in a letter to Marchand that approximately 20 per cent of the staff in the Department of Labour were bilingual and that the department had enjoyed excellent relations with the Quebec Department of Labour over the years.[6]

Starr spent much more time in the riding than in previous campaigns; an obvious change in his campaign strategy. Desperately needed in other parts of the country by the Conservative Party, Starr remained in the Ontario riding. He campaigned daily and his outside excursions were brief. Starr was still the perfectionist when it came to political campaigning and he rarely left anything to chance. Starr campaigned door to door, spoke at a number of political meetings, and he opened committee rooms in Ajax, Whitby and Oshawa. During some of his rare trips outside the riding, Starr introduced Prime Minister Diefenbaker at a rally in Port Hope and also addressed political rallies in Barrie and Galt—all in the province.[7]

In Oshawa, Starr told riding workers he was not satisfied with his 1962 majority of 2,963 votes over Aileen Hall, regardless of the political trends in other parts of the country.

---

5. Ibid., March 2, 1963.
6. LAC, George Vickers Haythorne Papers, MG31 E23, Vol. 1, File 1–2 (Correspondence, March 1, 6, 1963).
7. *Oshawa Times,* March 2, 1963.

Starr was expecting strong competition in this election. The PCs then redoubled their campaign efforts to strengthen their Oshawa city machine but so did the other political parties.[8] The NDP were making their most determined effort to win the riding by bringing in seasoned political campaigners such as Allan Schroeder, Education Director of the Canadian UAW, to direct Hall's campaign. The NDP were conducting an intensive door-to-door campaign in Oshawa and were concentrating more of their efforts in the Ajax-Pickering area, where trade-union representation was strong.[9] On March 15, Starr said he was aware the Ontario riding was a test riding for organized labour and its alliance with the NDP. He knew it was important to the NDP because they had brought in a campaign manager from Windsor and also had invited the NDP national leader, Tommy Douglas, to speak in the riding.

During some of his speeches hecklers interrupted Starr; professional hecklers, according to Starr, sent to disrupt and discredit his campaign and give him unfavourable publicity. On March 18, Starr opened a "million dollar" vocational wing to the Port Hope High School. This was part of what he called "the biggest school building program in history." Starr said, "It is one of the 468 projects approved since December 1960, at a total cost of $450,000,000 under which the federal government provides 25 percent of the capital outlay."[10] Since the Vocational and Technical Training Act of December 1960 was passed, Ontario's share of federal grants amounted to about $300,000,000. Starr said,

> The program aimed at arresting the drop-out rate in school and at reducing the 30 percent of the semi-and unskilled labour force for which job opportunities are fast diminishing. It is an investment in the future worth many times more than the money being spent on it. In previous years, Canada had never trained enough people to meet the demands of industry and with the drying up of workers because of European prosperity, government action became necessary. A training program has become a responsibility of government. We cannot afford to have large sections of the population enter the labour market without sufficient skill to find jobs in industry.[11]

On March 19, Starr predicted a Progressive Conservative victory to a cheering crowd of more than a hundred supporters in Claremont, north of Oshawa. Starr said,

> Since 1957, the Liberal Party policy has been to try to destroy the Prime Minister, a policy in which they have failed. They even went so far as to smear the name of the Prime Minister. This is what the Liberal Party descended to in their greed and lust to regain the power lost to them in 1957. The Liberals have obstructed the business of this nation, for what?—to win power? The Liberals were a government of good times who were kept in office by three wars. The Liberals were good time boys. They need a war to build up the economy. The Progressive Conservatives have built up the economy and don't have a war to help them.

---

8. Ibid., March 16, 1963.
9. Ibid.
10. Ibid., March 18, 1963.
11. Ibid.

Other candidates had to face serious obstacles while campaigning against Starr. Despite the fact Aileen Hall was teaching full time at her high school during the campaign, she managed to visit many parts of the riding. Neither she nor Norman Cafik were as well-known as Starr and they had to depend on their speaking skills and public appearances before election day.[12]

Starr was staking his political future on his personal reputation and his loyalty to Diefenbaker. His popularity was reinforced by the strong and experienced Conservative political organization in the Ontario riding. He was an experienced campaigner who knew elections were won on door-to-door campaigns and not primarily on national trends. Starr was sufficiently confident of his organizational ability that he lent part of his electoral organization to help the Conservative Party attempt to recapture the neighbouring Durham riding, where the Liberals had received a narrow majority in the previous federal election. Starr's approach to politics in the riding demanded a heavy personal-appearance schedule. He was a familiar figure on the coffee-party circuit and he was also involved in a vigorous door-to-door campaign, especially in the rural areas of the riding, where his popularity was always high.

Norman Cafik predicted Starr "will be lucky if he polls 19,000 votes. Mr. Starr never won an election because he was a Conservative but because he was Mr. Starr."[13] Starr knew losses at the local level during the last federal election were the result of less-than-effective riding organization and that this deficiency had to be remedied. Campaigning across the riding, Starr made a series of promises: the Conservative Party would strengthen Confederation on the national level and take other measures to build up Canada; new jobs would be created; the tax structure would be overhauled; a program of urban renewal would be undertaken; a national agricultural policy would be laid down; more vocational training would be provided; and a portable pension plan would be established.

The St. Gregory's Young People's Club and the Oshawa Jaycees co-sponsored a local political forum called Young Ontario Voters. During the speeches, the young audience was lively and showed its enthusiasm but was also polite and attentive. The audience was strongly in favour of Starr and showed their admiration for "Mike" by loudly cheering him at every opportunity. Aileen Hall continued her demanding schedule of coffee parties, public meetings, door-to-door canvassing and hand-shaking campaigns, in addition to her regular high-school teaching responsibilities. All these activities helped to acquaint more voters in the riding with the NDP campaign platform. Despite her strenuous efforts to obtain a more favourable voter response especially from the ethnocultural groups, a notice appeared in the *Oshawa Times* of April 3, 1963, which threatened to negate all of Aileen Hall's efforts. The notice read:[14]

> Vote for life—not for death
> Fellow Canadians: The issue before the voters is plain to see—will or will not Canada submit to U.S. pressure and accept nuclear arms? This, not a Liberal majority, is the real issue before the country. Labour must lead the nation to peace and independence

---

12. Ibid., March 28, 1963.
13. Ibid.
14. Ibid., April 3, 1963.

- By voting against all those candidates who advocate
  - nuclear arms
- By defeating the Liberal Party - the pro–American Party
- By electing a large group of NDP MP's pledged to oppose
  - nuclear weapons to the end

| Oshawa Club | National Committee |
| Box 442 | Communist Party of Canada |

This notice made public the pledge of support by the Oshawa Club of the Canadian Communist Party to the NDP in the Ontario riding. The notice further cemented the support of anti-Communist ethnocultural groups to the Conservative Party, to the disadvantage of the NDP.

Starr continued campaigning aggressively: he spent over 90 per cent of his time in the riding, personally calling on more than 2,500 homes—a strategy criticized by the other parties. The President of the Oshawa Liberal Association said that all Starr talked about was representing the people of the riding, and what a great personality he was, without saying a word about the Progressive Conservative policy.[15]

The NDP conducted a serious campaign in the riding, registering the largest number of posters and stickers, and conducting a more intensive door-to-door campaign compared to their previous efforts. The NDP brought in some of the best organizers from the trade-union movement to organize their campaign in Oshawa: Allan Schroeder, the aforementioned Education Director for the Canadian UAW, continued as a full-time campaign manager for the three weeks prior to the election.[16] The NDP organizers knew if Aileen Hall could make such an impressive showing in 1962 as a relative unknown, when the NDP party machine in the riding was not well organized, she would do much better with effective organization and concentrated effort under Canadian UAW direction. Starr was very aware of this well-organized labour-union offensive. On April 6, 1963, Starr published a full-page ad entitled "Workers Beware," in which he stated:[17]

> Workers beware of attempts to deceive you. I have been accused by left-wing political opponents of planning to sabotage unemployment insurance. My worker friends in Oshawa and district need only to look at my record to be assured that all my efforts for years have been for them and not against them.

The campaign was not without unpleasant incidents. Just prior to the election, the two larger front windows in Starr's home on Olive Avenue were smashed by bricks.[18] The leaded windows were struck with such force that they broke through the lead and landed twenty-one feet inside the living room, with glass scattered throughout the room.[19] At this time Starr received an anonymous letter from Lockport, New Jersey, threatening Starr that he

---

15. Ibid., April 4, 1963.
16. Ibid., April 6, 1963.
17. Ibid.
18. *Toronto Star*, April 10, 1963.
19. LAC, Peter Stursburg Papers, MG 31, D 78, Vol. 16, p. 16.

was in danger.[20] Starr suspected the threats came from a few union gangsters who were particularly opposed to the work of the Norris commission into Great Lakes shipping that Starr had initiated in July 1962.

On election day, April 18, 1963, Starr again won the Ontario riding but with a reduced majority. The votes were distributed as follows:[21]

Candidate	Party	Votes	Votes (%)
Michael Starr	PC	22,902	39.42%
Norman Cafik	Lib.	20,174	34.73%
Aileen Hall	NDP	15,020	25.85%

The electoral battle for the city of Oshawa was very similar to the outcome of the 1962 federal election. The results were as follows:

Candidate	Party	Votes	Votes (%)
Michael Starr	PC	11,241	38%
Norman Cafik	Lib.	9,593	32%
Aileen Hall	NDP	8,690	29%

Starr's majority in the city of Oshawa was 1,648 as compared to 2,918 votes in 1962. Starr's traditional vote strength was, as usual, in the municipalities. He won all the municipalities except Ajax and Pickering Township, which supported the Liberal candidate, Norman Cafik.

Aileen Hall was met by a standing ovation at the NDP campaign headquarters after the results were announced. She had continued to teach during the day and campaigned only after school hours; this was one of her major handicaps. Although Hall was better known in this election than in the previous election among the electorate, she was not as well known throughout the riding as Starr because she was a relatively recent immigrant, another handicap.[22] Hall was obviously disappointed with the results of the election, but said the campaign organization had "laid the foundation for a strong NDP in the Riding."[23]

According to Starr, there were several reasons for his victory and his share of the votes. He suggested the Liberals had a better riding organization and many Liberals who once voted for him had returned to the fold, and also some NDP votes went to the Liberals. Although Starr won the riding, Progressive Conservatives were not re-elected nationally. They had ninety-five seats compared to one hundred and thirty-three Liberal seats; only one short of the one hundred and thirty-four required for a majority. The NDP were

---
20. Ibid.
21. *Report of the Chief Electoral Officer, Twenty-Sixth General Election 1963*, Queen's Printer, Ottawa, p. 153.
22. Aileen Hall was born in 1930 and raised in Edinburgh, Scotland, and attended Edinburgh University. She immigrated to Oshawa in 1957 and was a candidate for the NDP in the 1962 and 1963 federal elections. In 1967, she was Executive Director of Planned Parenthood of Toronto. She returned to Britain in 1970 and was an instructor with the Good Food Guide. In 1984, she began writing about wine. She died on December 7, 2015. (Obituary: *The Guardian*, December 15, 2015.)
23. *Toronto Star*, April 9, 1963.

returned with seventeen seats; the Social Credit Party with twenty-four, mostly in Quebec. On April 23, John G. Diefenbaker ceased to be the Prime Minister of Canada, nor was Mike Starr Minister of Labour. The Conservatives were again in opposition, where, but for a brief sojourn under Prime Minister Joseph Clark, they would remain for the next two decades.

Senior officials of the Department of Labour held a luncheon for Starr at the Ottawa Hunt and Golf Club prior to his departure as minister, and presented him with a putter and golf balls.[24] After the defeat, the outgoing cabinet ministers had a few days to clear-out their offices. During his years as a minister, Starr had accumulated numerous files of documents, papers, correspondence and other material. At one point he had eight thousand open files. Starr however, did not know what to do with his personal papers and he was not aware of the services provided by the Public Archives of Canada. Faced with a deadline for vacating his office on Parliament Hill, he decided to destroy them.[25]

---

24. LAC, George Vickers Haythorne Fonds, MG31 E23, Vol.1, file 1–12, Departmental correspondence and memoranda-general.
25. LAC, Peter Stursburg Papers, MG 31, D 78, Vol. 16, pp. 46–47.

Chapter 15
Member of Parliament and House Leader, 1963–1965

For several weeks the results of the federal election were regularly debated in Canadian newspapers, including the ethnocultural press. Most newspapers deplored that Canada would again have a minority government, and several suggested the Conservatives were defeated because of their unrealistic defence policies. According to some election observers, the conflicts within the cabinet had fragmented the Conservative Party and Diefenbaker ran an essentially one-man campaign. There was no solid effort on the part of cabinet ministers for the Progressive Conservatives at the national level as there had been in previous elections. Instead they concentrated on their home ridings. The friction between Prime Minister Diefenbaker and President Kennedy regarding the Canadian response to the Cuban Crisis and the questions dealing with the acquisition of nuclear weapons by Canada made Kennedy more favourable to the Liberal Party. According to some sources, the Democratic Party offered the services of their pollsters and Madison Avenue public-relations specialists to the Liberal Party in this election.[1]

Ukrainian-Canadian newspapers noted with satisfaction that all five Ukrainian Conservative Members of Parliament, including Michael Starr, retained their seats. They also noted with regret that no Ukrainian Liberals were elected, nor were there any cabinet ministers of ethnocultural origin in Pearson's government. The *Homin Ukrainy* (Ukrainian Echo) claimed the new Liberal cabinet would be a coalition in the old tradition, between Anglo-Saxons and French Canadians, because there was no minister representing the "third force" in Canada. The newspapers noted, "It is a pity that Prime Minister Pearson has broken the tradition established by his predecessor."[2]

One inevitable result of the election was the increasing division within the Progressive Conservative Party regarding Diefenbaker's leadership. As political differences between Diefenbaker and some of his former cabinet ministers became more obvious to the press gallery, rumours were spread about Diefenbaker resigning from the leadership of the Conservative Party. After the election, Starr returned to Ottawa and resumed the role and responsibilities of a Member of Parliament but without the added burdens of a cabinet minister. Starr, who was the target of many political attacks by the opposition during the years of Conservative administration, now sat in the opposition benches and had the opportunity to criticize the Liberal administration. In his turn, he could now raise national

---

1. Denis Smith, *Rogue Tory, The Life and Legend of John G. Diefenbaker*, Macfarlane Walter and Ross, Toronto, 1995, pp. 496–499.
2. *Ethnic Press Digest*, "Views of the Ethnic Press on the Election and the New Government," Vol. 19, No. 5, May 1963.

and local issues and debate the actions or lack of action of the new Liberal government. Several issues were of particular interest and continued to receive special attention from Starr.

The first session of the twenty-sixth Parliament opened on May 16, 1963. Seven days later, Starr had his first opportunity to comment in detail on the Liberal government's new policies in a reply to the Throne Speech. Starr began by assuring the Liberal government of "a high degree of cooperation from the official opposition that is cooperation in all measures that take into account the realities of the situation and are designed to apply practical solutions to the problems."[3] He promised that, unlike the Liberals who disregarded and degraded the position of the previous Prime Minister, the Conservatives understood the enormous responsibilities that rested on the Prime Minister's shoulders and would not for merely partisan considerations forget that he was entitled to consideration and respect from all sides of the House.[4]

Starr believed the change from Conservative to Liberal government did not alter the vital issues facing the country and they had to be solved. According to Starr, the solutions to the economic problems of Canada must include the "initiative and energy of industry and labour" and that "above all, Canadians themselves may benefit to the maximum extent from the products of our labour and the exploitation of the resources of this country." Starr claimed his Progressive Conservative government had made the economy "move" and now it was up to the Liberal government "to keep it moving."[5] Starr congratulated Allan MacEachen, the new Minister of Labour, and added that he "can count on him [Starr] for a complete understanding of the problems with which he will be faced."

Starr shared with Walter Gordon, the new Minister of Finance, his concern about foreign control of Canadian industry. Starr said, "I agree entirely with his analysis of that problem. We can have no employment security in this country as long as we are a nation of branch plants, as long as managerial decisions affecting the course of our production and thereby the existence of jobs, continue to be made outside this country."[6]

He encouraged the Liberal government to support vocational training, municipal winter works programs and assistance to older workers displaced by automation. Starr strongly urged that the machinery of co-operation between management and labour "as the productivity council, be not allowed to lapse into rust and disuse."[7] Starr commented on the amount of criticism he had received for suggesting and implementing many similar measures. He said,

> I remember some of these hon. Gentlemen ... who showed a great deal of concern over the unemployment problem and certainly brought it to our attention with great vehemence. . . . It will be interesting to see what these gentlemen who now occupy the treasury benches and have the responsibility and opportunity are going to do about

---

3. *House of Commons Debates*, May 23, 1963, p. 181.
4. Ibid., p. 182.
5. Ibid.
6. Ibid., p. 183.
7. Ibid., p. 184.

those problems.... We will keep track of what is happening, what the situation is and what the results are.[8]

In the House, Starr expressed his concerns regarding the unemployment situation, vocational training, labour-management co-operation, automation, the school-building program and the municipal winter works program.

On June 7, 1963, the bill sponsored by the Liberals to create the Economic Council of Canada received first reading. It was proposed that this new council would initiate research projects in all areas of Canadian economic development, submit policy recommendations and absorb the functions of the National Productivity Council. The Progressive Conservative bill to establish a similar institution, a national economic development board had failed to survive second reading before the federal election was called in February 1963. Prime Minister Pearson stated that the Economic Council of Canada would be an instrument for creating "an economic consensus" and economic understanding "to make the best use of economic resources and maintain high levels of employment."[9]

During its short existence, the National Productivity Council was a pioneering project. It was the first attempt, other than under wartime conditions, to achieve national objectives by co-ordinating business, government and labour. This approach was an integral part of Conservative political philosophy that recognized the role of all segments of Canadian society in building Canada. The main underlying problem from the Conservative perspective was the partisan labour-union approach based on left-wing political philosophy. Some of the leaders of the national labour unions were influenced by Marxism and by a class analysis of Canadian society that included inevitable class conflict and questioned efforts at national co-ordination projects.[10]

The Liberal government announced the establishment of a manpower consulting service in the Department of Labour to provide financial assistance to employers and unions for research in manpower development and technological change.[11] These two objectives were included in the original Conservative act introduced in Parliament in November 1962, regarding the automation problem, which had never progressed beyond the resolution stage.

On July 11, 1963, Liberal Member of Parliament Maurice Lamontagne stated that the Liberal government supported the concept of planning which encouraged and motivated without limits and controls, because this was the only kind of planning that was desired and practical in Canada. He dismissed "imperative planning" as "practically unacceptable, economically undesirable and constitutionally unworkable." The NDP generally supported this legislation because it was viewed as a small step "along a road that we think is inevitable for this country."[12] The legislation received third reading on August 2, 1963.

---

8. Ibid., p. 183.
9. Ibid., June 7, 1963, pp. 791–794.
10. W. Craig Riddell, *Labour-Management Cooperation in Canada*, University of Toronto Press, Toronto, 1986, pp. 159–161.
11. *House of Commons Debates*, June 10, 1963, pp. 821–823.
12. *Canadian Annual Review for 1963*, pp. 185–187.

The Norris commission's report was tabled in the House of Commons on July 15, 1963.[13] The principal recommendation was the establishment of a government-controlled trusteeship over the Canadian maritime labour unions. This attracted immediate criticism from the Canadian Labour Congress and the Seafarers' International Union of Canada. Shortly after being tabled, the Liberal government established an interdepartmental committee to study the report. Allan MacEachen, the new Minister of Labour, later announced that the government had decided to implement the trusteeship recommendation in the Norris report. This action was received with unanimous support in Parliament and Starr commended the government.[14]

Despite the recommendations of the Norris commission, labour disputes on the Great Lakes did not cease. When the St. Lawrence longshoremen went on strike, Starr introduced a motion in Parliament for an emergency debate. He criticized the Liberal government for the lack of any effective action to stop this strike and prevent it from having an impact on the flow of grain to the Soviet Union.[15] Although Starr was an anti-Communist, he did not support any attempt to interfere with the food supply or to use food as a weapon even if the Soviet Union was the target. He knew all about the Soviet campaign to use food as a weapon to subdue the Ukrainian peasants in 1933 by orchestrating an artificial famine in Ukraine; a famine that resulted in several million deaths. The recommendations of the Norris report led to charges being laid against Hal Banks, head of the Canadian seafarers' union, resulting from a physical assault on a rival union leader, and he was eventually arrested. He was found guilty and later released on a bail of $25,000 but he skipped bail and escaped to the United States.

At the local level, the NDP lost the Oshawa riding in the Ontario provincial elections held on September 25, 1963, to Albert V. Walker, the Progressive Conservative candidate. Thomas D. Thomas represented the provincial ridings of Ontario from 1948 to 1955, and Oshawa from 1955 under the CCF banner and in 1963 as the provincial NDP candidate. His wife, Christine Thomas, served on Oshawa City Council and later as the first female mayor of Oshawa in 1961 and 1962.[16]

The Montreal Prosvita, the Ukrainian reading society, celebrated its fiftieth anniversary on November 16, 1963. Starr, whose parents had been among its earliest members, spoke at a banquet at the Windsor Hotel.[17] This celebration brought back fond memories for Starr. It was on the stage at the Prosvita Hall that he recited Ukrainian poetry and began with his parents his life-long involvement in the Ukrainian Canadian community. A memorial book celebrating this anniversary was published and Starr contributed a chapter describing his early years in Prosvita and in Montreal.

On October 2, 1963, the Liberal government introduced amendments to the Technical and Vocational Training Assistance Act that were passed on November 18, 1963. The

---

13. *Canada, Industrial Inquiry Commission Concerning Matters Relating to the Disruption of Shipping on the Great Lakes, the St. Lawrence River System and Connected Water, Report*, Ottawa, Queen's Printer, 2 volumes, 1963.
14. Kaplan, *Everything That Floats*, p. 138.
15. *House of Commons Debates*, October 4, 1963, p. 320.
16. Obituary of T.D. Thomas, *Toronto Star*, July 31, 1980; *The Globe and Mail*, July 31, 1980.
17. *Montreal Star*, November 18, 1963.

amendments, however, did not make any fundamental changes to the act. During this period, Starr was a member of the Standing Committee on Public Accounts and also the Standing Committee on External Affairs.

Because of the Liberal minority government, each vote in the House was critical and all Members of Parliament were expected to attend during all the sessions. Starr felt that his time would be much better spent in his riding than in Parliament waiting for a possible "snap" vote. He believed the value of a Member of Parliament was measured in his constituency and not by the time he sat in the Commons, except for certain ceremonial occasions. Starr felt that he was evaluated by the number of times he sat down to a church supper, a service-club luncheon, a veterans' banquet, a Boy Scout father-and-son "bean feed," or the frequency with which he made himself available at home and in his riding office to those of his constituents with tax, pension, job, or the hundred other problems with which each good MP was expected to concern himself. Starr sincerely believed that his constituents expected to see him working for and among them at home in his riding.[18]

In Ottawa, Starr was able to concentrate on his duties as Member of Parliament and enjoy in a more relaxed manner the camaraderie of fellow party members. A group of Progressive Conservatives who lived in Ottawa without their families usually had a corner table in the parliamentary restaurant, where they would have their meals in congenial company and discuss current political events. These meals became a fondly remembered custom for Starr. On Wednesday evenings, the group usually met to play poker. Jack Horner wrote in his memoir that "Mike Starr . . . was one of the few guys who could play poker all night and sit in the House the next day without falling asleep."[19]

At the annual Progressive Conservative banquet in Oshawa, Starr spoke about his trip to Washington, DC, and to Florida to visit Cape Kennedy (Cape Canaveral). The group of twenty-four parliamentarians left Ottawa on January 14, 1964. They stopped in Washington for two days and received a tour of the White House by Claudia "Lady Bird" Johnson. They then flew to Florida to visit the aerospace installations. Starr's trip was also reported in the local Oshawa press.

Opposition to Diefenbaker's leadership grew since the defeat of the Conservative government. The opposition spread to the Conservative parliamentary caucus where a small group of Members of Parliament began to plan a change in party leadership. The annual meeting of the Progressive Conservative Party Association was held in Ottawa from February 1 to 5, 1964. Over 1,500 delegates gathered at the Chateau Laurier. The meeting revolved around a bitter debate whether the traditional vote of confidence in the leadership of John Diefenbaker should be a secret vote. After an intense debate, the issue was decided in favour of an open vote. The newly elected President of the Progressive Conservative Association was Dalton Camp and Leon Balcer was appointed Quebec lieutenant and the Deputy Leader of the party. The threat to Diefenbaker's leadership was defeated.

On February 19, 1964, Starr was appointed Deputy House Leader and Gordon Churchill the House Leader. Starr was asked by Diefenbaker to take the position only a few hours before Parliament opened. A House Leader was appointed for each party in the

---

18. Press clipping from *Brantford Expositor*, December 3, 1963.
19. Jack Horner, *My Own Brand*, Hurtig Publishers, Edmonton, 1980, p. 32.

House of Commons; together they conferred about the order of presentations and the handling of business of the House. Starr's duties were to assist Churchill in these tasks.[20]

In April 1964, Starr spoke in the House on the question of the Electoral Boundaries Commission and the redistribution of electoral ridings. This issue had a special importance to Starr because his own riding of Ontario, a mixed industrial and rural area, was a prime candidate for reorganization. Starr agreed with the principle that redistribution should be taken out of the hands of the House of Commons, where in the past there were charges of gerrymandering. He also agreed with the proposed bill except for the provision dealing with tolerance levels. Starr felt that ridings should be more mixed and less uniform in social and economic composition than the tolerance levels proposed in the new legislation. According to Starr, low tolerance or a more uniform type of riding would create "a parochial type of member of parliament."[21] He argued that members of urban constituencies should also have ridings that included portions of agricultural areas. As a result, he felt that Members of Parliament would have ". . . a broader view and feel inclined as a matter of responsibility to take into consideration the agricultural side of life in Canada as well as the urban side."

During this debate on riding electoral boundaries, the question of political partisanship became an issue. Starr however, defended partisanship in the House of Commons and declared,

> I ran for parliament on a political platform representing a political party and I believe my duty in the House of Commons as a member of the opposition is to provide an alternative to the present government. Parliament is a place of politics and partisanship, that is the way I like it. That is the way it should be. That is why the democratic system works and when we end this system we will be on the road to dictatorship in this country.[22]

One of the more heated debates in the House during this period concerned the introduction of the new Canadian flag that was based on a maple-leaf design. Starr had originally not intended to participate but he felt compelled to express his views when the subject of French-English relations was introduced into the debate. Starr said, "I am not of British origin and I am not of French origin. I am proud to be of Ukrainian origin and I am also a good Canadian." He continued, "It makes me as a Canadian other than of French or English origin bleed to find the two founding races fighting between themselves causing disunity for political and partisan reasons."

Starr felt a new flag was being "rammed down" the throats of the people of Canada without their direct input, and he admitted to having a sentimental attachment to the Red Ensign—feelings that were shared by many of British ancestry in his Ontario riding. This flag also had a special significance to Canadians of Starr's generation. He added,

---

20. LAC, Michael Starr Papers, MG 32, B 15, *The Mike Starr Story*, Vol. 4; see also, *The Oshawa Times*, February 19, 1964.
21. *House of Commons Debates*, April 23, 1964, p. 2499.
22. Ibid.

> There are those in the House who feel the Red Ensign should be retained because it has served this country for so many years. Children have been born under it and immigrants have come here and found freedom under it. I speak as one whose parents came to this country at the ages of 17 and 16. They married here without a friend. Why did they come to Canada, Mr. Speaker? They came here to find freedom of opportunity, justice and liberty, things they never enjoyed in the country from whence they came. Because that flag gave them that opportunity, they worked hard. The opportunity was there and they were able to make a living in this country. There were able to set the foundation for people like myself to participate in the active life of this country, and they were as I am, good Canadians ... I come from people who believe in tradition and who do not throw tradition out the window when it has served its usefulness.

In Starr's opinion, this debate was "... one of the most important to come before this House since I became a member in 1952."

Starr admired the tolerance of "the British people" because he did not know what would have happened in another country if a symbol of the people's heritage was removed from the flag. The Red Ensign was a symbol of the people who came and built this country and provided the opportunity to those of other ethnocultural origins to come to Canada and enjoy the liberty provided under this flag.

Diefenbaker added, "Sir, the hon. gentleman who was speaking may not be speaking in a way that appeals to the sentiments of hon. gentleman opposite but if ever there was an hon. gentleman speaking with authority of heart and experience, it is the hon. gentleman for Ontario (Mr. Starr)." Starr continued,

> We believe this is a highly emotional issue and that the people of Canada should have an opportunity to voice their opinion. We will have a country of which we can be proud with a flag that will be chosen by the people themselves and not by politicians in the House of Commons who must knuckle under the whip of the party.

R.R. Southam, Member of Parliament for Moose Mountain, congratulated Starr "who made such an eloquent speech in defence of democracy."[23]

Another issue that continued to deeply interest Starr was unemployment. Starr was chairman of the Conservative Party's caucus committee on labour that met regularly to deal with labour issues. On July 27, 1964, Starr again raised this question in the House and accused the Liberal government of doing "literally nothing regarding unemployment." According to Starr, the Liberal government had claimed credit for the decrease in unemployment since it took office but he pointed out that unemployment had gradually decreased month by month since early 1961, when the Conservatives were still in office. Starr added, "This is directly as a result of the policies of the former government. This government has ridden on that wave of improvement and has endeavoured to take the credit but it has done nothing to try to improve the position substantially." Starr remembered when he was in office as Minister of Labour, Paul Martin, "the statesman for Essex East" continually "berated

---

23. Ibid. August 18, 1964, pp. 6963–6967.

us for not dealing, in his words, substantially with the problem." Starr referred to other Liberal members who attacked him day after day and as he remembered on one occasion, they spent eight days on one item to provide finances for the municipal winter works program, which at that time they "despised and criticized so much." Now, Starr said, the Liberals have adopted the program which they feel will cure unemployment.[24]

Later, when the Liberal government proposed regional development and other programs to eliminate poverty, Starr said, "The party to which I belong put these programs into effect when it was in office. When the Liberal government came into office a few years ago, it was quick to take up these programs, modify them and claim the credit for them. I wonder what else will be done in this regard by Government."

On Saturday afternoon, August 15, 1964, the annual Starr-Dymond-Walker Picnic was held at Helen Down's Farm in Whitby Township. Diefenbaker was invited to speak and he arrived at 3:00 p.m. with Mike Starr. Diefenbaker made his way slowly through the crowd of approximately 2,000 people. Followed by a large crowd of reporters and photographers, the former prime minister shook hands, stopped to talk, and listened to questions on various subjects. Diefenbaker gave a speech in which he attacked the "bulldozing" tactics of Lester Pearson in his efforts to promote the new Canadian flag. Diefenbaker stated that the new Canadian flag was Pearson's personal choice and not the choice of a majority of Canadians. He received a large cheer from the crowd when he said, "We are still fighting today for the right of Canadians to make their opinions known." When the crowd was asked to indicate their choice, they all raised their hands in support of the Red Ensign. When a small boy walked up to Diefenbaker and tried to present him with the new maple-leaf flag, Diefenbaker ignored him. A photographer who snapped the incident was sternly told by Diefenbaker "not to print that shot." Diefenbaker moved through the huge crowd for several hours chatting and shaking hands by the dozen. There were races and horse rides for the children. The Pickering Blue Notes marched and played for the crowd. There were also horseshoe-hurling contests and the nailhammering log event.[25] The picnic was a spectacular success.

In the House, Starr continued to defend his position on the new Canadian flag. He said, "We are doing what we believe the people in our ridings want us to do and that is to preserve the traditions of this country as well as its symbols.... We have traditions of which to be proud."[26] Starr was particularly annoyed with the attitude of the Social Credit Party members from Quebec, who opposed vigorously in the House any retention of British symbolism on the new flag. Starr said, "... they are doing something which is a discredit to themselves and to the province of Quebec and I say that by that sort of behaviour they are antagonizing the rest of Canada against them."[27] As the debate wore on, Starr admitted his impatience at some of the arguments in the House. He said, "I get carried away by what has been foisted on parliament and the people of the country instead of considering other matters more important to the economic situation than this symbol the government tries to camouflage as unity in Canada."[28] On December 9, 1964, Leon Balcer rose in the House

---

24. Ibid., July 27, 1964, pp. 6004–6005.
25. *The Oshawa Times*, August 17, 1964.
26. *House of Commons Debates*, December 2, 1964, p. 10781.
27. Ibid., p. 10782.
28. Ibid., p. 10785.

of Commons on a point of personal privilege and invited the Liberals to move closure and end the flag debate. The Liberal government subsequently applied parliamentary closure to cut off the Conservative debates against the proposed flag.

On February 12, 1965, Starr was chairman of the Progressive Conservative caucus meeting held in the West Block caucus room. Only ninety-eight out of a possible one hundred and twenty-eight caucus members were in attendance. Starr called the meeting to order and Diefenbaker made a speech on the need for loyal support. Some members rose and criticized Diefenbaker for his leadership and for alienating Quebec. The accusations, mixed with declarations of loyalty, disrupted the allready tense and angry meeting. However, a motion was moved supporting Diefenbaker's leadership in the House of Commons. Those who supported the motion were asked to stand. A majority stood but there was no official count. Starr as chairman declared, "That's it." Those members who were opposed were not requested to stand and declare their position.[29]

Debates among the political parties in the House of Commons became more and more bitter, providing the opportunity for personal attacks and innuendos. On February 16, 1965, Starr spoke in the House against various allegations of corruption at the highest government levels. Starr asked for the adjournment of the House so that the members could discuss

> a matter of urgent public importance, namely the great public unease which has arisen in all parts of Canada as a result of the allegations and disclosures of widespread corruption, marked by the intrusion of undesirable influences into several federal government offices, including that of the Prime Minister, which have disturbed and shocked the public conscience and called into question the conduct and public morality of those in authority and the advisability of the immediate constitution of a special committee of parliament for the purpose of making an unrestricted public inquiry into the foregoing.[30]

With Diefenbaker stubbornly staying in office, the national press speculated about his likely successors. Starr was personally loyal to Diefenbaker, but admitted his own riding executive had serious doubts about the PC leadership prior to the last two federal elections. He added that Oshawa was in the political sphere of influence of Toronto, where most of the opinion in favour of a leadership review was concentrated. A majority of his own riding executive believed that it would be to the advantage of the party if Diefenbaker stepped down.[31] Diefenbaker was aware of Dalton Camp's movement to replace him; the plotting and counter-plotting creating an atmosphere of suspicion and distrust. Diefenbaker was increasingly isolated from his former ministers and took advice, if any, only from Gordon Churchill, Alvin Hamilton and Mike Starr.[32] On April 7, 1965, Leon Balcer crossed the floor to sit as an independent Member of Parliament.

---

29. Patrick Nicholson, *Vision and Indecision*, Longmans, Don Mills, 1968, pp. 352–354.
30. *House of Commons Debates*, February 16, 1965, p. 11365.
31. *Oshawa Times*, March 24, 1965.
32. Fleming, *So Very Near*, p. 658.

In the House, Starr rose regularly to defend parliamentary traditions and his view of Canada. When the U.S. auto pact was negotiated, Starr rose in the House of Commons on April 8, 1965, to question the manner in which the agreement was approved and implemented. Starr said, "Canada immediately implemented her part of that agreement without coming to Parliament for approval of any kind. This was done either by Order-in-Council or by decision of the Cabinet. . . . Parliament has been the last to ratify or learn what this government intends to do or what this government is doing."[33] This agreement was of particular interest to Starr because it directly affected his riding and its huge General Motors plant.

Starr also spoke about the government's initial proposals regarding an official policy towards Canada's ethnocultural groups. Starr said,

> The Prime Minister made some reference to the two cultures and to bilingualism and biculturalism in Canada. He said that basically Canada is a nation of two founding races, and that these two founding races should be the cornerstone of our existence. No one has any quarrel at all with such a statement. During the flag debate, we in our party stood firm and fast for the view that the two traditional races should be depicted in some way on our flag. However, we were not successful in that regard.[34]

On Friday, April 22, 1965, Starr was appointed Opposition House leader replacing Gordon Churchill. Starr had also replaced Leon Balcer as Diefenbaker's seatmate in the House after Balcer left the Progressive Conservative Party to sit as an independent. Churchill had asked to retire as House Leader.[35] Rumours began to circulate in the press that Starr would be designated as a possible leader of the Progressive Conservative Party.[36] Churchill recommended Starr continue as House Leader ". . . as he was well liked by all."[37] Churchill was perceived as rather inflexible as House Leader and Starr was more relaxed and generally well-liked by members of all political parties. He was expected to be more flexible in his dealings with the other House Leaders.[38] Starr reluctantly accepted the position. He had earlier stated that he was not interested in the position and "in fact I would decline to accept it. I have never been greatly interested in procedural arguments and have no desire to become an expert on parliamentary rules."[39]

When questioned by the press about his attitude towards Diefenbaker, Starr said that as long as Diefenbaker was leader he owed his loyalty to him while remaining free to disagree on policy matters in caucus and in private meetings.[40] In the mainstream Canadian press, Starr was perceived as a possible leadership candidate whose main base of support were the Canadian ethnocultural groups. Starr resisted any attempt to portray him as a

---

33. *House of Commons Debates*, April 8, 1965, p. 111.
34. Ibid., pp. 113–114.
35. LAC, Hon. G. Churchill Papers, MG 32, B 9, Vol. 104, Memoirs, chapters 14–22, p. 273 (1973).
36. Stanley Westall, "Rising Starr a possibility for leadership," *The Globe Magazine*, March 6, 1965.
37. LAC, Hon. G. Churchill Papers, MG 32, B 9, Vol. 104, Memoirs, (1973), chapters 27, p. 1.
38. *The Province*, Vancouver, May 3, 1965.
39. *Oshawa Times*, March 24, 1965.
40. *Ibid.*, April 23, 1965.

representative of any special-interest group. He said, "I see myself as a Canadian born in Canada of Ukrainian origin.... I believe in Canadianism and participation in the life of Canada by all people regardless of their racial origin.... It is erroneous to portray me mainly as an ethnic spokesman."[41]

On May 11, 1965, Starr announced that he would be a candidate for the federal Conservative leadership whenever John Diefenbaker stepped down. Starr added that he did not know when that would be since there was no vacancy at that time and he did not expect one for some time. He said that he did not discuss his announcement with anyone, including Diefenbaker, or even with his wife.

Anne Starr learned of her husband's plans by reading his announcement in the newspaper. Starr was the first candidate to declare himself in the running for the Progressive Conservative leadership.[42] He had previously announced that he would run only if either George Hees or E. Davie Fulton were candidates. Although Starr's candidacy received the full support of his friends, the announcement was received with mixed reaction by some political observers, the national press and federal politicians.

In reviewing his political career, Starr felt that he did have some reason to aspire for the party's highest position. Philosophically, Starr was a Conservative of the traditional school, who sincerely believed in individualism and free enterprise, but throughout his political career he attracted popular support from various ethnocultural and working-class groups. Starr was instrumental in forming the "social justice" platform of the Conservative Party, particularly in issues relating to old-age security and unemployment-insurance benefits. Politically, Starr was one of the most popular speakers in the Conservative Party during the previous three federal elections. Since he had visited many ridings across the country, Starr felt that he would know most of the delegates at a national leadership convention. He was aware that he had established a good reputation as Minister of Labour when his term was recognized for efficiency and an enormous capacity for work. Throughout his political career, Starr had shown a talent for conciliation and this was demonstrated during the railway labour dispute in 1958. Starr felt that he could obtain support in western Canada, where he had campaigned regularly since 1952 among the vocal and active ethnocultural wing of Diefenbaker loyalists.[43]

Edward Nasserden, Member of Parliament for Rosthern, Saskatchewan, said that of all the declared candidates to succeed John Diefenbaker as party leader, Starr would have the convention support of a large percentage of Members of Parliament from the three Prairie provinces. He declared that Starr helped build up new communities in the west as they became more urbanized through the various Department of Labour programs. However, he added that if Manitoba Premier Duff Roblin or Alvin Hamilton were also candidates then the patterns of voting would change.[44] He was also respected by members of the other political parties and by most other members of the Conservative caucus. Starr, however, realized that his lack of a university education was a disadvantage, particularly with the Conservative Party intellectuals.[45] Starr said,

---

41. *The Province*, Vancouver, May 3, 1965.
42. *Toronto Star*, May 11, 1965.
43. *Toronto Telegram*, July 6, 1965.
44. LAC, Michael Starr Papers, MG 32, B 15, vol. 4, 1961-65 (July 1965).
45. Ibid.

I am grassroots, within the party leadership candidacy. I am my own man, running on my initiative. I made up my mind to offer myself on the basis of my background and experience. I feel it is in order for a man who has stood loyally with the party in good times and bad times, to offer himself for the party leadership when it becomes vacant as much as anyone who may have been in Parliament and then became an outsider building upon ambition to take over as leader.[46]

At the earliest stages of his campaign, Starr had been encouraged by Diefenbaker to run and he assumed therefore, that Diefenbaker would not be a candidate. Starr also assumed that Diefenbaker's encouragement implied his support. Diefenbaker also remarked that Starr could expect to be "knifed."[47]

Starr felt that his ethnocultural origins may be an asset in his campaign and he could win support in Quebec as a neutral. He was particularly concerned by the signs of disunity in Canada and felt the Royal Commission on Bilingualism and Biculturalism was "a $4,000,000 instrument of disunity." Starr stated that Canada "is no longer a country with just two main cultures. Our 20 million population breaks down about evenly into three groups, British origin, French-speaking and other ethnic groups." He asked, "Is the culture of the other ethnic groups to be meshed in or are such Canadians to abandon their culture and the contribution which they have been told in years past they could make to the nation?"[48]

Starr fully appreciated the role that French Canadians played in Canadian history and admired their long struggle to preserve their language and culture. He had the opportunity to express his appreciation in the House on the occasion of St. Jean Baptiste Day, on June 24, 1965. Starr said, "I join . . . in extending to our colleagues of the French language and to all French speaking Canadians our congratulations and best wishes on a day commemorating the existence and survival of their language for all French speaking Canadians but equally significant for all Canadians."[49] In retirement, Starr admitted that his contacts with ordinary French Canadians were limited. When involved with official business with representatives from Quebec, he always dealt with the leadership, who always spoke in English.[50]

On June 30, 1965, the third session of the twenty-sixth Parliament ended. During July and August Starr was a member of a fourteen-member Canadian parliamentary delegation visiting the Soviet Union for two weeks and Czechoslovakia for one week. Members of the delegation included Real Caouette from the Social Credit Party and Tommy Douglas from the New Democratic Party. The delegation also included another Ukrainian Canadian,

---

46. J.A. Hume, "Some answers from a man who wants Diefenbaker's job," *Ottawa Citizen*, May 29, 1965.
47. Ibid.
48. *Ottawa Citizen*, May 29, 1965.
49. *House of Commons Debates*, June 23, 1965. Despite these reservations by Starr and the criticism by many others especially from the French-Canadian community, this commission eventually produced book four of their recommendations, which laid the foundations for the official Canadian multiculturalism policy where Canada would have two official languages—French and English—but no official culture since all cultures in Canada were to be considered equal.
50. Ukrainian Canadian Research and Documentation Centre, "Memoirs of the Honourable Michael Starr" (1998).

Senator John Hnatyshyn, from Saskatoon. The delegation arrived in Moscow on July 19, 1965, and both Starr and Hnatyshyn delivered short speeches in Ukrainian during airport-arrival ceremonies. In Moscow, Starr and the other members of the delegation met with Soviet Premier Alexei Kosygin and President Anastas Mikoyan. Among other suggestions, Starr urged the Soviet leaders to loosen emigration machinery to permit the reunification of separated families in Canada. Mikoyan told the visitors that they were free to see anything except Soviet missile bases and they could see them only if Canada left the North Atlantic Treaty Organization (NATO). Starr replied, with a laugh, that perhaps if they saw the bases they would want to leave NATO. Mikoyan replied, "There's the irresponsible opposition speaking."

In Kyiv, the delegation was met by Alexander Korneichuk, the chairman of the Ukrainian Supreme Soviet. During a visit to a factory in Kyiv, Starr noticed that the signs with political slogans were in the Russian language. He inquired out loud why in a Ukrainian factory in the capital of Ukraine were there no slogans and signs in Ukrainian but in Russian. "Well, what did I tell you," was the reply of a member of the Soviet welcoming delegation to the other Soviet delegates.[51]

Senator Hnatyshyn requested authorization to visit Bukovyna, the land of his ancestors, and Starr had requested to visit Ivane-Puste, his father's village in western Ukraine.[52] When he reached the village, where all two hundred villagers gathered to welcome him, he was reminded of rural Ontario with its good rich farmland. To the consternation of his Soviet hosts, Starr also wanted to visit Pecharnia, his mother's village, which was not part of his planned itinerary. The village was about fifty kilometers from Ivane-Puste. After some negotiations Starr visited Pecharnia, which was on the slopes of the Dniester River with thick orchards of cherries, plums and peaches. The village was picturesque, with a few houses that still had thatched roofs. Starr had the opportunity to meet his two first cousins. During his visit, Starr was pleasantly surprised to see a newspaper clipping of himself from a Canadian newspaper on the wall in one of his relative's homes. Starr also had the opportunity to visit Zaluzia, near Lviv, where Anne Starr's mother was born. In Zaluzia, Starr met his wife's two aunts. During these visits, Starr had some opportunity to see life in a typical Ukrainian village without all the usual preparations that normally preceded visits by foreigners. In the Ukrainian villages, most people simply stood around at a distance viewing the visitors in silence as if they were from another planet.

The schedule for the entire trip was exhausting. The parliamentary delegation visited factories, heavy-industry plants, wine- and beer-making establishments and, in Moscow, they attended the Bolshoi Ballet. Everywhere the delegation received the red-carpet treatment and "too much hospitality." Starr travelled over 800 kilometers through Ukraine,

---

51. In 1967, the Association of United Ukrainian Canadians and the Communist Party of Canada (CPC) sent a delegation to Soviet Ukraine to study if Russification was taking place. They returned to Canada and wrote the "Kyiv Report" that, in fact, said the country was undergoing Russification. At the insistence of the Communist Party of the Soviet Union and then the CPC, the report was declared unofficial and shelved.
52. Ukrainian Canadian Research and Documentation Centre, "Memoirs of the Honourable Michael Starr" (1998).

visited the Black Sea region and saw the Dnieper and Dniester Rivers. Starr, who spoke Ukrainian, was often the interpreter for the delegation and was always in demand.[53]

During the summer the Liberals evaluated their political situation as a minority government and, by the beginning of September, they concluded that they had an opportunity to form a majority government. Parliament was dissolved on September 7 and a federal election was called for November 8, 1965.

---

53. LAC, Michael Starr Papers, MG 32, B 15, Vol. 4, 1961-65.

Chapter 16
The 1965 Federal Election in the Ontario Riding

When Prime Minister Lester B. Pearson called a federal election for November 8, 1965, thirty months had not yet passed since the previous, 1963, election. The announcement caught the local politicians in a state of semi-preparedness but Starr was confident of success and claimed that he had actually started to campaign the day after the last election. Although Starr began his campaign without being officially nominated, Oshawa Progressive Conservative Association President George Martin acknowledged the nomination meeting was "just a formality. We go with a winner." The Liberal candidate, Dr. Claude Vipond, was forming his campaign committee and poll workers were being organized. Vipond's campaign strategy was based on a personal campaign with only a few public meetings.[1] The New Democratic Party had not yet selected a candidate when the election was announced.

According to Robert Nicol, who was Starr's son-in-law and the co-chairman of the Conservative election campaign, Starr would conduct a door-to-door campaign as he had always done, with only occasional public meetings. On September 10, sixty-one people gathered in Oshawa for a four-hour meeting to discuss election strategy. Nicol claimed that the Conservative riding organization was completely mobilized.[2]

After Starr returned from his visit to the Soviet Union with the Canadian parliamentary delegation in the summer of 1965, he gave a series of slide presentations on his recent trip that he incorporated into his election campaign. On September 20 he spoke to the Oshawa Jaycees and on September 22 he gave a speech to the Ontario County Canadian Club. He also described his tour of the Soviet Union and Czechoslovakia to a capacity audience at a meeting of the Ukrainian Professional and Businessmen's Club at a local hotel.[3]

Although he was fifty-five-years old and slightly overweight, Starr felt physically fit for the campaign. He had a full schedule and had to attend nomination meetings in Guelph, Kitchener, Belleville, Aurora and Sherburne. He was scheduled to speak at a three-riding convention in Hamilton on September 27. Starr also had to visit and speak in western Canada in early October and travel as far as British Columbia. All this time, however, he had to spend more time in his riding, where his electoral majority had been declining.[4]

---

1. *Oshawa Times*, September 8, 1965. Much of this chapter is based on reports from the *Oshawa Times*.
2. Ibid., September 10, 1965.
3. Ibid., September 20, 1965; also, Archives of Ontario, Ukrainian Professional and Businessmen's Club.
4. Ibid., September 17, 1965.

On September 23, the Oshawa and District Labour Council voted that the funds of its political-action committee, which amounted to $3,400, be placed in the hands of the executive committee of the council with authority to "make such disbursements as are necessary to run a successful campaign."[5] The funds were used to support the NDP campaign and this link proved to be a crucial factor in future local and national elections.

At the Conservative nomination meeting, Starr again called on his party campaign workers to give him their full support. Starr did not want just a majority but he added, "I want you to get behind a steamroller and roll 'em down. I have confidence in you to work on my behalf. I will be away quite a few days, you are running, I am just carrying the torch. It is the Liberal government that is on trial." According to Starr, the various scandals in Ottawa were the "top issue" in this election.[6] Although this was his seventh campaign in thirteen years, Starr did at times feel nervous during this particular campaign. It was important for Starr to stay in the riding but he was committed to thirteen nomination meetings in western Canada and in Ontario. Starr said, "It is difficult to brush aside all the requests, and the responsibility on my part to win all seats possible and return to honesty and integrity is great."[7] One large and important event was the annual Starr-Dymond-Walker Picnic, then on September 25 on Helen Down's Brooklin farm. This picnic enabled Starr to renew old friendships and rally the important support of the rural areas of the riding. On September 29, 1965, the NDP were able to present their candidate, Oliver Hodges, a fifty-year old fruit farmer from Winona, Ontario, and former union executive.[8]

The debate regarding Diefenbaker's leadership of the Conservative Party became a national issue that reached the Ontario riding. On October 1, Dr. J. E. Rundle was rumoured to be running as an independent Conservative in the Ontario riding. This news was well received by the Liberal candidate, Dr. Claude Vipond, who said,

> I think it is a splendid thing for someone to come forward and give the Conservatives who are dissatisfied an opportunity to protest against Mr. Starr's persistent support of the discredited and indecisive Mr. Diefenbaker. I think this man represents a flood-tide of dissatisfaction among disgruntled Conservatives in this riding and across Canada.[9]

This news was also well received by the NDP candidate, Oliver Hodges, who stated,

> An unexpected Conservative candidate here is another manifestation of their disunity. It is not at all surprising when the Conservative Party is sundered and shattered in the country. Dr. Rundle and his backers probably want to split the Conservative vote here too. I think this is an offshoot of the whole movement to get rid of Diefenbaker.[10]

---

5. Ibid., September 23, 1965.
6. *Toronto Star*, September 28, 1965.
7. *Oshawa Times,* September 25, 1965.
8. *Globe and Mail,* November 4, 1965.
9. *Oshawa Times*, October 1, 1965.
10. Ibid.

Starr made no comments about any of his opponents or the possible candidacy of Dr. Rundle, who was his doctor.[11] Starr repeated that he stood on his record of the past and his platform for the future. On October 2, Dr. J. E. Rundle confirmed his intention to run as an independent candidate and added that he sought no established political-party affiliation. He stated,

> I feel that more independent members at Ottawa would militate against splinter groups and lead to a return to two-party government. I have long had political aspirations but because of my continuing high regard for the Honourable Mike Starr I did not contest the 1963 election.[12]

The election campaign in Oshawa gradually gathered momentum. Hodges and Vipond were handing out leaflets and shaking hands at city plant gates. Hodges, the NDP candidate, was at the Duplate Plant campaigning and reminding workers to attend the political meeting where the NDP leader, Tommy Douglas, was to speak on October 6 at the local high school. Vipond, the Liberal candidate, was at the General Motors South Plant distributing coffee from a mobile wagon and shaking hands. Hodges met with NDP Party workers in Bay Ridges to discuss canvassing plans for the area. He also spoke to UAW union officials from General Motors at the UAW Hall in Oshawa, where he won their unanimous endorsement.[13]

NDP leader Tommy Douglas visited Oshawa on October 6 and spoke to a large audience of 600 people at a local high-school auditorium. He spoke on financial assistance and free tuition for university students, the auto free-trade agreement, and he received the loudest applause when he suggested that car prices and wages paid to autoworkers be equalized between Canada and the United States.[14] Continuing his campaign, Starr spoke to about fifty party workers on October 6 at both Ajax and Bay Ridges campaign headquarters. On October 8, Starr canvassed in Oshawa and Whitby. The next day, he made television clips that were to be shown across the country. He made two speeches in Winnipeg on Thanksgiving Day and flew back to Oshawa on October 11. The following two days, Starr continued campaigning in Oshawa and Whitby.

The Ontario riding had increased considerably in population since the last federal election. The riding now had a total population of 152,500 spread out across 1,320 square kilometers. The riding's number of total eligible voters on November 8 was 78,468 as compared to 70,303 in 1963, representing an increase of 8,165 votes. In the city of Oshawa, the total eligible votes were 40,412 as compared with 36,175 in 1963, an increase of 4,337 votes. This increase of 8,165 votes in the riding was crucial.[15]

The NDP was determined to take advantage of the voter increase. But in spite of good candidates, willing workers, strong finances, and plenty of enthusiasm, the NDP always seemed to fall short of victory in the Ontario riding because it lacked proper and permanent organization. To remedy this situation, the NDP obtained the services of William Cumptsy,

---

11. *Toronto Star*, October 4, 1965.
12. *Oshawa Times*, October 2, 1965.
13. Ibid., October 5, 1965.
14. *The Globe and Mail*, October 7, 1956.
15. *Oshawa Times*, October 12, 1965.

one of the best NDP organizers in the country. Cumptsy began the organization of the riding for the NDP in a positive and realistic manner. In order to properly build the riding organization, Cumptsy often worked late into the night on the many and varied details of a successful riding organization.

Starr was very aware of the NDP organization offensive and increased his own campaigning. By October 13, Starr had canvassed over 350 homes in the Ajax area. In so doing, Starr came to a number of conclusions about the opposing parties. Starr said,

> It would seem to me that the NDP candidate is a political unknown from outside the riding and this fact seems to bother some people—as far as the Liberals are concerned, the scandals of people in high places has left the people of this riding aghast.[16]

On October 14, Starr met with his campaign executive and discussed the details of the final three-week campaign. The following day, he canvassed the new subdivisions in the Oshawa area and later met with his chairmen, who formed "the backbone" of the Conservative organization in the riding.[17]

Judy LaMarsh took a swing at Starr in a speech, although she did not mention him by name. She said:

> Are you ever worried about the sitting member, that backer of Diefenbaker? Any member's first loyalty is to his riding and when the paths diverge, you can't serve two masters. Or can you? Apparently in this riding you have a choice between a Diefenbaker Tory and a non-Diefenbaker Tory.[18]

LaMarsh also made reference to Dr. James Rundle running as an independent candidate. Unemployment was still an issue and she quoted Dominion Bureau of Statistics figures showing unemployment at 2.5 per cent. LaMarsh said, "Every economist says three percent is full employment. Your member never produced that kind of record."[19]

One of the more important issues in the election campaign in the Ontario riding was the auto trade pact with the United States. The Liberal candidate, Dr. Vipond, challenged Starr to either "put up or shut up" about the pact. When Dr. Vipond was addressing a Liberal Party rally at Bay Ridges, he criticized Starr because he had claimed that the agreement had many secret clauses in it. Vipond said, "This is not true. Mr. Starr has been casting innuendos at the Auto Trade Pact for some time and the time has come for him to get his facts straight."[20] Starr stated that he generally favoured the auto pact. He added:

> But the pact was signed in the United States without submitting it to Parliament. Canada put it into effect three days later. The United States waited 19 months. What people can't understand is why car prices are not lower ... I want to see it work—but

---

16. Ibid., October 13, 1965.
17. Ibid.
18. Ibid., October 15, 1965.
19. Ibid.
20. Ibid., October 18, 1965.

should we not be fearful of it? How many will lose jobs? Will there be adequate provision for those who are sacrificed?[21]

According to Starr, the main issue in this election campaign was honesty and integrity. On the question of Confederation, Starr supported the Conservative platform for Canadian unity. Starr said, "We propose an open Confederation Conference for unity through equality and the drawing up of a new Constitution if necessary."[22] Starr was critical of the Liberal government's handling of the vocational-school-building program which he helped to establish. He claimed the 75 per cent construction grant program for vocational and technical schools introduced in 1961 had deteriorated into a measured pause. He promised that this would be changed by a Conservative government, because, according to Starr, there was nothing more important than the upgrading of the labour force. He was in favour of Medicare and added it was the Conservative government that had appointed the Hall commission, under Justice Emmett Hall, which produced a 900-page report on Medicare.

During his speaking tour of western Canada, Starr spoke in Edmonton on October 19 and 20. On October 21, Starr spoke in Vancouver before returning to Oshawa. With his provincial and national speaking commitments completed, Starr began intensive local campaigning. On Saturday evening, October 23, Starr attended a dinner at the Oshawa armoury. He was a guest at a Ukrainian banquet for 400 people on Sunday afternoon and, in the evening, spoke to campaign workers.[23] On Monday morning, Starr was canvassing door to door and main-streeting. In the evening, a Mike Starr Night was held. Over 500 party workers and supporters from all parts of the riding gathered at the Hotel Genosha for a combined dinner and dance. On October 26, he was campaigning in Ajax and Bay Ridges accompanied by his rural campaign manager, William Newman.[24] The next day, about 80,000 pieces of literature were mailed to voters in the riding. The pamphlets explained Conservative policies and gave biographical information on Starr.

Oliver Hodges said a NDP Party worker canvassed by Starr was told that if the NDP candidate, who was from Winona, outside the riding, was elected, he would not be around the riding anyway. In defence, Hodges emphasized:

> I have said many times and it has been reported in the press that when I am elected I will move here. This is a fool piece of political campaign talk he is circulating. There are other more important issues to discuss. I am thoroughly annoyed at him.[25]

On October 28, the Conservative Party campaign manager, Robert Nicol, dismissed as just another gimmick the Liberal's plan to open a full-time office in the city after the voters ". . . receive the representation they deserve."[26] The Liberals planned to open an office where the public could bring their questions and problems for discussion. Nicol remarked:

---

21. Ibid., October 19, 1965.
22. Ibid.
23. Ibid., October 25, 1965.
24. Ibid.
25. Ibid., October 27, 1965.
26. Ibid., October 28, 1965.

> It makes it rather impersonal for the people to have to go to an office and make an appointment to see the candidate or have a secretary send a registered letter for you to Ottawa. Mr. Starr has always had his door open at home for the people of his riding. Many people from every walk of life have brought their problems to Mike at his home.[27]

On that same day, Starr was canvassing in the Townships of Whitby and East Whitby and in the evening attended the anniversary banquet of the B'nai B'rith. On the evening of October 30, he held a rally at the Legion Hall at Uxbridge, where former Ontario Premier Leslie Frost was the speaker. Vipond responded to Starr's intensive campaigning by hiking the length of the twenty-two mile riding.

On November 1, Starr claimed Prime Minister Pearson was threatening Canadian voters with another election in a year or eighteen months if he did not get a majority. He said, "It was no fault of the Conservatives that an election was called, Pearson disbanded Parliament." Starr added that two and a half years ago the Liberals said that they wanted a stable government. He added, "Well, they got a stable government and now the stable has to be cleaned out on November 8th." Starr charged that the Liberals had been indulging in scandals, featherbedding and corruption. He promised that the Conservatives would clean up the mess in this country.[28]

The next day Starr attended the Ukrainian Youth Association annual graduation ceremonies.[29] The following day he campaigned in Port Perry, Prince Albert, and Uxbridge. On November 4 he was in Whitby and on the following day he visited about 240 homes in Bay Ridges. Starr ended his campaign in Oshawa on November 6.

On November 5, Dr. J. E. Rundle, the independent Conservative candidate, said that if he could not get elected, he hoped and prayed that his votes would go to Mike Starr. Despite Liberal claims, he insisted he had entered the political scene to oppose Starr and his Conservative principles. He said,

> I am not out to cut his throat. I am simply maintaining my independence and I feel it would be a shame if Dr. Vipond gets elected. Mr. Starr has a more genuine interest in the individuals in this riding than either of the two other candidates I oppose.[30]

Starr did not reply to Dr. Rundle's statements but said that his personal motto ever since his first election to the Oshawa City Council twenty-one years ago had been: "Getting along with people gets things done."[31] Starr's campaign manager Robert Nicol announced that Starr's second grandchild, born during the previous week, would be named Michael. Starr made a strenuous effort during this campaign and his popularity among all the ethnocultural groups in the riding remained high. He canvassed personally and used large numbers of campaigners on a door-to-door canvass throughout the riding.[32]

---

27. Ibid.
28. Ibid., November 1, 1965.
29. Ibid., November 2, 1965.
30. Ibid., November 5, 1965.
31. Ibid., November 6, 1965.
32. Ibid., November 9, 1965.

In the November 8, 1965, federal election the Liberals were returned nationally but without a majority. The result was at best a stalemate: the Conservatives had 97 seats and the Liberals 131 seats, compared to the 129 seats they won in 1963. In the Ontario riding the results were similar to the 1963 election:[33]

Candidate	Party	Votes	Votes (%)
Michael Starr	PC	22,752	37.61%
Claude Vipond	Lib.	20,515	33.91%
Oliver Hodges	NDP	16,207	26.79%
James E. Rundle	Ind.	1,026	1.70%

The votes in the city of Oshawa were distributed as follows:

Candidate	Party	Votes	Votes (%)
Michael Starr	PC	10,807	35.4%
Claude Vipond	Lib.	10,075	33%
Oliver Hodges	NDP	8,995	29.5%
James E. Rundle	Ind.	621	0.02%

Starr won sixty-eight city polls and tied three; Vipond took forty-seven polls and also tied three; Hodges took forty polls and tied two. According to Vipond, the rain and the low turnout of voters worked against the Liberals.[34]

Starr felt he had never worked harder than in this campaign, and he produced 2,237 more votes than his nearest rival, which compared well to the 2,800 advantage he had in 1963. Several local Progressive Conservative executive members claimed that they had expected Starr to increase his majority to 5,000 or 6,000 votes. But as one commented, they always think positively. Starr restated his belief that this was a useless election and that the Liberals' tremendous drive for power had been denied by the Canadian people.[35]

On November 9, 1965, Hodges issued a statement announcing the NDP had a "solid and growing base" in the Ontario riding. He believed the trend in future elections would be toward the NDP, adding:

> Another election in my opinion will put an NDP member in the House of Commons. Redistribution will be a factor, but the principle reason will be that there will be a great deal of organizational work done before the next election. The NDP program appeals to those who know it ... we have a job of communication to do and we will do it.[36]

---

33. *Twenty-Seventh General Election 1965, Report of the Chief Electoral Officer*, Queen's Printer, Ottawa, 1966, p. 158
34. Dr. Vipond continued his medical practice in Oshawa until 1974 and then served as medical director of rehabilitation services at Oshawa General Hospital until he retired in 1985. Throughout his career, he was active in various medical and community organizations. He passed away in Oshawa on October 18, 2016. (Obituary: *Queen's Alumni Review*, Issue 1, 2017.)
35. *Oshawa Times*, November 9, 1965.
36. Ibid.

It was expected that the riding would be redistributed prior to the next federal election, a process that would make the city of Oshawa much more important in future election results. In the last federal election, Starr's majority in the city had been reduced to 689 votes over the Liberals, and the NDP was not far behind. Starr's majority was 1,648 votes in the city over the Liberals in 1963, as compared with 2,918 votes in 1962. While Starr's city majority decreased, he did slightly better in the rural areas north of Oshawa that traditionally supported the Progressive Conservative Party.

The NDP riding association sought to learn from the lessons of previous elections and ensure that its electoral machine was even better organized for the next federal election. In this election campaign, it was generally acknowledged in the local press that the NDP had wasted much valuable time selecting an appropriate candidate. When the NDP did obtain a candidate who could appeal to voters, especially to trade-union members, there were only four weeks left in which to campaign. The problem of time was compounded by bad planning. Another handicap which was heavily emphasized by the other political parties and by the local press was that Hodges was an outsider and, therefore, unfamiliar with local issues. William Cumptsy, NDP organizer for the Ontario riding, outlined on November 16 at the Oshawa and District Labour Council some of the political action needed to win the riding for the NDP. Cumptsy said:

> I started work here seven weeks before the last election with no organization, no committee rooms, and no funds. We ended up with NDP representatives in 156 of the 195 polls. That was good but we need a better organization to win the riding.[37]

Cumptsy outlined the strategy needed to put three NDP supporters in each poll district. He stated that they would be able to discuss party policies and inform people about the NDP. As part of this program, Cumptsy said the local NDP would open offices at the "Four Corners" in the centre of the downtown district of Oshawa. Keith Ross, Oshawa and District Labour Council Secretary, emphasized the importance of Cumptsy's work in the riding. He said:

> We could have picked up 2,000 or 3,000 votes in the election if we had informed the misinformed. The day of the mass-appeal is over—we saw that when T. D. Thomas was beaten in the provincial election—we have got to get some door-knocking done to get our message across. Oshawa knows what it wants and we can get the job done. We can get this riding back provincially and with redistribution, get it back federally.[38]

William Blasczuk, a Local 1817 United Steelworkers delegate, said that the NDP should start preparing for the next election by getting the political-action committee of each union active immediately.[39] The Ontario riding NDP, therefore, decided that the campaign should be an everyday and year-round effort. One problem was that too many party workers "went into retirement" immediately after each election. There was a definite need for a strong and

---

37. Ibid., November 17, 1965.
38. Ibid.
39. Ibid.

effective poll organization in the riding. There was also the need to replace the old-fashioned mass-appeal and indirect political campaign with a more intimate and personal approach. From their experience in the Ontario riding, the NDP realized that the door-to-door canvass was the foundation of any successful campaign. The NDP won a larger percentage of the vote where the party members were able to personally meet the voters, and the NDP always led the polls where the polls were properly canvassed. The NDP were determined to fight Starr with Starr's political tactics.

Chapter 17
The Leadership Race, 1967

The first session of the twenty-seventh Parliament opened on January 18, 1966. In Ottawa, Starr continued serving as Progressive Conservative House Leader in the House of Commons and reaffirmed his intention announced earlier to seek the Conservative Party leadership if Diefenbaker resigned.[1] There were rumours Diefenbaker would resign within two years of the election but Starr said that he had not heard from Diefenbaker regarding his retirement plans.

Although Starr was among the first to declare his candidacy for the leadership of the Progressive Conservative Party, Diefenbaker, who sat beside him in the House, continued to remain on the best of terms with him. Diefenbaker did not demonstrate any hostility towards Starr as he sometimes did the other declared candidates. Starr, in turn, continued to be loyal to Diefenbaker, defending him when necessary both inside and outside the House. On one occasion, when the attacks by the Liberal Members of Parliament against Diefenbaker became too frequent, Starr moved a motion "[t]hat this house call upon the Minister of Justice to substantiate the charges and allegations which he has made against the Leader of the Opposition and members of the Privy Council of the former government." The motion was ruled out of order.[2]

The Munsinger affair was one issue that revealed profound divisions between the Liberal and Conservative parties that had taken root during Diefenbaker's tenure as Prime Minister.[3] The alleged sex and security scandal story was introduced to the House of Commons on March 4, 1966, and led to heated exchanges that continued for several weeks. During one parliamentary exchange, the suggestion was made that Diefenbaker and Davie Fulton, while Prime Minister and Justice Minister respectively, were guilty of impropriety. The House exploded in accusations and counter-accusations. Erik Nielsen, the MP from Yukon, later stated, "Mike Starr was our House Leader, and God bless Mike, he is the kindest dearest soul, but he is no in-fighter in the House of Commons."[4] Erik Nielsen led the debate for

---

1. *Globe and Mail*, November 9, 1965.
2. *House of Commons Debates*, March 11, 1966, p. 2543. As a result, Peter C. Newman in his book, *A Nation Divided, Canada and the Coming of Pierre Trudeau* (Alfred A. Knopf, New York, 1969, p. 94), described Starr as among the "Diefenbaker die-hards" and "lesser lights."
3. Gerda Munsinger (1929–1998) emigrated from Germany to Canada in 1955. Munsinger was the central actor in a national political sex scandal. She was alleged to be a Soviet intelligence agent and was involved with several cabinet ministers. She returned to Germany in 1961. For a detailed and deeper description of the Munsinger affair, see Peter C. Newman, *The Distemper of Our Times: Canadian Politics in Transition, 1963–1968*, McClelland and Stewart, Toronto, 1968, chapter 28. Also see Bryan D. Palmer, *Canada's 1960s, The Ironies of Identity in a Rebellious Era*, University of Toronto Press, Toronto, 2009, chapter 3.
4. LAC, Peter Stursberg fonds, Interview of Erik Nielsen by Peter Stursberg, March 5, 1973, p. 34.

the Conservatives in the House. Eventually, a report was prepared on the Munsinger affair by Mr. Justice W.F. Spence and published on September 23, 1966.[5] This affair later became the subject of jokes, including in the Starr family, where Starr was teased if he was also personally involved in the sex scandal.

As House Leader, Starr raised a variety of questions that concerned the party and, in some instances, spoke on issues of personal interest. Starr questioned the Liberal government's new legislation to reorganize the various federal government departments in an effort to make them more efficient. He was particularly concerned with the reorganization of the Department of Labour and felt that the new legislation would weaken the work of this department. Regarding the reorganization of government departments, Starr said, "Their effectiveness can only be brought about through the leadership of the government, depending in turn on the ministers who will head the departments and how effective they are in taking a leading role in the policy-making of their departments."

Starr reviewed the history of the Department of Labour. He stated:

> In 1957 the Department of Labour was considered a poor second cousin to all other departments ... having under its jurisdiction only Industrial Relations and Disputes Investigations Act and a few other minor acts. Over the years, because of our activity in government, this department rose to a very important position and played a very important part ... so much so that the personnel of the department felt they had now taken their rightful place in the administration of the country. The Department of Labour plays a prominent part simply because labour is a very large and important segment of the Canadian population. Because of that the Department of Labour should and must play a significant role ... and it deserves recognition and attention. Now ... in the year 1966 this government is dismembering the department. All of the programs instituted since 1957 are being taken away and it is being relegated to a very insignificant role. ... The morale of the personnel left ... is low and all interest has been lost. In 1957, they felt they were second cousins but they now feel they are third cousins to other departments.[6]

He was also concerned that levels of immigration to Canada in the new government reorganization would be tied to labour-market demands. Starr said, "After all, we are dealing with people. We are not dealing with so many ciphers on the labour market. One is led to believe that the new manpower policy will deal with members of the labour force and with immigrants as ciphers only. The humanitarian aspect of things seems to have gone out of style with this government."[7]

Starr also spoke out during the continuous debates on "bilingualism and biculturalism" in Canada. On June 9, 1966, the House debated the composition of the board of directors of the new National Arts Centre in Ottawa. An amendment was proposed that the directors be nominated to reflect the "bilingual character" of Canada. Starr rose to criticize this

---

5. *Report of the commission of inquiry into matters relating to one Gerda Munsinger*, Ottawa: Queen's Printer, 1966. (Commissioner: The Hon. Wishart F. Spence).
6. *House of Commons Debates*, May 24, 1966, pp. 5433–5434.
7. Ibid., p. 5435.

amendment and spoke from a Ukrainian-Canadian perspective that lay outside the traditional French-English polarity. He said,

> As I understand it, if this amendment passes, the members of the board would be composed of people who represent the two cultures of Canada. Bilingualism has that connotation at this time. That is my understanding. I think that this would be the worst type of discrimination which could be entered on the statute books of this country. After all, there are some six million Canadians who have ethnic backgrounds other than French or English, who are proud to be Canadians, who want to participate in the cultural life of this country, and who have a great deal to offer, both in culture and in tradition, by way of stimulating our country now and for the future. . . . By this amendment, I feel that these people would be discriminated against. If they had the ability, and it was recognized that they would make good members of the board and would have something to add, this amendment would entirely eliminate them from consideration. This would be a crying shame and any action of this sort by this parliament would tend only to divide the country more. . . . What we would be doing, irrespective of whether we are of French origin, English origin or any other origin, is working together as Canadians, all for the benefit and good of this country . . . I must vote against this amendment . . . because I do not think it gives a fair opportunity to every Canadian who wants to be a Canadian, has proved himself to be a Canadian, and who wants to work for the Canadian way of life.[8]

On October 18, 1966, Starr took part in the Commons debates on medicare. Starr was particularly aware of the "troubles and worries of Canadian workers and citizens brought about by the expense of illness and adversity."[9] Although he supported the bill, he did not support medicare on a compulsory basis "because Canadians are not prepared to accept compulsion. . . . The Canadian people are resentful of compulsion."[10]

Earlier in the year, on May 19, 1966, Dalton Camp, now President of the Progressive Conservative Party of Canada, made a speech at the Albany Club of Toronto calling for a leadership review. Camp crossed the country on several occasions holding press conferences declaring that he wanted to "democratize" the party. Newspapers across Canada quoted Camp and other prominent Conservatives campaigning for a leadership review and, in effect, for an opportunity to replace Diefenbaker as leader of the party. Camp made a similar speech on September 20 to the Toronto Junior Board of Trade that was also widely quoted in the press. Camp's campaign set in motion various factions and forces within the Conservative Party that shook this organization to its foundations for the next decade.

Dalton Camp's criticism of Diefenbaker aroused strong emotions among some of Diefenbaker's most loyal followers. At one point, Camp feared Starr would run against him for the presidency of the party.[11] Arthur Maloney from Toronto was particularly

---
8. Ibid., p. 5435.
9. Ibid., October 18, 1966, p. 8811.
10. Ibid., p. 8812.
11. Peter Stursberg, *Diefenbaker: Leadership Lost, 1962–67*, University of Toronto Press, Toronto, 1976, p. 167.

annoyed. On October 17, Jim Johnston, the National Director, mentioned that Starr had recently informed him about Maloney's reaction and that he had severely criticized Camp's action. On October 20, a quick survey of the Conservative Members of Parliament showed support for Maloney. The Diefenbaker loyalists in Ottawa supported Maloney's nomination as the best candidate to oppose Camp for the presidency of the party. Starr, one of Maloney's closest friends, went to Toronto to persuade Maloney to declare his candidacy for the presidency.[12] Maloney agreed to run, but it was only three weeks before the annual meeting. A long list of Members of Parliament declared their support for Maloney against Camp.[13]

While Starr was attempting to rally the support of Diefenbaker loyalists in Ottawa, he was faced with a serious crisis in his own riding. On October 12, 1966, General Motors announced a layoff of 2,600 workers. Other reductions made a total decrease of 3,350 in the automobile industry. This caused serious concern and strong representations were made by the city of Oshawa to the federal government regarding the detrimental effect of the automotive free trade agreement on the local economy.[14] The agreement had been in effect since January 1965. Prior to the agreement, from 1961 to 1965, employment in Oshawa increased more rapidly and more sharply than in any other Ontario city for which statistics were compiled. As a result, these layoffs had a particularly devastating effect on the population, where previous fluctuations in the labour force were accepted as the normal variations occurring in an industry that was highly sensitive to changes in the entire economy. Starr rose in the House to express his concern. He asked, "based on the serious lay-offs because of the Canada-US automobile pact, can the Minister advise whether the proposal that Oshawa should be designated a special area for the purpose of tax concessions to industry, so that a diversification of industry can take place in that city, is receiving favourable consideration?"[15]

The annual Progressive Conservative Party convention was scheduled for November 14 to 16, 1966, at the Chateau Laurier in Ottawa. Maloney's campaign was based on loyalty to Diefenbaker and no leadership review. He summarized his position in a statement to the delegates, "When John Diefenbaker enters a room, Arthur Maloney stands up."[16] Unfortunately, the Liberal government had scheduled a debate in the House of Commons on a proposed change of rules regarding financial matters. This debate coincided with the opening of the convention, which meant loyal Diefenbaker supporters such as Starr and Churchill could devote only a limited amount of time to campaign on his behalf.[17]

---

12. LAC, Hon. G. Churchill Papers, MG 32, B 9, Vol. 104, Memoirs, p. 313. See also Peter C. Newman, *A Nation Divided, Canada and the Coming of Pierre Trudeau*, Alfred A. Knopf, New York, 1969, p. 136.
13. James Johnston, *The Party's Over*, Longmans Canada Ltd., Don Mills, Ontario, 1971, pp. 129–130.
14. LAC, RG 26 Series A-1-d, Volume 150, file 8-41-8/4; A Brief to the Government of Canada Presenting the Position of the City of Oshawa resulting from the Canada-United States Automotive Agreement (October 5, 1966).
15. *House of Commons Debates*, October 24, 1966, p. 9027.
16. Ibid., p. 159.
17. Patrick Kyba, *Alvin, A Biography of the Honourable Alvin Hamilton, P.C.*, Canadian Plains Research Center, Regina, Saskatchewan, 1989, p. 259.

When Diefenbaker made his speech to the assembly of delegates on November 14, he was heckled and interrupted. Starr claimed most of those present making anti-Diefenbaker statements were not voting delegates. Starr said, "No voting delegate in his right mind would show such disrespect for the office of Party Leader, and no one, no matter how strongly he feels about Mr. Diefenbaker as leader, should ever act in this way."[18] These actions received prominent coverage in the national press and further divided the Conservative Party. In the contest between Arthur Maloney and Dalton Camp for the position of President of the Conservative Party, Camp won by sixty-two votes, 564 to 502 votes. The anti-Diefenbaker forces received a further boost to their campaign.

As the anti-Diefenbaker forces consolidated their strength, Gordon Churchill circulated a "Declaration of Loyalty" statement which read, "We, the undersigned Members of Parliament of the Progressive Conservative Party, request that the Right Honourable J. G. Diefenbaker continue as Leader of our Party." The statement was dated Ottawa, November 15, 1966. Mike Starr was one among the seventy-one Progressive Conservative MPs to sign this statement.

On Tuesday evening at 10:00 p.m. a special meeting was called in Churchill's office on Parliament Hill. Ten MPs were invited, including Starr. Recent events were reviewed and plans for future actions were discussed. Diefenbaker had decided to remain as party leader rather than resign immediately, but divisions within the party were growing and becoming regular stories in the national press and on the national television news. Finally, in January 1967, Diefenbaker called for an immediate leadership convention.[19]

A testimonial dinner was organized for Starr in Oshawa and Diefenbaker was invited to be the main speaker. Before 400 guests, he praised Starr as possessing "the abiding quality of loyalty." He said, "The Conservative party has a message with men like Michael Starr. It is a people's party and with men like him it will remain a people's party." But Diefenbaker made no direct reference to the leadership in his speech.[20]

On February 20, 1967, Starr entered the Conservative Party leadership race; he felt he had just as good a chance as anybody else and he did not believe Diefenbaker would contest the leadership, so he reaffirmed his plans to run only if Diefenbaker was not a candidate.[21] Diefenbaker did not discourage him and said that Starr's candidacy was "great." He said much the same to the other candidates.[22] Over the next few months, George Hees, Alvin Hamilton, Donald Fleming, Davie Fulton, Wallace McCutcheon and Duff Roblin announced their respective plans to run and began actively campaigning across the country.

Starr's candidacy presented several difficulties: his motives for entering the leadership race were considered by some political observers as "most mysterious"[23] and not many voters could imagine him either as PC leader or as a potential prime minister. Starr had an

---

18. Donald Peacock, *Journey to Power, The Story of a Canadian Election*, The Ryerson Press, Toronto, 1968, p. 33.
19. Robert C. Coates, *The Night of the Knives*, Brunswick Press, Fredericton, 1969, p. 203.
20. *Toronto Telegram*, February 11, 1967; *Oshawa Times,* February 11, 1967, "Tory Chief Leads in Tribute to 'Mike' Starr."
21. *Toronto Star*, February 21, 1967.
22. LAC, Peter Stursburg Papers, MG 31, D 78, Vol. 16, p. 44.
23. Newman, *A Nation Divided*k, 1969, p. 155.

easygoing nature that gave him a regular-guy image, which most people associated with a municipal politician and who shared most of their ambitions. Journalist Doug Fisher compared Starr to the other leadership candidates and wrote that Starr's greatest weakness was his "easygoing" nature and his greatest strength was that he was "likeable."[24] His lack of higher education was perceived as an impediment by some MPs: he lacked a background as an intellectual, nor did he have a degree from Oxford or Harvard, as did Pearson. Starr also had difficulty making a good speech and, when he did speak, he still had a trace of a Ukrainian accent. Even if he could meet all the required qualifications for the position of Prime Minister, the underlying difficulty, according to some newspaper reports, was Starr's ethnocultural origin. The level of political evolution in Canada had not yet reached the point where a first-generation Canadian could aspire to be the Prime Minister of his country.

Another difficulty with Starr's candidacy was his view of the French-English relations in Canada. Also, Starr did not speak French. Starr knew that many Canadians had found it difficult to understand the French-English problem and he admitted that he was also more than a little confused. He said:

> The word "Canadian" in my opinion is big enough to embrace everybody. We could have a great nation, working hand in hand, all of us, forgetting the fact that we're going to be superior one over the other. We should work on an equal basis as Canadians who are going to build a nation. Canadians should be given every opportunity to be bilingual or polylingual if they choose, and French and English will remain the dominant languages. But unhyphenated Canadianism should be good enough for everybody.[25]

As a leadership candidate, Starr was interviewed by several newspapers and had the opportunity to express his views on a large number of issues. In response to their questions, Starr said he had supported an NDP sub-amendment urging a halt to the United States bombing of North Vietnam while some of the other Conservatives had opposed it. Although Starr disagreed with the bombing, he continued describing the United States as "the bulwark on behalf of democracy in fighting the spread of communism." Regarding the questions of pensions and medicare, he opposed the compulsory aspects of these programs but described himself as "not so far to the right that I wouldn't help the needy." About the flag issue, which had dominated Canadian politics for many months, Starr said that although originally opposed to it, he now liked the maple leaf flag "because it's our flag." Concerning the on-going debates on federal-provincial relations, especially the issue of Quebec's role within Confederation, Starr suggested that provincial and federal governments should sit down together during the centennial year for what he termed a "family conference."[26] On more than one occasion, Starr stated that the "family model" was a basic concept of Canadian conservatism.

The only policy declaration Starr made which attracted media attention during his leadership campaign was another controversial event. He proposed a freeze should be placed on wages and prices by the government to counter inflation, and that income tax should

---

24. *Toronto Telegram*, May 1, 1965.
25. *The Globe and Mail*, July 22, 1967.
26. *The Brandon Sun*, May 30, 1967.

be abolished and replaced with a general sales tax on all goods and services, except on some essentials such as food and clothing. Starr drew cheers and criticism from a Progressive Conservative seminar held in April when he called for the abolition of income tax and a temporary wage and price freeze. He also called for the expropriation of land held by speculators to lower land costs and a capital-gains tax on quick profits made in stock-market "gambling."[27] Starr felt personal income tax was an unfair way to raise funds and he would work to establish a federal trading tax instead of the existing system. One negative comment came from George Peck, a Progressive Conservative representing the Scarborough East riding in the Ontario Legislature. He could not understand how a member of a free-enterprise political party could advocate "pure socialist dogma." On April 11, 1967, the *Telegram* stated:

> The temporary wage and price freeze Mr. Starr is advocating might be possible to implement in wartime, but hardly in peacetime. Such federal decrees would just not be practical. What the government could do, however, is set realistic guidelines for wages and prices. But it would be up to the public to match prices and wages in the light of present-day supply and demand. It has to be this way to maintain the free enterprise system. It cannot be done by government edict. If wages and prices were to be frozen, there would have to be a form of rationing as well.

The *Toronto Star* published the headline, "Mr. Starr is in Fantasyland" and reported that he was putting forward proposals more extreme than anything the NDP had ever advocated and,

> more extreme, indeed, than any program the Canadian Communists have announced publicly in recent years. The trading-tax Mr. Starr suggests as an alternative would be a real block-buster. To compensate for the lost revenue from the income tax, the rates would have to be sky-high. They would inevitably give a sharp boost to the cost of living—thus countering the effect of Mr. Starr's price-wage freeze.

The *Toronto Star* found it difficult to understand why a politician of Starr's experience would seriously propose such measures. Starr's proposals also spread some confusion among the UAW members in Oshawa, where the union was entering into negotiations with General Motors for wage parity with the United States.[28] Starr, however, defended his proposals as being the only answer to the current economic difficulties, and added that he was receiving letters of support from ordinary Canadians who were concerned about supporting their families while the cost of living was continually increasing. Starr said that this situation obliged everyone to demand higher and higher wages when people really wanted stability.[29]

Starr's leadership campaign was plagued by persistent rumours that he was going to withdraw from the race, reports he had to continually deny. He felt there was an organized

---
27. *Toronto Star*, April 10, 1967.
28. Ibid., April 11, 1967.
29. *The Globe Magazine*, July 22, 1967.

campaign to persuade him to withdraw. Starr also had to deny reports that he had decided to support Donald Fleming, the former Conservative Finance Minister. Starr said, "Mr. Fleming is trying to swing the party to the far right. I believe in a middle course between Mr. Fleming and Alvin Hamilton."[30]

When the organizers of the 1967 Progressive Conservative convention inquired with Starr regarding his contact person and organization on June 1, 1967, Starr replied, "I have no organization set up as yet and as a result cannot give you any name for contact purposes."[31] Starr was faced with several other difficulties in his leadership campaign across the country. Despite his many previous campaign trips, he was not sufficiently well-known nationally among the general public. His skill as a platform speaker, television performer, and respondent at press conferences was considered by political observers to be no more than adequate when compared to the other leadership candidates. On August 11, 1967, all the leadership candidates except Starr attended four days of policy discussions during the Quebec "thinkers" conference.[32] One of the major policy recommendations at this conference was the support of the "two nations" concept of Canada.

In the local press and among political observers, there was a general consensus that on the more positive side, Starr did maintain some prominence in opposition as Conservative House Leader since early 1965 and as a hard-working and aggressive critic of Liberal government policy. Starr was also well liked for his quiet dignity, warmth, frankness, appeal as a prominent member of a large ethnocultural group and the competence with which he handled the Department of Labour in the Diefenbaker government. Starr's reputation as a "nice guy" enabled him not to be personally associated the way Diefenbaker was at that time, with the high unemployment rate during his tenure as Minister of Labour from 1957 to 1963. Starr was generally remembered by members of the party as a good minister.

On August 21, 1967, Erik Nielson was announced as Starr's campaign manager. Starr also stated, "I will be guided by the ideas of Senator Allister Grosart. He had had a lot of experience in this field and handled the campaigns of the Hon. George Drew and Mr. Diefenbaker." His campaign would be "low-key" and, he added, "I am unable to arrange a vast campaign as others have. The reason is obvious—financial. My main campaign is going to be centered at the convention." Starr would try to meet all 2,400 delegates before the voting in the last four days. But, he added, "If the delegates are committed there isn't much I can do about it. But I think 50 to 60 percent will not be committed. I have a chance with them."[33] Starr's strategy was to mobilize Diefenbaker's supporters. During his many trips to western Canada to enlist the support of the large ethnocultural groups for the Progressive Conservative Party, Starr felt that he had established a relatively solid base of support among party members from these groups, especially the Ukrainian members who normally would have supported Diefenbaker. Starr would not make any predictions but he did say that Diefenbaker's entrance as a leadership candidate was a 50–50 proposition.

---

30. *Toronto Telegram*, July 21, 1967.
31. LAC, Progressive Conservative Party Collection, MG 28, IV-2, Vol. 253, file — Convention 1967 — Candidates.
32. *Oshawa Times*, August 11, 1967.
33. Ibid., August 21, 23, 1967; see also, *Toronto Telegram*, August 21, 1967.

The five delegates from the Ontario riding all pledged their support for Starr.[34] Anne Starr said, "We're not too excited; Mike is running a quiet campaign." She said that they maintained what she called "our ordinary family life" and would leave election fever to others. At this time, Anne Starr was an honorary vice-regent of the Imperial Order Daughters of the Empire Golden Jubilee chapter to which she had belonged since 1945. She also worked whenever possible with the Oshawa hospital ladies auxiliary.[35] On weekends they were regularly invited to various social events in Oshawa. Starr usually relaxed by playing a few rounds of golf at the Oshawa Golf Club every week, by watching John Wayne movies, and reading political-science and James Bond books.[36]

While other leadership candidates campaigned across the country, Starr's lack of a campaign budget obliged him to refuse speaking engagements unless his expenses were paid.[37] Starr campaigned by making long-distance phone calls to delegates, answering letters and planning strategy. When Starr spoke to the Toronto Progressive Conservative Businessmen's Association, he received loud applause when he rejected the idea of any special privileges for Quebec. He agreed with Diefenbaker that there was no room in Canada for a "two-nation" concept. Starr believed that all provinces had an equal place but not under the two-nation idea. Starr opposed the concept of a "special status" for any one province. He felt those wishing to speak French should have the opportunity to do so by choice and not by compulsion.

In a public poll conducted by the *Toronto Star* at the Canadian National Exhibition, Starr ranked seventh of the nine candidates most likely to succeed John Diefenbaker.[38] When informed of the poll results, Starr said that the surveys represented only a small percentage of the population. He said that his apparent low rating was probably due to the lack of publicity that he had received. People did not have the opportunity to know him as well as some of the other candidates, but he felt that things would be different at the convention. Starr said that he was much better known among Progressive Conservatives because of past associations and elections.[39]

Starr planned to make a personal appeal to each of the 2,400 delegates before the voting began on the last of the four days. He felt his traditionally effortless ability to quickly gain friends and supporters would be a major advantage in his campaign. He said:

I feel that I'm the type of candidate who represents the ordinary citizens of Canada. They know . . . they have faith in me. They know I will always do what is best for the ordinary working man and the ordinary citizen in this country, the typical Canadian. I don't represent any one faction like some of the others probably may.[40]

---

34. Ibid.
35. *Toronto Telegram*, August 31, 1967; *Oshawa Times*, August 31, 1967.
36. *Oshawa Times*, August 23, 1967.
37. Michael Vineberg, *The Progressive Conservative Leadership Convention, 1967*, MA thesis, McGill University, 1968, p. 56.
38. *Toronto Star*, August 23, 1967, "Ex-Poll '67."
39. *Oshawa Times*, August 25, 1967.
40. *The Globe Magazine*, July 22, 1967.

According to Starr, the typical Canadian was "the salaried employee worried about the cost of living, the home-owner concerned with raising his family, the good neighbour who works for his community." Starr continued, "Most people still admire the virtue of loyalty. I think this sort of thing appeals to people because they practice it in their own lives. I think it is up to people to decide. They listen to me. I meet them and I leave it to their good judgement to decide whether I merit their support or not."

The planned campaign organization would include approximately a hundred people. Robert Nicol was responsible for the organization under Erik Nielson, and his main responsibility was to keep in contact with "all delegates coming in from across Canada to support Mr. Starr."[41] Nicol was also planning a "mass demonstration" at the convention. He had produced a four-sided pamphlet that promoted Starr as the next Progressive Conservative leader to bring "unity in our party" and "victory at the polls." Compared to the other candidates who were spending up to $100,000, it was rumoured that Starr would spend between $10,000 and $20,000 on his campaign.

Erik Nielson stated that personal contact would be the basis of the whole Starr leadership campaign. Nielson's basic function was "to bring together the delegates and Mike." In order to promote this campaign strategy a reception room would be established in every major hotel in Toronto during the leadership convention. Nielson said Starr would not make any speeches or personal appeals for votes to the delegates but he would merely meet with them. If they wanted to talk then that was fine--but Starr would not force himself on them. Personality was generally recognized as Mike's strong factor and he spoke plainly and bluntly. According to Nielson, Starr was one of the few politicians the ordinary guy could understand. The campaign tactic was obvious. It was hoped that Starr's subtle quietness would contrast visibly with the vocal sales approach of the other candidates and in this way appeal to a number of delegates. On September 5, 1967, Starr reiterated he had no intention of withdrawing from the Conservative Party leadership race even if Diefenbaker declared himself as a candidate.

As the date of the convention approached—it was to be held at Maple Leaf Gardens in Toronto the week after Labour Day—the official slogan of the Starr campaign "For Unity in our Party, For Victory at the Polls" was replaced by the more easily remembered slogans like "Starr Light, Starr Bright" and "Hitch Your Wagon to A Starr." On September 7, before the convention, Starr said, "today I feel my campaign is just beginning to roll and my supporters are rallying around. We have just begun to fight." Starr had been promised support from at least fourteen Conservative Members of Parliament and he noted, "That's a lot more than some of the front runners have."[42] In addition, four Ontario provincial cabinet ministers were expected to sign his nomination papers and wear Starr buttons. Among his supporters were George Wardrope, Allan Grossman, John Yaremko, Dr. Matthew Dymond and Dr. Hugh Horner. Peter Savaryn, from the Alberta Progressive Conservative Party and a prominent Ukrainian community leader, was also a declared supporter.

Starr received expressions of support from delegates from every province of Canada. He received strong and visible support from many western delegates. Even some Quebec delegates told Starr that they would support him. He had not expected to receive much

---

41. *Oshawa Times*, August 31, 1967.
42. Ibid., September 7, 1967.

support from Quebec and, as a result, had made little or no effort to obtain supporters from the province. The Starr campaign was expected to gather further momentum when many Oshawa and district supporters were supposed to pour into Toronto. They were expected to lend active and moral support, and also vocal background at Starr's nomination and when he made his speech to the convention. He had no plans to try to direct his supporters to any of the other leadership candidates and said, "The truth is that I haven't yet made up my mind who I will vote for if I am eliminated. My supporters will make up their own minds. I won't be wearing any other candidates' badges. Right now the whole situation is a question mark."[43]

When Diefenbaker appeared at the convention, the leadership candidates including Starr visited him in the vice-regal suite on the sixteenth floor of the Royal York Hotel. On the way, Starr met reporters waiting for leadership-campaign scoops; Starr said simply that he was merely dropping-in to "say hello" and see how Diefenbaker was feeling. In reply to a question whether he would ask Diefenbaker for his support, Starr replied, "He knows I'd appreciate it if he gave it to me. It's up to him." Starr added, "I haven't asked anybody for support." A reporter then asked, "Who are you going to throw your support to if you get knocked off the first or second ballot?" Starr quickly replied, "Well, there wouldn't be much support to throw anywhere, would there?" And everyone had a good laugh.[44] Diefenbaker was in his pyjamas and he told Starr to sit down. Starr sat on the other bed and Diefenbaker asked, "Do you think I should run again?" Starr replied, "Oh, my God, no!" and then he got up and left the room.[45]

On the night of Thursday, September 7, after the impassioned Diefenbaker plea against the two-nation theory, Starr and his supporters were even more optimistic. Of all the leadership candidates only Starr had declared himself strongly against the two-nation concept already endorsed by the convention's policy committee. He now hoped to gain added strength from those Diefenbaker supporters who agreed with the old "Chief" that the two-nation policy was unacceptable. Starr said, "I think Mr. Diefenbaker's speech would have hurt Stanfield, Roblin and all the other candidates who have favoured some form of two-nations in Canada." Late that same evening John Diefenbaker formally decided to let his name stand in the leadership race. Diefenbaker's last-minute entry into the leadership contest severely limited Starr's hopes. Much of his delegate strength was in the prairies where many of the delegates were now going to return to their first loyalty, the "Old Chief." Because Starr had made commitments to his supporters and some financial obligations were incurred, it was simply too late to withdraw his candidacy. Candidates for the leadership of the Progressive Conservative Party required the signatures of at least two delegates on his nominating papers. On Friday at 8:58 a.m., Mike Starr filed his papers.

Starr was nominated after a eight-minute-long address by Dr. Philip Bernard Rynard, the former Member of Parliament for Simcoe East. His seconder was René Létourneau, a former Member of Parliament from the Quebec riding of Stanstead, who spoke for four minutes. On Friday, September 8, Starr marched in at the head of a banner that bore a

---

43. Ibid.
44. LAC, National Film, Television and Sound Archives, Hail and Farewell, CBC Canada-1967, 01V1CV, 2, 3 and 4.
45. *Oshawa/Whitby This Week*, October 28, 1987.

Figures 17.1 and 17.2 Images from the Starr leadership campaign (Grant Harper material). Starr ran a modest leadership campaign based on his previous federal and municipal experience and also on his popularity among the ethnocultural groups. He had originally expected that John Diefenbaker would not run as a candidate. However, when Diefenbaker declared his candidacy, Starr's hopes that he may emerge as a possible kingmaker in the leadership race were shattered.

Canadian flag and the slogan "One Canada" and he was followed by some 200 demonstrators, only a few of whom appeared to be wearing the delegate's ribbons. Rynard said "He serves his country with great ability, unfailing success and above all unquestionable loyalty," and Létourneau said Starr's election as leader would win seats for the Conservative Party in Quebec.[46]

Starr made an emotional appeal for support to the convention. He told the 10,000 people at Maple Leaf Gardens that if the party could not settle its own differences, it had no right to seek national support when Canada's major problem was one of national unity. He asked this audience to put the past behind them. Starr spoke of his own background and experience and projected the image of a sincere and simple man.[47] He reminded them he earned $5.00 a week in his early working days and now he was seeking the leadership of a national political party. Starr emphasized, "Only in a country such as Canada could this happen to a man whose parents came here as immigrants." Starr said that he had no gifts with which to attract delegates and he had not wined and dined them. His duties as House Leader prevented him from campaigning across the country. He admitted that a campaign of that nature would be out of character for him. However, he made it clear that he knew something about winning in his own elections and also helping many other Conservative candidates in recent elections. He said the task was to organize and unite Progressive Conservatives, to lead the opposition in the Commons with experience, to clarify the policies of the party and make them understandable to all Canadians and, finally, to become the Prime Minister. On the unity issue, Starr said that immigrants came to Canada not as English or French Canadians but as people who simply wanted to be

---

46. *The Globe and Mail*, September 9, 1967.
47. Newman, *The Distemper of Our Times*, p. 176.

Canadians. He stated, "The world is big enough to include all of us." Starr was also the only leadership candidate who raised the threat of communism for the consideration of the convention. Although most of the candidates spoke in both French and English, Starr spoke only in English. At the end of his speech, Anne Starr joined her husband on the podium to acknowledge the applause of the delegates.[48]

Compared to other leadership candidates, Starr ran practically without money, publicity or an elaborate campaign, and he finished accordingly. He received just 45 votes on the first ballot. Robert Stanfield led with 519 votes, Roblin had 349, Fulton 343, Hees 295, Diefenbaker 271, McCutcheon 137, Hamilton 136 and Fleming 128. On the second ballot Starr received 34 votes and, as a result, was eliminated. At the end of the voting, Robert Stanfield was elected the leader of the Progressive Conservative Party.

Starr admitted the entry of John Diefenbaker and the strong showing of Alvin Hamilton had seriously reduced his total vote. He had no way of knowing how many votes he would have received if Diefenbaker had not entered the leadership race but "guessed" that he would have received around 100 votes on the first ballot. Starr admitted that he was "pretty bitter" immediately after the voting because he had had definite commitments prior to the election which amounted to much more than forty-five votes. Starr claimed it would have been "nonsense" for him to try to swing his supporters to any other candidate because, under the voting system, "you don't know where your support really is." Starr was not approached by other candidates for support and did not indicate to his supporters an alternative preference. Although many political observers suggested Starr supported Duff Roblin after his own elimination, Starr declined to comment; he did, however, admit some of his delegates later supported Stanfield. The other candidates' election machines were too strong and Starr did not have the necessary financial support to organize a successful campaign. However, Starr enjoyed the convention and he felt that he had conducted a good, dignified campaign.[49] Starr believed that if Diefenbaker had declared his candidacy at an early date he would have been a formidable candidate at the convention. The votes that Alvin Hamilton, Donald Fleming and Starr received, in addition to Diefenbaker's own votes, would have amounted to over 400 votes on the first ballot. The results of the leadership campaign and Canadian politics could have been different.[50]

In reviewing his candidature, Starr knew that he would not emerge as the winner but he felt that he had the opportunity to be a "power broker" within the Conservative Party. He later stated that he ran because he wanted to open doors for other politicians with similar ethnocultural backgrounds who had leadership ambitions. If Starr tried and failed, he had, at least, pointed others in the direction where they would hopefully succeed.

---

48. *Oshawa Times*, September 9, 1967; see also, LAC, Sound Archives, Progressive Conservative Party Convention, 1967, ACC 1968-31, Tapes 623–626.
49. *Oshawa Times*, September 11, 1967.
50. Stursberg, *Diefenbaker: Leadership Lost*, p. 194.

Chapter 18
The 1968 Federal Election

Starr knew his future as Conservative Party House Leader would be decided by Robert Stanfield, the newly elected leader and, on September 11, 1967, said he did not plan to do anything until hearing from Stanfield. After a Conservative caucus meeting on September 25, Stanfield announced Starr would be interim Opposition Leader of the Conservative Party and also the House Leader until Stanfield took his seat in the House of Commons.[1] Prime Minister Lester Pearson rose in the House to congratulate Starr on his appointment as acting leader of the Opposition. Pearson said,

> He is an old friend and a doughty foe. We on this side—and I am sure that this is true of members of the House on whatever side they may sit—appreciate his quiet, sincere and effective service to his party, to Parliament and to his country. In short he is a good man and a fine public servant.[2]

As he had Diefenbaker, Starr fully supported Robert Stanfield as the new leader of the Progressive Conservative Party. In a speech in the House, Starr clearly stated his loyalty and described Stanfield as

> a man of integrity, thoughtfulness and reason, one who has projected his image in a most acceptable way in Canada and the members of this party in this chamber as well as throughout Canada are looking forward to his entry into the House of Commons as soon as possible. I must say emphatically that we are all united behind him to form an effective and forceful opposition.[3]

Starr's candidacy and his position within the Conservative Party further increased the awareness of the new leadership of the role of the ethnocultural groups in Canadian political life. Stanfield spoke to more than 2,500 Ukrainian Canadians at a centennial concert sponsored by the Ukrainian Canadian Committee at Massey Hall in Toronto. He said that the two groups that founded Canada, the English and the French, were obliged to respect each other in order to achieve Confederation. All the ethnocultural groups that contributed to the building of Canada now had to respect each other if Canada was to survive in the future. Stanfield, who spoke during the intermission of the concert, was applauded, but a standing ovation was reserved for Starr who had introduced Robert Stanfield to the audience.[4]

---

1. *The Globe and Mail*, September 26, 1967; *Oshawa Times*, September 25, 1967.
2. *House of Commons Debates*, 2nd Session, Vol. III, September 25, 1967, p. 2399.
3. *House of Commons Debates*, September 25, 1967, p. 2400.
4. *The Globe and Mail*, October 30, 1967.

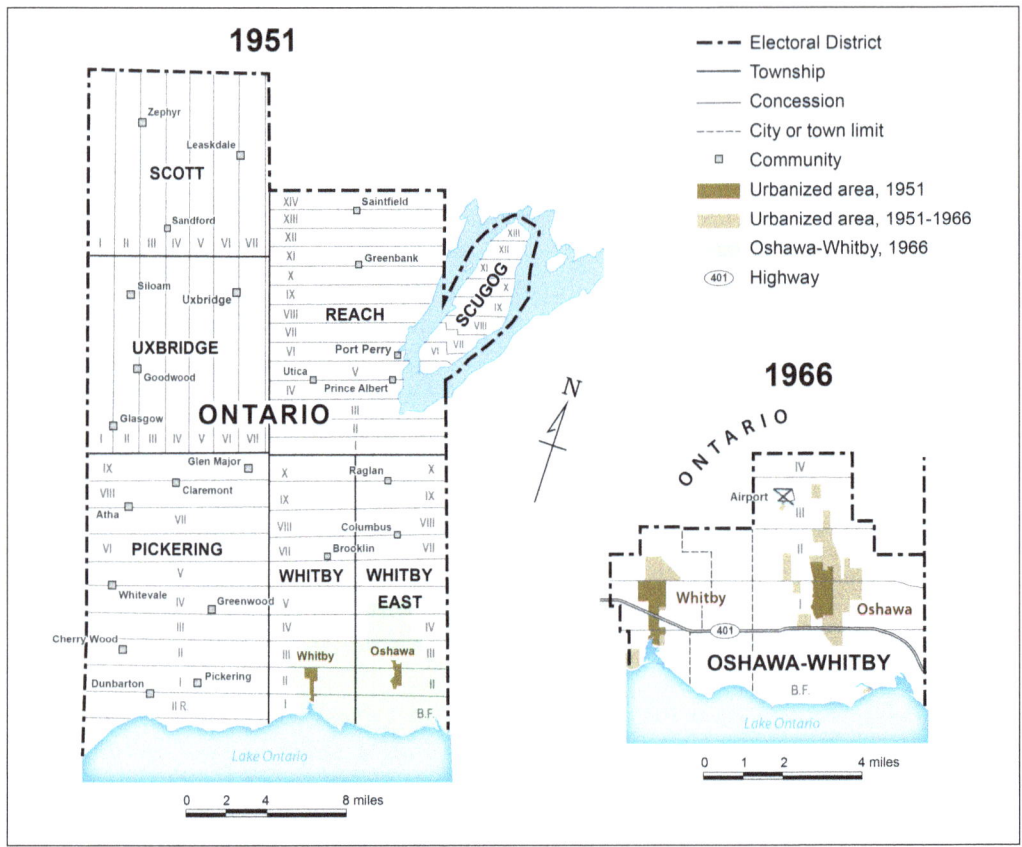

Figure 18.1 Electoral map of the Ontario/Oshawa-Whitby riding. The Ontario riding that first elected Mike Starr in 1953 had a large rural component that provided a steady base of support for Starr. In 1967–68, redistribution created the new riding of Oshawa-Whitby, composed of urban areas, centres of strong union support. This redistribution was a major factor in the outcome of the 1968 federal election.

The redistribution of the electoral ridings that was debated at length in the House of Commons in 1964 was finally implemented and the riding of Ontario was divided into two ridings, one composed of the rural townships and another of the largely urban areas. On October 18, 1967, Starr moved in the House that the new electoral district be named "Oshawa-Whitby" rather than "Oshawa." The motion was accepted and the bill read the first time. The rural areas of the riding remained as Ontario Riding.[5]

In the few short weeks that Starr led the Progressive Conservatives in the House, he was considered by political observers to have performed well, asking many probing questions during the daily question period and making one major speech on the Liberal government's manpower policies. Stanfield was elected to the House of Commons on November 6, 1967 and took his seat on November 15. Starr remained Opposition Leader and sat immediately to the left of Stanfield.

On November 14, 1967, Starr's last day as leader of the Opposition, Lester Pearson again offered his congratulations, telling the House

---

5. *House of Commons Debates*, October 18, 1967, p. 3221.

I hope he will not misunderstand me when I offer the congratulations of the House on the way he had carried out his responsibilities. Of course, Mr. Speaker, there have been times when he has been quite unreasonable and strong headed in his criticism of the government, but he seems to get away with that sort of thing, yet maintain the regard, respect and affection of us all. Let me say, Mr. Speaker, that he will move over in a political but not in a physical sense and we are delighted that he will still be around.[6]

Starr continued to maintain his contacts and interests in the Ukrainian-Canadian community. The fiftieth anniversary of the Bolshevik Revolution was approaching and opposition to this event united the Ukrainian-Canadian anti-Communist organizations. Approximately 350 protestors organized large protests on November 7, 1967, in front of the Soviet Embassy in Ottawa while a similar demonstration was held at the Soviet consulate in Montreal.[7] The protestors included Ukrainian Canadians and other ethnocultural groups tracing their origins to Central and Eastern Europe; some Canadian-born participants also attended. These demonstrations were of unprecedented size and duration and particularly annoyed the Soviets.[8] What aggravated the situation was the presence of Yaroslav Stetsko, president of the Anti-Bolshevik Bloc of Nations and a leader of the Organization of Ukrainian Nationalists.[9]

The various national Ukrainian committees and organizations had been discussing the need for an international umbrella organization to represent their political interests at the international level. In November 1967, the First World Congress of Free Ukrainians was held in New York City to unite the various anti-Communist Ukrainian organizations throughout the world in their protest against the policies and practices of the Soviet Union in regards to Ukraine. The congress attracted over 1,000 delegates from twenty-two countries. John Diefenbaker and Mike Starr were invited to address delegates. Starr was the main speaker at a four-hour freedom rally in Madison Square Garden on Saturday, November 18. Addressing the delegates in Ukrainian, Starr spoke about the fifty years of Communist rule in Ukraine and in Eastern Europe and said that whatever material progress Communists had made, they had not progressed one step beyond the political philosophy of the Tatars, the Ivans, the Peters and the Catherines. No tsar was ever more absolute than the men in the Kremlin. He added, "The surest blow we can strike in today's world is the repeated blow of truth. The truth about the foreign dominations imposed by Moscow. It may not be in our power to force freedom from the tyrant by arms. But it does lie in our power to fight for a free Ukrainian state by a relentless war of words, deeds and demonstrations."[10]

---

6. Ibid., November 14, 1967, p. 4233; *Oshawa Times,* November 14, 1967.
7. *The Globe and Mail*, November 8, 1967.
8. "Stiff Soviet note of protest charges Canada connived in embassy violence," *The Globe and Mail*, November 17, 1967.
9. Robert A. D. Ford, *Our Man in Moscow, A Diplomat's Reflections on the Soviet Union*, University of Toronto Press, Toronto, 1989, p. 104. Yaroslav Stetsko, headquartered in Munich, Germany, was head of the Stepan Bandera faction of the Organization of Ukrainian Nationalists, perhaps the most militant section of the Ukrainian nationalist movement. The League for the Liberation of Ukraine was the Canadian organization representing this movement.
10. LAC, The Hon. Michael Starr Papers, MG 32, D 15, Mike Starr Story, Vol. Five (1965-1983); for an edited and abbreviated version, see speech by Michael Starr in *First World Congress of Free*

Two thousand people marched on the Soviet mission at the United Nations and stormed to within fifty feet of the mission before being thrown back by more than 150 policemen.[11] This event made the front pages of the international press, including all of the Ukrainian-Canadian newspapers. Diefenbaker spoke about Soviet colonialism at the closing banquet of the congress on the evening of Sunday, November 19.[12]

Starr's skill and experience as House Leader became evident on February 19, 1968. Progressive Conservative members were in good spirits with the recent election of their new leader. Prime Minister Lester Pearson had announced his retirement and was holidaying in Jamaica; a campaign for a new leader of the Liberal Party had been launched. Liberal Members of Parliament who were leadership candidates were campaigning across the country. Robert Winters was the interim Prime Minister and Mitchell Sharp, as Minister of Finance, was shepherding Bill C-193 through the House of Commons. This bill introduced a number of amendments to the Income Tax Act. It soon became obvious the Liberal Party did not have sufficient members in the House to pass the amendment. The debate started at 3:00 p.m. and continued after the dinner break. The bill to amend the Income Tax Act was then submitted for a third reading. Starr, as the Conservative House Leader, asked the Deputy Speaker to call the yeas and nays. When the yeas and nays were counted, the vote was eighty-two in favour of Bill C-193 and eighty-four against. The Liberal government had been defeated.[13]

Starr told Stanfield that he would soon be the next Prime Minister but noticed Stanfield paled at the thought. The new leader, however, was not keen to pursue this victory; Stanfield was convinced that a new election would seriously ruin Canada's reputation for political stability with negative consequences for the Canadian economy. Pearson rushed back to Ottawa from his vacation and the Liberal government remained in power.[14] Stanfield's lack of determination to defeat the Liberal government damaged the morale among the members of his party. Starr's aggressive action in the House was in sharp contrast to his actions the previous year during debates about the Munsinger affair.

In the Ontario provincial election held on October 17, 1967, NDP candidate Cliff Pilkey won the Oshawa riding.[15] The Progressive Conservative campaign manager, Robert Nicol, attributed the defeat of the Conservative candidate mainly to a "remarkable" NDP job of electioneering. Cliff Pilkey was grateful that William (Bill) Cumptsy, the federal NDP organizer, had been loaned to the Oshawa NDP organization for the provincial election. Cumptsy, who had been the full-time area NDP organizer in Oshawa for two years, had

---

Ukrainians – Proceedings, Winnipeg, 1969, pp. 108–109; also *Ukrainskyi Holos* (Ukrainian Voice), December 6, 1967.
11. *The New York Times*, November 19, 1967.
12. LAC, The Hon. Michael Starr Papers, MG 32, B 15, Mike Starr Story, Vol. Five (1965-1983).
13. *House of Commons Debates*, February 19, 1968, pp. 6893–6899; see also, Newman, *A Nation Divided*, p. 451.
14. Newman, *A Nation Divided*, p. 451
15. Cliff Pilkey was elected in 1963–1966 as an alderman to Oshawa City Council. He was elected to the Ontario Legislature as the NDP MPP for Oshawa in the 1967 provincial election and served until 1971, when he was defeated. In 1976, he was elected President of the Ontario Federation of Labour and held this position until he retired in 1986. He passed away on November 17, 2012. His son, Allan Pilkey was NDP MPP for Oshawa from 1990 to 1995. Obituary: *The Globe and Mail*, December 12, 2012.

been recalled to Oshawa from Ottawa for the election. In September 1967, Gordon Graylish replaced Cumptsy, who had returned to Ottawa to work for the federal NDP. Despite the problems of divisions within the Oshawa UAW local, the NDP riding organization was effective in mobilizing their supporters. The NDP prepared a thorough and detailed organization for the provincial election. The NDP political machine was well-organized and kept gaining momentum toward election day.[16] The NDP won both the city of Oshawa and the town of Whitby. This provincial victory greatly encouraged the NDP federal riding organizers and raised their hopes for the next federal election.[17]

The federal Liberal Party elected Pierre Trudeau as their new leader on April 6, 1968, and he was sworn in as Prime Minister on April 20. Trudeau had been the centre of media attention at the Liberal leadership convention and this launched a political momentum that exploded across Canada: Trudeaumania.[18] With nationalism in Canada and political discontent in Quebec on the rise, many Liberals, and increasingly many Canadians, felt only Trudeau could effectively lead the country. The second session of the twenty-seventh Parliament ended on April 23, 1968, and the new Prime Minister called a federal election for June 25.

On May 5, 1968, the NDP fielded the first official candidate in the new federal riding of Oshawa-Whitby when delegates chose Edward Broadbent to represent them in the federal election. Broadbent was thirty-two years old and an assistant professor of political science at York University.[19] He had been born in Oshawa, where his father worked for General Motors and was a member of the United Autoworkers Union. Many people still remembered "Eddie" as a paperboy and a dedicated student. As a youth, he won a trip sponsored by the Rotary Club to Ottawa and was given a tour of the Parliament Buildings by his Member of Parliament, Mike Starr.[20] He literally had to work his way through college[21] but Broadbent graduated first in the class of 1959 with a bachelor of arts in philosophy from Trinity College, University of Toronto. He went on to earn a master of arts in philosophy and a doctorate in political science. Broadbent taught English for a year at O'Neill Collegiate before attending the London School of Economics in 1962–63 on a Canada Council scholarship. The Oshawa NDP felt Broadbent's education and working-class family background made him an ideal candidate to represent their party in Oshawa-Whitby.[22]

In his nomination speech, Broadbent spoke about the problem of the transfer of power in society from elite groups to the majority. The speech was partly based on the subject of his PhD dissertation, and he summarized his political philosophy by stating, "No boy or girl should begin life with a political or economic advantage over others."[23] He explained this meant providing education for both children and adults without fees at any level, ensuring economic well-being, including housing and complete medical protection, and

---

16. *Oshawa Times*, October 18, 1967.
17. *Oshaworker*, June 6, 1968.
18. For an analysis of this phenomenon, see Paul Litt, *Trudeaumania*, UBC Press, 2016.
19. *Oshawa Times*, May 3, 1968.
20. *The Globe and Mail*, "Broadbent's Progress," October 31, 1987.
21. *Oshaworker*, June 6, 1968. For a detailed biography, see Judy Steed, *Ed Broadbent, The Pursuit of Power*, Viking (Penguin Group), Markham, 1988.
22. Ibid.
23. *Oshawa Times*, May 6, 1968.

guaranteeing French- and English-speaking Canadians the equal right to use their language in legal and educational institutions. However, some of the union members had difficulty understanding Broadbent's nomination speech and felt that there were too many "50-cent words."[24] Broadbent later admitted that "I really was too academic in my approach."[25] He also had to be careful not to aggravate the internal divisions with the Local 222 branch of the UAW union. The union was divided between two factions: autoworkers and democrats. The autoworkers tended to be more right-wing in their politics while democrats were more supportive of the NDP.[26] In later years the democrats increased their influence to the benefit of Broadbent. This division however, with its origins in the early 1950s, was a matter of special concern for Broadbent,[27] and he knew he had to keep on good terms with both caucuses when he was involved in local political issues.[28]

Early in the election campaign, Broadbent predicted a NDP victory: "In the weeks ahead both Mr. Starr and the Liberal candidate are in for a surprise."[29] He began his campaign in earnest on May 9, 1968, when he opened a committee room on Simcoe Street North. On the same day, Desmond G. Newman, the mayor of Whitby, won the Liberal nomination for Oshawa-Whitby by acclamation.[30] The following day, the seventy-five members of the expanded executive of the Progressive Conservative Federal Riding Association reviewed the election campaign in detail. Robert Nicol, the Conservative publicity director, described the event as the largest executive meeting ever held in Oshawa. Starr was officially nominated as the Progressive Conservative candidate for Oshawa-Whitby on May 14, 1968, at a meeting held in Whitby where there were free bus rides and a rock-and-roll band.

In his nomination speech, Starr criticized Pierre Trudeau for degrading the office of Prime Minister to a state of mania. He said,

> This is not a time for clowning, but a time for clear thinking, thoughtfulness and action. ...There are 11 cabinet ministers from Quebec holding 15 portfolios and Ontario has eight ministers holding six portfolios. The rest are scattered across the country. Is this the concept of a just society?[31]

Starr defined the major issues of this campaign as high interest rates, the shortage of housing, and unemployment—all of which were the direct result of the Liberal government's inability to govern.[32]

---

24. *The Globe and Mail,* August 13, 1988.
25. *Toronto Star,* June 22, 1970; LAC, Signature Series, Guy Bertiaume, Librarian and Archivist of Canada in conversation with the Hon. Ed Broadbent, [Public Discussion], February 7, 2017.
26. LAC, Communist Party of Canada fonds, MG28 IV 4, Volume 29, File 29-54, Correspondence, Oshawa Region, 1963, 1965, 1969; Judy Steed, "The first hurdle, an upset victory launched a future leader's career," *The Globe and Mail,* August 13, 1988.
27. Steed, *Ed Broadbent,* p. 114, 121.
28. *The Globe and Mail,* "In Ed Broadbent's old riding, the candidates are in the home stretch," August 10, 1990.
29. *Oshawa Times,* May 6, 1968.
30. Ibid., May 9, 1968.
31. Ibid., May 15, 1968.
32. Ibid., May 10, 1968.

All three candidates in Oshawa-Whitby had opened their official campaigns with personal canvassing. Broadbent was assured of the support of the Oshawa and District Labour Council when he explained his campaign platform.[33] He was able to gain the support of both left and right factions of the UAW local. The support of the UAW union continued to be an important factor in Oshawa political elections. Robert Nicol said that, among the Conservatives, the preliminary work in Starr's campaign was completed and canvassing began in the "corridor" area between Whitby and Oshawa.[34] Desmond G. Newman, the Liberal candidate, had maintained a hectic pace by campaigning sixteen hours per day since he received the nomination. He had planned an extensive door-to-door campaign in Oshawa. The Liberals began their meetings before the election was called. On March 6, 1968, the Oshawa Liberal Club invited Toronto MP Dr. Stanley Haidasz to speak in Oshawa in the hope that his Polish origins would influence the vote of the large Polish community in Oshawa.[35]

Early in the election campaign, the outcome of the Oshawa-Whitby election was already seen as one of the closest three-way races in the country. With a spread of only 2,237 votes between the Liberals and the Progressive Conservatives in 1965 and approximately 5,800 new voters, all candidates had a solid chance of victory. The new riding of Oshawa-Whitby had 53,339 eligible voters. Newman expected to gain votes on the strength of the Trudeaumania generated by the exciting new Prime Minister. The Liberals invited Trudeau, who appeared from the heavens in a helicopter at the Oshawa Shopping Centre. A vast crowd listened to him speaking about building "a just society" before he got back into the helicopter, rose again into the air, and disappeared.[36] NDP supporters always voted faithfully for the NDP regardless of the conditions and it seemed likely Trudeaumania was going to harm Starr more than Broadbent.

Starr was under severe pressure to maintain the previous majority of 2,237 votes if the trends in the previous ten years combined with the result of redistribution were considered as serious factors. He could no longer depend on the traditional Conservative vote in the northern rural section of Ontario County, where he had always maintained a comfortable margin over the Liberals and was always well ahead of the NDP. Starr was not, however, discouraged and felt he would benefit from the new riding boundaries because, without the large rural area to cover, he could focus his efforts and campaign more effectively in the urban centres of Oshawa and Whitby. He claimed to be not too concerned about the effects of the redistribution: Starr had lost Oshawa only once, in 1957, and had won Whitby in each of his seven elections. Also, he was not as heavily involved in the national Progressive Conservative campaign as in previous elections, so he had more time to spend in his own riding.

Broadbent knew redistribution was definitely helping the NDP, especially after the electoral victory in the provincial election. He studied public-opinion polls in the Toronto area since the last election and they showed an increase in the percentage of trade unionists voting NDP. The same trend was observed all over Ontario and in Oshawa. According to Broadbent,

---
33. Ibid., May 17, 1968.
34. Ibid., May 21, 1968.
35. LAC, Hon. Stanley Haidasz fonds, Volume 9, file 23, Oshawa Liberal Association – 1968.
36. Michael Bliss, *Writing History, A Professor's Life*, Dundurn, Toronto, 2011, p. 120.

new people in the riding were more likely to be trade unionists and the younger generation did not have the personal attraction to Starr. There were rumours among younger voters that Broadbent was seen driving a motorcycle and wearing a black leather jacket on the streets of Oshawa. Newman, on the other hand, saw redistribution as a minor factor in relation to the final outcome. He felt that the election would be won by the candidates' policies.

As the campaign progressed, the Conservatives became seriously concerned with the growing popularity of the rival political parties. On June 3, 1968, Progressive Conservatives put into action a special squad to visit homes displaying Liberal or NDP party signs. They had over two hundred door-to-door canvassers working for Starr in the residential and business districts in Oshawa-Whitby. They felt that the previous provincial election was lost because they did not get the votes out,[37] and thus this was the most highly organized drive ever mounted by the Conservatives in the riding. The Conservatives had plans to post 8,000 signs and distribute over 250,000 items of election literature before election day. There were seventy-five Conservative campaign workers in three offices and arrangements were made to have six hundred workers with three hundred cars to transport voters to the polls.

The NDP were also campaigning heavily in the riding. By May 25, Broadbent had knocked on at least 2,500 doors and, by June 6, approximately 95 per cent of Oshawa homes had been visited. The NDP were hoping for total coverage. Broadbent's committee rooms were continually crowded and busy; walls were covered with charts recording the poll canvasses, coloured maps of the poll-by-poll votes in the past elections, and election posters. University students home from school campaigned for Broadbent and young girls in miniskirts greeted workers at plant gates with NDP campaign literature as they left for home. Party workers also campaigned in local beer parlours where workers congregated after their shifts.[38]

On June 6, 1968, Starr was speaking in Regina during a campaign trip across Canada. He claimed that if Trudeau was elected as Prime Minister then "Quebec will get all it wants." He added that Trudeau was "kidding the public" on the issue of strong central government. Starr felt Trudeau talked about one central government but did not illustrate it.[39] On June 7, 1968, Starr was in Yorkton, Saskatchewan, where he described Trudeau as a socialist who should frighten every Canadian: "I'm frightened when you read the background of this man who is a socialist with two other socialists, Mr. Marchand . . . and Mr. Pelletier joined the Liberal Party so that they could put into effect their philosophy. It should frighten every Canadian."[40] Starr returned to the Oshawa-Whitby riding, where he continued his door-to-door campaign. On June 10 he attended a political rally in Scarborough where Robert Stanfield was the main speaker.

Tommy Douglas visited the Oshawa-Whitby riding during his cross-Canada campaign tour, a visit that greatly boosted the morale of local NDP workers. Broadbent claimed his party had enough of an early lead in the campaign to ensure victory.[41] He told a meeting

---

37. *Oshawa Times,* June 3, 1968.
38. LAC, Signature Series, Guy Bertiaume, Librarian and Archivist of Canada in conversation with the Hon. Ed Broadbent [Public Discussion], February 7, 2017.
39. *Oshawa Times,* June 6, 1968.
40. Ibid., June 11, 1968. Igor Gouzenko had published a fifteen-page pamphlet entitled *Memorandum: "Trudeau, a potential Canadian Castro"* that may have influenced Starr.
41. *Oshawa Times,* June 11, 1968.

of the Oshawa and District Labour Council that it was absolutely clear the NDP could win Oshawa-Whitby. Although the NDP had a good organization that worked well, Broadbent warned "if we stop now we're dead." He urged voters to forget Mike Starr was a nice guy; it was, in his opinion, irrelevant in politics and voters had to remember the Conservative policy was "reactionary."[42] The NDP issued a campaign brochure entitled "Compare the Candidates" that emphasized the differences between Broadbent and the other candidates. The NDP stressed they had Cliff Pilkey representing Oshawa in the Ontario Legislature and that Broadbent was born in Oshawa, had a record of academic achievement, served in the Canadian Armed Forces, was part of the under-thirty-five generation and was, therefore, in touch with young people every day.[43]

Starr's supporters openly referred to the NDP candidate as "Dr. Broadbent" hoping to attract attention to his intellectual background and emphasize the distinction between him and the working-class voters.[44] In a speech at the Kiwanis Club meeting in Hotel Genosha, Starr again stressed his experience—as alderman, mayor of Oshawa, and Ontario riding Member of Parliament for sixteen years. He stressed that he had won respect in the House of Commons as Minister of Labour, Conservative House Leader, and as official Opposition Leader before Robert Stanfield took his seat. Starr, who lived in the riding most of his life, felt that this time he could campaign without a campaign manager. His election committee included seventy-six people, each responsible for some small part of the election campaign, from signs, ethnocultural committees, coffee parties, to radio publicity. Starr claimed he had about 200 workers, 1,500 lawn signs, 1,500 telephone pole-posters and 200 billboards. Most of his campaign workers had a poll to canvass at least once and Starr canvassed personally where he felt it was necessary.

Broadbent, who had a campaign fund of $7,000, erected 6,000 of his 10,000 lawn signs, and completed two of the planned four canvasses of every house. Broadbent's riding machine included six full-time workers and over five hundred volunteers. Four of those full-time workers were on loan from the UAW, a fact that annoyed Liberal candidate Newman, who had to personally pay his five full-time workers. Newman felt poll captains were unnecessary and he attempted to apply his managerial skills to create a task force to mass canvass several polls in a single effort. Newman claimed he had about 200 volunteers but, according to the local press, his large committee rooms were often deserted.[45]

The General Motors main shift change was at 6:00 a.m. and every morning at that time both Broadbent and Newman, along with their supporters, were at a different gate trying to speak to workers. The press reported both had problems communicating with workers: Broadbent because he was an academic, and Newman because he was a businessman. However, Broadbent made a deliberate effort not to speak like a professor, and Newman spoke like an academic.[46] The UAW network inside the General Motors plant made a determined effort to enlist support for Broadbent and the NDP. Each worker was approached by union officials

---

42. Ibid., June 12, 1968.
43. LAC, The Hon. J. Edward Broadbent Papers, MG32 C83, Vol. 92, File 1, Election Campaign, 1968.
44. Steed, *Ed Broadbent*, p. 121.
45. *The Globe and Mail*, June 15, 1968.
46. Ibid.

and encouraged to vote NDP. This link between the local UAW and the NDP was a determining factor in local, provincial and federal elections until the mid-1990s.

Continuing the tradition established in previous elections, the Progressive Conservative campaign stressed its main asset—Mike Starr. In the *Oshawa Times* of June 22, 1968, the following notice appeared which described the Conservative approach and rationale in this election:[47]

> I am neither a Conservative nor Liberal or NDP but I made my decision very easily. Let's decide with logic. . . . If we elect an NDP candidate he will be a backbencher of a minority party. (Surely the number of signs his party distributed in the area is no indication of his ability.) If we elect a Liberal candidate—well, he may be a member of a party in power, but still a backbencher without much influence. Let's leave him as a Mayor of Whitby for a few more years . . . let him learn. Then there is Mike, a man with experience, with influence, a man with all doors open for him in Ottawa. He is a Member of Parliament well liked and respected by senior members of other parties and by their leaders.
> I am voting for Mike Starr.
> Your Neighbour

During this campaign Starr had the opportunity once again to explain Conservative Party political philosophy. He stated that,

> The principles and objectives of the Conservative Party are . . . the paramount importance of the individual, equality of opportunity, responsibility and treatment. Individual liberty within a free society. Continuity in development and progress. One nationality, one Canada. On the basis of these principles, the aims and objectives of the party are therefore: To place national unity and the national welfare above fleeting political advantage, recognizing that Confederation was founded and rests upon unity in equality between the two basic races of Canada with every Canadian—regardless of race or creed—having equality of opportunity for human betterment and economic progress. . . . To respect the rights and initiative of the individual that he may have the opportunity of improving his own lot starting from a common national point of equal opportunity and equal treatment. To encourage the enterprise of the individual and stimulate free enterprise as the best means of creating national prosperity.[48]

The automobile free trade agreement had been in effect since January 1965 and Oshawa continued growing and prospering. In 1968, the city's population reached 74,194. An important factor contributing to industrial growth in Oshawa was the Canadian government's tariff policy. This expansion began when protective tariffs were imposed against the United States. The policy provided Canadian industries with a sheltered home market and encouraged the establishment of American branch factories such as General Motors in Oshawa. These factories had access not only to the Canadian market, but also to markets

---

47. *Oshawa Times*, June 22, 1968.
48. Ibid., June 18, 1968.

in Commonwealth countries.[49] But, in October 1966, General Motors announced the layoff of 2,600 workers and, with other reductions, made a total decrease of 3,350 workers in automobile employment. In Oshawa, all three candidates lamented the loss of auto jobs. Locally, Starr was particularly concerned about the auto pact. He said:

> The Auto Pact was put into effect by the present government without reference first to Parliament. The United States on the other hand gave themselves an opportunity for a complete one-year study of the pact's effect on their industry and economy. I have insisted continuously in Parliamentary committees to ascertain its impact on our economy and employment. The government has continuously refused such a study . . . The people of Canada have a right to know where the government stands on this matter because it's not sufficient to say the pact has brought more unemployment. Prior to the agreement being signed, employment in the auto industry was increasing yearly on a satisfactory basis.[50]

Starr had fought against the large layoffs taking place at General Motors because of the auto pact.[51] He would continue speaking on this issue and insisted the whole auto pact and its implications be reviewed. The UAW Local 222, in Oshawa, however, blamed Starr for doing nothing to prevent the layoff of Oshawa workers, an accusation repeatedly raised by the union newspaper, *Oshaworker*.[52]

Election day was June 25, 1968. Despite the rainy weather and overcast sky, 81 per cent of the electorate turned out to vote. The writing was on the wall at Starr's headquarters at the Genosha Hotel the minute the results of the first poll were posted: Starr was trailing by two votes. At the end of the day, the results were as follows:

Candidate	Party	Votes
Edward Broadbent	NDP	15,232
Michael Starr	PC	15,119
Desmond Newman	Lib.	14,819

Because of the extremely narrow margin, Starr refused to concede victory until the results of the resident Canadian Armed Forces' vote were known, which meant a delay of about one week. NDP officials said the military vote would not change the final outcome but Starr felt otherwise. He said, "There's still one poll to hear from and that is the Service vote. On the basis of that we will have to decide what we will do." The Conservatives, including Starr, concluded that they had split enough of the vote with the Liberals to enable the NDP to "sneak in."[53] The phenomenon of Trudeaumania sweeping English Canada extended into

---

49. Regional Studies Program, *Research Publication Number Three, Population COJPB, Oshawa, 1967*, Ontario, p. 36.
50. *Oshawa Times*, June 22, 1968.
51. *Toronto Telegram*, August 30, 1966.
52. *Oshaworker*, June 20, 1968.
53. Ibid.

Oshawa and increased the vote for the Liberals to the point where it created a three-way split from which Broadbent emerged as the winner. It may be speculated that some of the older voters did not vote for Starr because they respected John Diefenbaker and did not appreciate his treatment during the Progressive Conservative leadership campaign.[54]

Broadbent won the election because of the efforts of the riding NDP organization that began in earnest at the time of the provincial elections. Broadbent said, "And I would like to think that my policies had something to appeal to the voters. We appealed to a much greater section of the population than the NDP has ever done. We've had lawyers and teachers and all kinds of middle-class people taking an active part in the campaign which we have never had before."[55] Gordon Graylish, regional organizer for the NDP, added, "We believe the Party organization brought out the vote. This is the first time the issues have really been brought to the public and they were brought by a very good candidate."[56] Broadbent attributed his victory to the fact he talked to autoworkers about their on-the-job problems and about the housing shortage while Starr campaigned primarily on his past record. The large Broadbent clan was also mobilized to support Ed, as he was known. Although they may have previously supported other political parties, the clan put "family first" and all voted for Ed and the NDP.[57] Broadbent's appeal extended into the Ukrainian community and made, in one case, a crucial impact: Nestor Pidwerbecki, who had earlier worked for Starr in previous elections, began to work for Broadbent. He later became Broadbent's constituency representative for a decade.[58]

On June 29, 1968 the votes were as follows:

Candidate	Party	Votes
Edward Broadbent	NDP	15,208
Michael Starr	PC	15,118
Desmond Newman	Lib.	14,881

The NDP's election night lead was announced as 113 votes but it was reduced to 62 votes when it was found in the revised count that some votes had been credited to the wrong candidate. The forces' poll result had further reduced the NDP margin to 20 votes.[59] The Armed Service vote was divided as follows:

Candidate	Party	Votes
Desmond Newman	Lib.	60
Michael Starr	PC	51
Edward Broadbent	NDP	9

54. Kyba, *Alvin*, p. 283.
55. Ibid.
56. Ibid.
57. LAC, Signature Series, Guy Bertiaume, Librarian and Archivist of Canada in conversation with the Hon. Ed Broadbent, [Public Discussion], February 7, 2017.
58. Steed, *Ed Broadbent*, p. 279. Pidwerbecki also began his long career as a municipal politician, and in 2014–16 he was Deputy Mayor of Oshawa.(*Oshawa This Week*, September 14, 2014).
59. Ibid., June 29, 1968.

On July 3, Broadbent was still optimistic he would be upheld as the winner. Starr confirmed that he would seek a recount of the ballots.[60] During the recount, it became obvious that it was the use of ballpoint pens that cost Starr his seat in Parliament after representing the area riding for sixteen years. The election law stipulated that a ballot must be crossed with a black pencil and anything else is rejected. On July 13, Starr said, "The ballpoint pen ballots were my problem. They cost me about 50 votes that had been passed by the Deputy Returning Officers." Starr confirmed the actual recount was done thoroughly and fairly and that, in the final analysis, the people had spoken. Starr added, "I had to go to a recount for the sake of the people that worked for me and voted for me. I owed it to them."[61] The recount climaxed the tense and close race that started when the polls closed on June 25. The official recount also revealed errors in the preliminary vote statements. This resulted in a further loss of votes by Broadbent that cut his lead at one point during the recount to a precious eight votes. The final official total of the vote was as follows:[62]

Candidate	Party	Votes	Votes (%)
Edward Broadbent	NDP	15,224	33.58%
Michael Starr	PC	15,209	33.55%
Desmond Newman	Lib.	14,899	32.87%

When reporters asked Starr about his plans for the near future, he replied that it was much too soon to tell.[63]

---

60. Ibid., July 3, 1968.
61. Ibid., July 13, 1968.
62. *Twenty-Eighth General Election 1968, Report of the Chief Electoral Officer*, Queen's Printer, Ottawa, 1969, p. 121.
63. *Oshawa Times*, July 13, 1968.

Chapter 19
Public Service, 1968–1973

The various political factors that influenced the federal election in Oshawa had a much stronger impact in the rest of Canada. Trudeaumania in particular was credited for the substantial Liberal victory. The results of the 1968 federal election were as follows:

Party	Seats
Liberal	155
Progressive Conservative	72
New Democratic Party	22
Social Credit	14
Independent	1

Many prominent and well-known Conservative politicians were defeated. In addition to Mike Starr, there were Wallace McCutcheon and Dalton Camp in Ontario, Roblin in Manitoba, Hamilton in Saskatchewan and Fulton in British Columbia. Only three of the candidates who had contested the party's leadership only ten months before had survived—Stanfield, Diefenbaker and George Hees. Stanfield later said that it was his misfortune in 1968 that ". . . all the 'bonks' got elected while all the good members were defeated."[1]

The Progressive Conservative national headquarters contacted Arthur Maloney about a possible application to the Ontario Court of Appeal concerning Starr's narrow defeat. Maloney, Starr's former Parliamentary Secretary, was a prominent Toronto lawyer. An appeal was filed under section 55 of the Canada Elections Act and adjourned until August 1, 1968. The appeal was based on the approximately 125 ballots under dispute during the recount.[2] When Starr heard about this recount, he gave it some thought then decided he would not support it. On July 23, he instructed Arthur Maloney to withdraw the court appeal.[3] Starr then left with his family to a small cottage near Orono, not far from Oshawa, for a well-deserved rest.

On August 7, 1968, the *Toronto Daily Star* reported that former Labour Minister Mike Starr was without a job.[4] The article suggested Starr was in difficulty because he had "no wealth or advanced education." Starr, who was recovering from the election battle, became deeply annoyed with this story and described it as "bunk" and "not factual." He then refused

---
1. Geoffrey Stevens, *Stanfield*, McClelland and Stewart Ltd., Toronto, 1973, p. 226.
2. *Oshawa Times*, July 22, 1968.
3. Ibid., July 23, 1968.
4. *Toronto Daily Star*, August 7, 1968.

to grant any more interviews to reporters.[5] This event, at a deeply emotional time in Starr's life, heightened his suspicion of reporters and journalists. As far as Starr was concerned, the journalists were mainly interested in furthering their own careers rather than providing accurate reports and he maintained this attitude for the rest of his life. Robert Stanfield gave considerable thought to Starr's position and future prospects. He felt Starr's defeat was a very serious blow to the party and to him personally,[6] and there were rumours that Starr would receive an executive position within the national Progressive Conservative office in Ottawa. In the meantime, Starr had received several offers of employment but he did not make any definite decisions and preferred to "take it easy."

With the election over, Starr had the opportunity to analyze and evaluate the results of this particular election. In addition to considering general influences such as the riding redistribution and the effects of Trudeaumania, the extremely small number of votes which determined the final results obliged Starr to also evaluate every poll and practically every vote. A few more votes, especially from the Ukrainian community, would have made a great difference in the final results. Also, there was the distinct possibility that Starr would have been elected had he been a candidate in the old riding of Ontario.

On September 27, 1968, Gérard Pelletier, the Secretary of State in the new Liberal government, informed the press, in a surprise announcement, of Starr's appointment as Judge of the Citizenship Court for York and Ontario Counties and the cities of Toronto, Oshawa and Barrie. Starr was to assume the position immediately and serve for a period of seven years. Citizenship Court judges held hearings for persons seeking Canadian citizenship, questioned them on their knowledge of Canada, and administered the oath of citizenship. The Citizenship Court judges were part of the administrative system of the Department of the Secretary of State. Norman Cafik, the newly elected Liberal Member of Parliament for the redrawn Ontario riding, was delighted at Starr's appointment and said that it was an indication of the federal government's appreciation for his services and contributions in the past.[7] Starr, who had received a number of offers from business and industry, felt that this position was more "in his line" and knew that he would enjoy it.

When Starr was appointed Citizenship Court Judge, he decided to continue living in Oshawa and commute to Toronto. He began by trying to find out where the court was: he found the address in the telephone book; it was on the eighth floor of a federal building in Toronto. When Starr visited the building, there were little paper signs with directions that eventually led Starr to the men's washroom but there were no signs on the outside of the building informing the public that it was the offices of the Citizenship Court. Starr felt the conditions inside the building were crowded and lacked dignity.[8]

Starr wanted to ensure that Canadians of Ukrainian descent, including those who were members or former members of Ukrainian left-wing organizations and the Communist Party of Canada, were aware of the opportunity to apply for Canadian citizenship. In the past, these individuals encountered various obstacles in applying for Canadian citizenship. This became a serious issue among members of the Association of United Ukrainian

---

5. *Oshawa Times*, August 8, 1968.
6. Ibid., August 10, 1968.
7. Ibid., September 27, 1968.
8. *Oshawa This Week*, October 18, 1972.

Figure 19.1 On September 27, 1968, Starr was appointed as Judge of the Citizenship Court for York and Ontario Counties and the cities of Toronto, Oshawa and Barrie. Starr enjoyed this position and did his best to encourage old and new immigrants to apply for Canadian citizenship. He proved to be a very popular Citizenship Court Judge. He held this position until 1972, when he resigned to run again as a Progressive Conservative candidate in Oshawa.

Canadians for many years. Starr even encouraged some individuals to contact him personally to normalize their citizenship status.

A Citizenship Court session held in October 1970 was typical: Starr, as judge, presided on the eighth floor of the federal building located on St. Clair Avenue East in Toronto. On this particular occasion, there were seventy-two applicants, from nineteen countries. Starr, dressed in ceremonial robes, was accompanied by RCMP Constable Miles Tymchyshyn; behind him was a large, gold, Canadian coat-of-arms on a blue background, and he was flanked by two Canadian flags. Starr said to the audience,

> You are all acquainted with the words of the oath of allegiance, an oath which removes all service and loyalty you once owed to another country and government. As a Canadian, as well as the freedoms you assume, you also take on a corresponding duty to observe the law and your civic duties and to promote the common good. Remember that freedom also demands a level of self-control and mutual responsibility.

Starr then handed each applicant their certificate and shook hands with them. All stood and sang "O Canada" and "God Save the Queen."[9]

---

9. *The Toronto Telegram*, October 30, 1970

Reflecting on the nature of Canadian citizenship, Starr said,

> Canadians are not a nation of flag-wavers, which is a shame because Canada is a country to be proud of. I try to convey this sense of pride to those becoming Canadian citizens. I speak of the opportunities that can be found in Canada. Everyone can play some part in its development.

Starr generally supported Canada's evolving policy of cultural pluralism and opposed the popular American melting-pot model. He added, "You can't really melt cultures and people in a pot; the black people in the United States are rebelling against this concept."[10]

He proved to be a popular judge who was personally interested in citizenship and immigrant issues and had his own plans to promote greater interest in the problems immigrants faced with attaining Canadian citizenship. Starr was able to co-operate with Ontario's Minister of Citizenship John Yaremko in awarding certificates to new citizens. He held sessions in high-school auditoriums in front of students where dozens of new Canadians received their citizenship papers. To welcome the largest possible number of applicants, Starr even held a citizenship ceremony in June, 1971, in the Steelworkers Union Hall on Cecil Street in Toronto. On this occasion, he presented certificates to fifty-one new Canadians.[11] Starr presided over the largest citizenship court district in Canada and issued over 12,000 certificates a year; about 45 per cent of the total for Canada. Plans for further sessions where hundreds of new citizens received their documents were discouraged by the Department of Secretary of State because they were considered innovative and without precedent.

Starr had another opportunity to express his views about Canadian citizenship in a speech to the annual convention of the Canadian Corps Association, Ontario Command, held in November 1971 in Oshawa. At this event he said that too great a percentage of Canadian citizens take their citizenship for granted and their community responsibilities all too lightly. He was "appalled" at the number of Canadians who did not vote in elections. He believed the country needed citizens who were willing to sacrifice time and energy for the common good. Starr outlined the qualities of his ideal citizen. He said:

> Our task is to build Canadians of integrity, Canadians who will have a love of country but not a selfish love; Canadians who are willing to give of themselves for the good of others and yet not count the cost; Canadians who are prepared to work toward standards of excellence rather than drift with the crowd, and finally, Canadians who will emphasize dignity, nobility and freedom of all men rather than the excellence of a self or specific group.

The convention responded with a standing ovation.[12]

Although Starr was no longer involved in politics, people still phoned and visited him at his home with their various problems—employment for family members, income-tax problems, pensions—as they did when he was in Parliament. He continued his involvement

---

10. Ibid.
11. *Toronto Star,* June 18, 1971 (with photograph).
12. *Oshawa Times*, November 22, 1971.

Figure 19.2 An editorial cartoon from October 18, 1972, depicting Stanfield as King Kong holding Macpherson's everyman, batting at Mike Starr who flies at him in a biplane with a machine gun firing. Library and Archives Canada, Mikan 2862315.

in local community affairs and served as Chairman, Board of Trustees, of the McLaughlin Art Gallery of Oshawa from 1968 to 1972.[13] His term on the citizenship bench was a well-deserved rest from the political arena but he missed the challenge of political life. When the next federal election was called, in 1972, Starr resigned from his position as judge to run against Ed Broadbent. Starr announced his intention to run on September 11, 1972, because "there were so many things that I wanted to do . . . that the current government would not do, so I resigned and ran again."[14] Starr was also running against Peter Connolly, a former executive assistant to Bryce Mackasey, Minister of Manpower and Immigration. Connolly had been nominated as the Liberal candidate but, as a non-resident of the riding, he knew that he had only a very limited chance. The Communist Party of Canada also fielded a candidate, but Starr's real competition came from Broadbent. Since 1968, Broadbent

---

13. Kieran Simpson (ed.), *Canadian Who's Who 1989*, Volume XXIV, University of Toronto Press, p. 840.
14. *Oshawa This Week*, April 16, 1980.

had maintained a year-round community office in Oshawa with a direct telephone line to Ottawa. He also provided regular newsletters from Ottawa explaining his own positions, and requesting opinions from the constituents.[15]

Since his election to Parliament in 1968, Broadbent had acquired a national reputation, helped by his unsuccessful bid for the NDP leadership in 1971. He attempted to follow a political position between the moderate socialists and the so-called Waffle, a militant left-wing faction of the NDP, and, as a result, alienated convention delegates from both camps and lost the leadership campaign.[16] David Lewis, the new NDP leader, won based on his long political experience and ability to manoeuvre among the party's various factions. In Oshawa, the two rival caucuses in the United Automobile Workers Union Local 222—democrats and autoworkers—continued dividing the union. This political division between right and left factions had always weakened the local NDP organization as the two rivals could never agree on a candidate. Broadbent was different: he had not risen through either faction and convinced both to work for him. He was, as a result, able to build a formidable election machine in 1968. Broadbent learned early that he had to avoid being identified with one or the other rival groups and he continued following this policy in 1972. Broadbent, however, admitted that he had some difficulty understanding the autoworkers. At that time, he was driving a Swedish-made Volvo, which did not go over well in a General Motors town. Broadbent also had difficulty avoiding being labelled as a political radical. In March 1969 he suggested that a series of public talks about social democracy be organized to counter references to him as "Ed the Red."[17] Broadbent said later "It was a good place to learn consensus-building. My experience with the union was very important in my political maturation."[18]

But Broadbent began his 1972 election campaign with serious problems. Although his unsuccessful bid for the NDP leadership gave him national exposure, Broadbent was obliged to spend less time in his riding. His first campaign manager left after a disagreement and Broadbent had difficulty finding a replacement. After two weeks of campaigning his prospects did not improve. The NDP headquarters in Ottawa became concerned about his campaign and sent Jo-Anne McNevin to assist him. Within a week, the veteran NDP organizer from British Columbia restructured Broadbent's campaign and reorganized his riding organization.[19]

Despite his 1968 defeat, Starr was optimistic about his prospects in 1972. Starr said, "I'm not discouraged by my defeat in 1968 because I lost only by a slim margin while many of my colleagues lost very substantially." Although he lost to an NDP candidate, Starr blamed his defeat on the Trudeaumania phenomenon that drew away his votes to the Liberals. In this election, the Liberals had to import a candidate from outside the riding and this was a sign of their weakness.[20]

---

15. Ibid., October 18, 1972.
16. *Time*, October 28, 1974, p. 8, "A Socialist of the Center."
17. LAC, The Hon. J. Edward Broadbent Papers, MG32 C83, Vol. 52, File 6, Oshawa-Whitby NDP Riding Association, 1968-1973.
18. *The Globe and Mail*, October 31, 1987.
19. Jeffrey Simpson, *Discipline of Power*, MacMillan of Canada, Toronto, 1984, pp. 304–306; see also, Steed, *Ed Broadbent*, p. 175.
20. *Oshawa This Week*, September 20, 1972.

As in previous election campaigns, Starr emphasized his long record of service to Oshawa.[21] He assured voters he would have "front-bench" status in any future Conservative government. During his many years in Ottawa, Starr developed many personal contacts that would cut through government bureaucratic obstacles. He defined politics as the art of the possible and believed this was best achieved in a quiet, sober, and reasonable way.[22] At his nomination meeting, Starr said he would support the Progressive Conservative Party's national platform. He expected votes from his traditional areas of support, including the local Ukrainian and other ethnocultural groups. Starr continued maintaining his interest in Ukrainian community activities and was the President of the Oshawa branch of the Ukrainian Canadian Professional and Businessmen's Federation.[23] He claimed he would attract votes from all age groups and backgrounds and felt his biggest appeal was that he "represents all sectors" in the riding. Starr's campaign manager was John Muha, a local businessman.

There were a number of developments to Canada's political landscape in 1972 that may have had an influence on Starr's campaign. The atmosphere began to change among the younger electorate including the Ukrainian Canadians. The political views of the Canadian-born Ukrainians, especially those of the baby-boom generation, were shaped by contemporary events and developments in the rest of Canada and also, the United States. Many of this Canadian-born generation began to attend universities across Canada and also in other countries, and were open to the political ideas of the "New Left." To some of these new voters, the traditional issues represented by Starr dimmed in their appeal.[24]

On October 8, 1971, Prime Minister Trudeau announced the federal government's multiculturalism policy in the House of Commons. He announced this policy the next day at the Ukrainian Canadian Congress Convention in Winnipeg. The Ukrainian community, led by Senator Paul Yuzyk, had campaigned for this policy for several years. The announcement of this policy was considered a political victory for Ukrainian Canadians and, as a result, membership of the younger generation of Ukrainian Canadians increased in the Liberal Party.

The Pickering Airport project was one of the more controversial issues in the riding during this election. Starr generally supported this project because it meant more jobs for the Oshawa area. However, it was generally known that Robert Stanfield did not support this project.[25] After much debate it remained dormant. Starr was proud of the support he received from labour and campaigned as their future representative in Ottawa. He described his political position as the "middle way" between "Professor" Broadbent of the NDP and Trudeau of the "fat-cat" Liberals. To promote the prosperity of Canada, Starr recognized

---

21. *Oshawa This Week*, October 4, 1972.
22. Ibid., September 27, 1972.
23. *Panorama, National Executive, Ukrainian Canadian Professional and Businessmen's Federation,* May, 1972.
24. For a good description of the political issues of the "New Left'" at that time, see Myrna Kostash, *Long Way From Home, The story of the Sixties generation in Canada,* James Lorimer and Company, Toronto, 1980.
25. *The Globe and Mail*, October 13, 1972.

the duties and responsibilities of labour, the contribution of corporations and, at the same time, the rights of taxpayers.[26]

Starr claimed that some Oshawa constituents had been unable to contact Ed Broadbent, their local MP, so they turned to Starr for help and he never turned them away.[27] During the campaign, Anne Starr continued her practice of opening her house to anyone with questions or problems. The Starrs enjoyed meeting people and were constantly surrounded by family and friends. Anne said, "We can't live for just the two of us. After Mike lost in the last election, he was able to relax and have more of a family life than we could for a long time. For the first two years, he was fine but then he started to get restless. Some people are born to be a doctor, he was born for politics." Anne Starr knew politics was the "love of his life" and he was happiest in the middle of it. As in previous elections, she supported Mike "all the way."[28]

In the 1972 election the votes were distributed as follows:[29]

Candidate	Party	Votes	Votes (%)
Edward Broadbent	NDP	23,757	41.81%
Michael Starr	PC	22,933	40.36%
Peter Connolly	Lib.	10,027	17.65%
Russ Rak	Communist	98	0.17%

Starr's popularity with the electorate remained high and Broadbent won the election by a little more than 800 votes, or just one percent of the total votes more than Starr, his closest rival. The margin was relatively tiny but it was still larger than in the 1968 federal election.

Nationally, Progressive Conservatives were able to dramatically increase their votes but the Liberals returned to power with a minority government. The results of this election, according to members of parliament elected, were as follows:

Party	Seats
Liberals	109
Progressive Conservatives	107
New Democratic Party	31
Social Credit	15
Independent	1

Broadbent credited his victory to hard work and canvassing. He also credited the support he received from young voters aged eighteen to twenty-five who had not voted four years earlier when he narrowly defeated Starr by only fifteen votes. He claimed many "old line"

---

26. Panorama, National Executive, Ukrainian Canadian Professional and Businessmen's Federation, October 4, 1972; also *Oshawa Times*, October 25, 1972.
27. *Oshawa This Week*, September 20, 1972.
28. *Oshawa Times*, October 26, 1972.
29. *Twenty-Ninth General Election 1972, Report of the Chief Electoral Officer*, Information Canada, 1973, Ottawa, p. 151.

Liberals and Conservatives voted NDP in this election and also pointed to his parliamentary record, his involvement in a number of local projects and the strength of his campaign organization.[30] However, shortly after this election, the NDP organization decided that it could no longer afford a full-time organizer in the Oshawa area.[31]

John Muha, Starr's campaign manager said, "I'm disappointed but we feel we did a good job. People obviously wanted to give Broadbent another term in office. Many polls which we thought were Liberal and would vote Conservative, voted for Broadbent."[32] Starr was once again without a job and faced an unknown future.

---

30. *Oshawa This Week*, November 1, 1972
31. LAC, The Hon. J. Edward Broadbent Papers, MG32 C83, Vol. 52, File 6, Oshawa-Whitby NDP Riding Association, 1968-1973.
32. *Oshawa This Week*, November 1, 1972.

Chapter 20
Public Service, 1973–1988

On January 5, 1973, Ontario Premier William Davis asked Starr to participate in a task force established to investigate the Workmen's Compensation Board (WCB) of Ontario. The WCB had acquired many of the negative characteristics of a faceless bureaucracy, neglecting many aspects of public service, avoiding change and with an unmotivated staff. Starr's appointment was criticized by an NDP member of the provincial legislature as "obvious Conservative management bias." Starr replied that he was certainly not management.[1] Starr served seven months on the task force, which submitted its report at the end of August, 1973. The report recommended twenty-nine major proposals for the restructuring of the board.

Starr was appointed acting chairman of the WCB on September 4, 1973, replacing Bruce J. Legge. The press suggested Legge had to resign because WCB reforms were no longer possible under his leadership.[2] The appointment surprised and pleased Starr. His major challenge was board restructuring, a project estimated to take about one and a half years. The board had the authority to establish the assessment policies of the WCB, review the Workmen's Compensation Act, and recommend amendments and revisions. It considered and approved annual operating and capital budgets, reviewed and approved investment policies, as well as any major changes in board programs. In addition, the board established, maintained and regulated various advisory committees, including a joint consultative committee representing labour, management and the public. The chairman was the full-time chief executive officer,[3] yet Starr commuted to the WCB offices in Toronto from Oshawa.

Shortly after being appointed, the press acknowledged that Starr, as chairman, was a popular choice and he had given the WCB a more human face than it showed under his predecessor.[4] Soon after Starr was appointed, an injured worker who was a frequent previous visitor, entered the WCB headquarters in Toronto to discuss his compensation problems. After he left, the injured worker said with a smile and a bit of astonishment, "You know what, they gave me free coffee."[5]

Starr viewed his role as that of an ombudsman and if injured workers were dissatisfied with a decision regarding their claim his door would always be open to them. He established a WCB policy that gave the benefit of doubt in cases of injury on the job, when evidence was less than complete, to the worker. The board accepted reasonable doubt on the balance of evidence.[6] Injured workers were generally aware that the actions and program of the

---

1. *Oshawa Times*, January 5, 1973.
2. Ibid., September 5, 1973.
3. The Workmen's Compensation Act, Toronto, 1974, pp. 29, 31.
4. *Oshawa Times*, September, 6, 1973; *The Globe and Mail*, February 26, 1978.
5. Jonathan Manthorpe, "Crisis of Change at Workmen's Compensation Board," in Donald C. MacDonald (ed.), *Government and Politics of Ontario*, MacMillan of Canada, 1975, p. 89.
6. Based on the article in *The Globe and Mail*, October 7, 1976.

WCB were limited by legislation, but once they realized Starr was open and accessible to them, their attitude to the WCB changed.

However, not all Canadians involved in the labour movement praised Starr for his work on the WCB. The pro-Communist Association of United Ukrainian Canadians, at their thirty-third convention in 1975, stated in their report:

> The do-nothing attitude of the Workmen's Compensation Board is scandalous. One sees silicotic miners in Elliot Lake doomed to die of lung cancer while Rio Algom makes a profit of over 50 million dollars. Why doesn't Mike Starr who was supposed to clean up the Workmen's Compensation Board do something?[7]

Some injured workers continued to feel they were not receiving adequate compensation. On November 21, 1977, thirty injured workers, who were members of the Toronto Chapter of the Union of Injured Workers, began a twenty-four-hour occupation of the seventh-floor offices of the WCB headquarters in Toronto. The demonstrators demanded to speak with Mike Starr about ". . . their questions and complaints." When Starr came down from his office, the demonstrators shouted and accused the WCB of arbitrarily cutting off compensation supplements to injured workers and complained about unfair legislation. Starr told the demonstrators there was nothing he could do about the legislative changes demanded by the injured workers. He pointed out that it was the provincial Minister of Labour and the Ontario government that were responsible for the necessary changes to the Workmen's Compensation Act. A demonstrator confronted Starr and claimed that workers should continue to receive supplements even while on vacation. Starr shrugged his shoulders and said, "What can you do?" Another worker who was not part of the demonstration told Starr, "You're doing a good job here. You don't deserve this." He shook Starr's hand and left. The demonstrators then demanded to see the Ontario Minister of Labour and decided to occupy his office for the night.[8]

Workers' complaints provided members of the Ontario Legislature of all political parties with busy workloads. Regardless of these problems, Starr liked and enjoyed his work. He knew that despite the constant criticism the WCB had made significant improvements in services to injured workers since he took over. Although Starr listened, was friendly and tried his best to alleviate the injured workers' personal issues, he could not increase their pensions.[9] The WCB dealt with over 400,000 cases a year. Starr admitted that a small percentage of cases still had problems with "red tape." On one occasion, Starr even managed an intervention in Ottawa. Although Starr did not have any direct contact with the Ottawa bureaucracy for some years, he was able to put pressure on Statistics Canada to reinstate a work-injury survey that was cut along with three positions during the federal government's budget reductions in 1978.[10]

In Ottawa, Progressive Conservatives recommended a number of proposals to deal with the economic situation in Canada. Inflation had reached record levels and became a

---

7. LAC, Association of United Ukrainian Canadians fonds, MG28 V154, Volume 1, file 14, Proceedings AUUC Convention, 1975.
8. Based on the article in *The Globe and Mail*, November 22, 1977.
9. *Toronto Star*, February 7, 1979.
10. *The Citizen*, February 19, 1979.

Figure 20.1 An editorial cartoon depicting Starr with his foot in his mouth in a hospital emergency ward, where Stephen Lewis is the attending physician. Stephen Lewis, the Ontario NDP Leader, accused Starr of participating in the Ontario provincial elections when Starr defended the role of the WCB against charges by the NDP that the WCB was not responding to the needs of injured workers. Library and Archives Canada, Mikan 2866136.

serious national problem. As leader of the federal party, Robert Stanfield proposed legislation in February 1973 for the immediate implementation of a ninety-day price and wage freeze followed by two years of controls. The Liberals and the NDP were opposed to any legislation that required rigid controls. It was with reluctance that Stanfield supported this economic proposal because inflation had become a serious national problem and he felt that it could be restrained only through direct federal government action. Stanfield supported this proposal only as a temporary measure and because it was absolutely necessary.[11]

Although initially opposed to the proposal, the federal Liberal government established the Anti-Inflation Review Board on October 14, 1975. Legislation to control inflation in Canada was approved in the House on October 27. The federal Anti-Inflation Act established a control system for three years and all companies with 500 or more employees, on all federal employees and on most other public-sector employees; all were subject to wage controls. The price and cost markups of large firms were also subject to profit-margin

---

11. Stevens, *Stanfield*, p. 44.

controls. Although this control legislation and its effects are still subjects of academic debates, the restrictions did reduce inflation to some degree in 1975–76.

Starr was amused—and more than a bit puzzled—that his proposal for wage and price controls during the Conservative leadership campaign in April 1967 was now federal Liberal government policy. It had met with strong opposition among Progressive Conservatives for being socialist, and Starr felt his proposal had had a negative effect on his leadership campaign,[12] yet it became a main plank within the party in 1973 and then adopted by the Liberals in 1975.

Starr knew he would eventually be replaced as WCB chairman but he did not look forward to the prospect of retiring. At one point he asked, "What the heck am I going to do at my age? Stay at home and eat pirohy?"[13] Already in September 1978, *The Globe and Mail* had reported that the Ontario government was quietly searching for a new chairman to replace Starr—if the provincial government could find someone capable of assuming this position.[14] However, Starr received a two-year extension of his appointment and, in January 1980, there were again reports in the *Globe and Mail* that the provincial government was looking for a replacement for Starr.

Norman Cafik, who ran unsuccessfully against Starr in the 1962 and 1963 federal elections, was elected as the Liberal MP for the Ontario riding in the 1968 election. Cafik ran unsuccessfully in 1973 for the leadership of the Ontario Liberal Party. In 1977, Prime Minister Pierre Trudeau appointed him Minister of State for Multiculturalism, making him the second Canadian of Ukrainian descent appointed to the federal cabinet. He was eventually defeated in the 1979 federal election and resumed his business career.[15] The Oshawa riding was again won in the 1979 federal election by Ed Broadbent, who had been elected NDP leader in 1975.

The Progressive Conservatives under Joe Clark won the 1979 federal election, ending sixteen years of Liberal governments. The PCs won 136 seats but only two seats in Quebec; a minority government six seats short of a majority. On June 4, 1979, Clark was sworn in as Canada's youngest Prime Minister, and led the first Conservative government since the defeat of John Diefenbaker's government in the 1963 election. Among the federal cabinet ministers appointed were Donald Mazankowski, Steven Paproski and Ramon Hnatyshyn, the son of former Senator John Hnatyshyn from Saskatoon, all claiming Ukrainian and Polish heritage.

In addition to many other honours, Starr was appointed honorary Colonel of the Ontario Regiment on October 18, 1979. This militia unit had a long and distinguished record in Oshawa and during the Second World War, fought in Italy, France, Netherlands and Germany. In peacetime, the unit played an important role in the social life of the community. R. S. McLaughlin was among the previous honorary colonels.[16]

In February 1980, Prof. Paul Weiler of Harvard University was appointed to study the Workmen's Compensation Act of Ontario. Weiler was the former Chairman of the British

---

12. *Oshawa/Whitby This Week*, October 28, 1987.
13. Pirohy is a traditional Ukrainian and East European dish.
14. *The Globe and Mail*, September 26, 1978.
15. *Canadian Parliamentary Guide*, 1979, p. 39.
16. *Oshawa Times*, October 18, 1979.

Figure 20.2 An original cartoon depicting Lincoln Alexander talking to a disbelieving injured Ontario worker about the just practices of the Workmen's Compensation Board. Library and Archives Canada, Mikan 33015902.

Columbia Labour Relations Board. He submitted his report in December 1980 and generally recommended a thorough reorganization of the WCB system. In particular, he recommended changes in the system of compensation and also suggested amendments to promote investment in safety and rehabilitation. The reactions to these recommendations in the business community and in the press were mixed. Major criticism ranged from the increasingly high cost of the WCB system to the constant fears that some workers would abuse the system.[17]

In April 1980, the Ontario government announced the appointment of Lincoln Alexander as the new Chairman of the Workmen's Compensation Board.[18] Alexander was the Conservative labour critic in Ottawa and was briefly the Minister of Labour in Prime Minister Joseph Clark's administration. So, to some extent, Alexander followed the political route pioneered by Starr. Just as Starr had been the first Ukrainian, Alexander was the first Canadian of African ancestry to hold this position.

---

17. *The Globe and Mail*, December 30, 1980.
18. *Oshawa This Week*, April 16, 1980.

Starr officially resigned his position on the Workmen's Compensation Board on June 1, 1980.[19] On leaving the board, Starr suggested that legislation concerning the WCB should allow the WCB to increase benefits to keep pace with the coat of living, make lump-sum payments to claimants and compensate workers for 100 per cent of their lost income rather than some percentage. He added that it was time for Ontario to examine other compensation plans and, if necessary, make some radical changes.[20] He remained as a consultant to the WCB until the end of the year.

Starr was proud of his record as chairman, but he was also realistic. He admitted that it was not always possible to satisfy everyone and he concluded that according to his experience, some people would never be satisfied. Starr looked forward to enjoying the relief from pressure and responsibility.[21] On June 25, 1980, Starr was honoured by the Ontario government.[22] Starr said, "They can still use my services in government—maybe they will reappoint me to another position." Starr was approached by a number of Oshawa citizens who asked him to run for the position of mayor but he declined.[23] He also declined to run in the federal election in the Oshawa riding.[24]

Starr continued to serve as an example and inspiration for other members of the Ukrainian community to enter politics. In the Ontario provincial election held on March 19, 1981, the candidate for the Progressive Conservative Party was Robert (Bob) Boychyn. He was thirty-four years old, a second-generation lawyer born in Canada and a former city council member, from 1976 through 1978.[25] Despite some signs of division within the Conservative ranks, Starr supported Boychyn and had "a gut reaction" that he would be successful.[26] The results of this election were:

Candidate	Party	Vote
M. Breaugh	NDP	10,307
B. Boychyn	PC	7,836
T. Wallace	Lib.	3,311

Boychyn came second with a respectable number of votes. He ran against Mike Breaugh, an experienced NDP candidate, and this was another challenge in local Oshawa politics. Breaugh's campaign manager was Nester Pidwerbecki, a seasoned local campaigner. From the beginning of Breaugh's electoral campaign, he had the support of Ed Broadbent.[27] Despite these results, Starr remained optimistic that Boychyn would be more successful in the next election.[28]

---

19. *Oshawa This Week*, June 1, 1980.
20. *The Globe and Mail*, June 6, 1980.
21. *Oshawa Times*, August 8, 1980.
22. *Oshawa This Week*, June 25, 1980.
23. Ibid., April 9, 1980.
24. *Oshawa Times*, August 8, 1980.
25. *Toronto Star*, March 12, 1981; obituary of George Boychyn, February 1, 2002.
26. *Oshawa Times*, March 16, 1981.
27. Ibid., February 9, 1981.
28. Ibid., March 20, 1981.

On May 7, 1981, Starr was appointed to the Liquor License Board of Ontario (LLBO) for a three-year term. On the LLBO, Starr sat with six other members and heard applications for liquor licenses and transfers from establishments across the provinces. He received an honorarium per day plus expenses while on commission business.[29] He also served as the part-time vice-chairman. Starr commuted to Toronto to attend the meetings of this board.

At the local level, Starr was the "honoured guest" of the Cystic Fibrosis Celebrity Roast on May 5, 1982, at the Oshawa Kinsmen Hall. "Roasters" came from Oshawa, Toronto and also from Ottawa. These included former Ontario Ombudsman Arthur Maloney, former Oshawa Mayor Ernest Marks and Durham Regional Police Chief Jon Jenkins. Erik Nielson took time from his busy schedule in Parliament to add a few comments during the roast. One of his best lines referred to Starr's favourite pastime—playing card games. Nielson said that Starr, when he was in Ottawa, held so many Liberal IOUs "that they didn't dare attack him in the House."[30]

At the end of 1981, the Oshawa branch of the Ukrainian Canadian Committee organized a "Ukrainian Day" to celebrate the ninetieth anniversary of the arrival of the first Ukrainian pioneers to Canada. The events took place at the Dnipro Hall, the Ukrainian community centre, and included a prayer service, greetings, concert and dance. Among the local dignitaries were representative of the Durham Region, City of Oshawa, and local Ukrainian churches, with Mike Starr at the head table. The ceremony included a presentation on the history of Ukrainians in Oshawa, who first settled in this area about 1905. By 1981, Ukrainian Canadians numbered over 6,000 in Oshawa.[31]

The economic profile of Oshawa began to change during these years. The various industries that hired immigrant labour requiring basic skills were gradually closing. Malleable Iron, Houdaille Industries, Pedlars People and Robson Leathers had all closed by the beginning of 1981.[32] General Motors continued to be the main employer in Oshawa but the gradual introduction of automation required that the workers have, in some cases, a post-secondary education. There were also some changes at the community level. The Association of United Ukrainian Canadians' Hall on Bloor Street was sold to the Maltese Canadian Falcons Soccer Club in 1977.[33] The members of the AUUC continued to meet in private homes and financially supported their newspaper and headquarters in Toronto. The Hetman Hall became a social centre for Ukrainian senior citizens.

On June 1, 1983, the provincial government of Ontario officially opened its new revenue building in Oshawa and it was named in honour of Michael Starr. Located in downtown Oshawa, at the corner of King and Centre Streets, the new seven-story building provided offices for 1,600 workers. The official opening took place at a ribbon-cutting ceremony in the presence of Ontario Premier William Davis. There were numerous guests and a crowd of several hundred. Premier Davis, in his brief remarks, outlined Starr's political career, where he emphasized his contributions to the political life of Canada. He added that Starr never gained the recognition that he truly deserved for his political contributions.

---

29. Ibid., May 7, 1981.
30. Ibid., March 6, 1982; *Oshawa This Weekend*, May 8, 1982.
31. *Ukrainian Voice/Canadian Farmer*, April 28, 1982.
32. *Oshawa Times*, February 14, 1981.
33. Sharon Young, *Oshawa Folk Arts Council 1961–1981*, Oshawa Folk Arts Council, 1982, p. 126.

Davis remembered Starr's tenure as the federal Minister of Labour and his program to encourage the building of vocational schools in Ontario, including some in Oshawa. The Premier called Starr a man of "tremendous sensitivity" and said that he was a "political partisan who had respect for his political opponents."[34] Premier Davis and Mike Starr then unveiled a plaque with an inscribed dedication.[35]

On July 7, 1983, Prime Minister Pierre Trudeau appointed Mike Starr and Mitchell Sharp to the joint chairmanship of a task force that would review and or establish conflict-of-interest and post-employment guidelines.[36] The task force was created in part as a response to a series of questionable events in Ottawa that suggested unethical behavior among politicians and senior public servants. Starr was appointed co-chairman because he had the reputation of being a politician of personal integrity and respected by all political parties. He was also a veteran politician with years of experience at all levels of government—municipal, provincial and federal. The purpose of the Task Force on Conflict of Interest was to examine and report on the policies and practices that should govern the conduct of ministers, parliamentary secretaries, exempt staff, full-time Governor-in-Council appointees and public servants. According to the Prime Minister, it was of particular importance that the task force confirmed public confidence in the integrity of the government process and the need to attract competent Canadians to government positions.[37] The task force submitted its report on May 1984 in the form of a 276-page document entitled, "Ethical Conduct in the Public Sector."

The report listed numerous recommendations, including detailed information regarding arrangements to allow individuals to avoid conflict of interest. Another important recommendation concerned the establishment of an Office of Public Sector Ethics. This office would clarify questions of interpretation and also investigate and resolve accusations of conflict of interest. Also, the office would provide information that promoted public awareness of ethical issues. The recommendations were prepared with the concern that guidelines regarding conflict of interest would not impose "unnecessary sacrifices on those in public office" and would not discourage competent people from entering political and public life.[38] On May 28, 1984, Prime Minister Trudeau wrote in a letter to Starr and Sharp that he would leave it up to his successor to decide what to do with their report. It did not seem that any of their recommendations would be implemented before the next federal election.[39] The press generally ignored this report and it sat on the shelf for several years, to Starr's dismay.[40] Some of their recommendations were accepted by later Liberal and Conservative governments; it was only in 2007 that the Office of the Conflict of Interest and Ethics Commissioner was established in Ottawa.

---

34. *Oshawa Times*, June 2, 1983.
35. *Ukrainian Echo*, July 6, 1983; also *The Times*, June 2, 1983.
36. Mitchell Sharp, *Which Reminds Me… A Memoir*, University of Toronto Press, Toronto, 1994, pp. 254–256.
37. *Ethical Conduct in the Public Sector*, DSS, Ottawa, 1984, p. 5, "terms of reference."
38. Review of Report by Kenneth M. Gibbons in *Canadian Public Administration*, pp. 329–330, vol. 291, no. 2, Summer 1986; also *Ethical Conduct in the Public Sector*, pp. 269–276.
39. *The Citizen*, May 29, 1984.
40. Ukrainian Canadian Research and Documentation Centre, "Memoirs of the Honourable Michael Starr" (1998).

The second session of the thirty-second Parliament was dissolved on July 9, 1984, and a federal election was called for September 5. In Oshawa, Progressive Conservatives made a determined effort to mount a serious campaign against Ed Broadbent. The various Ukrainian community organizations were mobilized and succeeded in nominating Alex Sosna as the Conservative candidate. Sosna was a thirty-five-year-old lawyer whose family was active in the local Ukrainian community. Dr. Bob Starr, Mike's son, became involved in organizing the Conservative nomination convention. Starr did not intervene publicly in support of any of the Conservative nominees because he felt he had to maintain neutrality in this part of the campaign. However, once Sosna was nominated, Mike Starr gave his full support to the new candidate. Starr revived his old network of formal and informal supporters, phoned Conservatives across the riding and, for all practical purposes, became the campaign manager. The management of the local campaign was greatly facilitated by the use of new computer technology that linked the Progressive Conservative riding headquarters with the national headquarters and provided the latest information on policy and programs. The election campaign was conducted in the new Oshawa riding, created in 1976, and consisted of the City of Oshawa and parts of Durham, Ontario and Oshawa-Whitby ridings.

National opinion polls suggested a Progressive Conservative sweep, which increased optimism among local PCs; Sosna felt he had a chance to defeat Broadbent on the strength of the party's national campaign combined with a good grassroots effort. Sosna, however, remained realistic regarding his hopes. In the previous two federal elections of 1974 and 1979, Broadbent won with an impressive 51 per cent of the vote and had the best showing of any NDP candidate in Canada, and in July 1975 he won the federal NDP leadership. Sosna admitted Broadbent had not only his national stature to his benefit but also had "a tremendous staff here that looks after the little problems of people." In support of his own position, Sosna argued the riding would benefit even more if the sitting Member of Parliament for the Oshawa riding sat on the government side in Parliament. The NDP felt that they may be losing some support to the Conservatives but were gaining from the Liberals. The Liberal candidate, Terry Kelly, did not receive much assistance from the national campaign of the Liberal Party and, in effect, ran a low-profile riding campaign.[41] The NDP realized they were involved in a very close campaign and quickly rushed more campaign workers into the riding.[42]

On election day, September 5, 1984, the results of the voting in Oshawa[43] were as follows:

Candidate	Party	Vote	Vote (%)
Edward Broadbent	NDP	25,092	42.30%
Alex Sosna	PC	23,028	38.82%
Terry Kelly	Liberal	10,719	18.07%
Others		489	0.80%

41. *The Globe and Mail*, September 1, 1984.
42. *The Globe and Mail*, "In Ed Broadbent's old riding, the candidates are in the home stretch," August 10, 1990.
43. *Thirty-Third General Election 1984, Report of the Chief Electoral Officer*, Supply and Services, Canada, 1984, p. 220.

Although Broadbent won this election, his majority over his closest rival, Alex Sosna, was only 2,064 votes or 3.4 per cent of the vote. This was certainly a remarkable achievement for Sosna, a relatively unknown first-time candidate running against a well-known figure in national politics. The Conservative landslide across Canada, combined with a thorough grassroots organizational work, especially through the mobilization of the local Ukrainian organizations, seriously threatened Broadbent's hold on the Oshawa riding. The important element in the surprising Conservative results was the participation of Mike Starr as the campaign manager. Starr's involvement brought back fond memories of the Conservative riding victories in the 1950s and 1960s. Also, this campaign gave Starr the opportunity to return to the political fight that he first lost by a tiny margin in 1968.

Progressive Conservatives swept the country in a landslide election reminiscent of the 1958 Diefenbaker sweep—under Brian Mulroney's leadership, the party formed a significant majority government. They were, however, unable to regain Oshawa. In this election, the Members of Parliament elected according to political parties were as follows:

Party	Seats
Progressive Conservative	211
Liberal	40
New Democratic Party	30
Independent	1

When Prime Minister Brian Mulroney formed his cabinet, Ramon J. Hnatyshyn and Harvie Andre, two Canadians of Ukrainian descent, were appointed. It was a measure of the progress in the evolution of Canadian political culture that, on this occasion, as had been the case in 1979 when Joe Clark formed his cabinet, there were no headlines in any major Canadian newspaper or television news broadcasts emphasizing the ethnocultural backgrounds of these new cabinet members. The pioneering efforts of Mike Starr in the 1950s to reach the highest political offices in Canada were now an integral part of the Canadian political experience.

On March 20, 1985, Starr and his wife were invited to Ottawa to attend an event with cabinet ministers and MPs who were of Ukrainian descent. A special effort was made by the Ottawa branch of the Ukrainian Professional and Business Association to ensure Starr and his wife were present. Prime Minister Brian Mulroney welcomed the participants that included Ukrainian religious and community leaders from across Canada. The evening was organized to celebrate Ukrainian contributions to Canadian political life. By 1981, Ukrainian Canadians could claim ninety provincial members, twenty-six federal members and five senators, for a total of 121 parliamentarians.

Among federal cabinet ministers attending were Ramon Hnatyshyn, Harvie Andre and Steve Paproski. Also present were Senator Paul Yuzyk and Senator Martha Bielish. Members of Parliament present were Alex Kindy, William Lesyk and Andrew Witer. Judge Michael Baryliuk, who represented the Ukrainian Canadian Committee, was the main speaker. He reviewed Ukrainian Canadian political history and spoke about discrimination against Ukrainians during the early years of settlement in Canada. He also spoke about current events and the accusations against Ukrainian-Canadian individuals and the community as a whole for harbouring "war criminals." He mentioned the perilous cultural situation of Ukrainians under Soviet rule. The parliamentary evening provided politicians and community leaders with an opportunity to discuss current community problems, a sense of a national Ukrainian community spirit, and a chance to celebrate their achievements.[44] Starr had the opportunity to renew friendships and acquaintances, friendships that in some cases originated during the first years of his political career when he travelled the prairies organizing support for the Progressive Conservative Party. Young adults who helped organize local meetings and events were now themselves Members of Parliament or ministers. The community that was the subject of discrimination and alienation was now represented at the highest levels of Canadian government and felt totally at ease celebrating their achievements on Parliament Hill.

In the May 1985 Ontario provincial election, Bob Boychyn was again the Progressive Conservative candidate. Boychyn ran against Mike Breaugh, the NDP candidate, who was the sitting member in the provincial legislature, representing the riding since 1975. The results of this election were:

Candidate	Party	Votes
M. Breaugh	NDP	12,686
B. Boychyn	PC	7,528
J. Neal	Lib.	5,034

According to Breaugh, the NDP won this election due to a combination of solid riding organization and "basic street politics." It didn't hurt, too, that the local NDP had strong support from federal NDP MP and party leader Ed Broadbent.[45] Boychyn claimed his loss was due to low voter turnout and a general anti-Progressive Conservative attitude across the province.[46] After this election, Boychyn continued his involvement in local community activities and became a member of the regional council, Chair of the Durham Regional Police Services Board and, later, Justice of the Peace.[47]

On September 24, 1985, Anne Starr died after a short illness at the Oshawa General Hospital. She was in her seventy-first year and the news shocked her many friends and acquaintances. The funeral service was held at the St. George Ukrainian Catholic Church and she was buried at the St. Wolodymyr and St. Olha Cemetery near Oshawa. Her death was a great loss to Starr, who described his wife as a "great asset" to him: Anne had served throughout Starr's long political career as his most faithful and trusted advisor, campaign worker, secretary, receptionist and archivist. She was also loved by many people and could make friends very easily. Starr claimed that after he retired from politics and they would go shopping, his wife knew more people than he did.[48]

On August 10, 1986, the Ukrainian Canadian Committee, Alberta Provincial Council, hosted a Ukrainian Day at the Ukrainian Cultural Heritage Village near Vegreville. The

---

44. *Novyi Shliakh* (The New Pathway), April 20, 1985.
45. *The Globe and Mail*, May 3, 1985; *Toronto Star*, March 12, May 14, 1985
46. *Oshawa Times*, May 1, 4, 1985.
47. *Toronto Star*, December 8, 1994; November 6, 1997; August 1, 2003.
48. *Oshawa/Whitby This Week*, October 28, 1987.

event honoured Michael Luchkovich, the first Ukrainian Canadian elected to the federal parliament, in 1926. Before a crowd of 10,000 people, Luchkovich's political career and accomplishments were remembered and praised. Various speakers outlined his contributions to Canada and the Ukrainian-Canadian community. Deputy Prime Minister Don Mazankowski referred to Luchkovich as "a proud Canadian and clearly the focus of his thoughts was on his Ukrainian heritage. He spoke out on minority issues, especially those affecting Ukrainians." Also speaking on that day was the Honourable Ken Kowalski, Minister of Environment for Alberta, and Laurence Decore, Mayor of Edmonton. A major event of this celebration was the awarding of the Michael Luchkovich Public Service award. The award was established as an annual presentation to Ukrainian Canadians who had distinguished themselves in Canadian public services as representatives of their constituencies and of Ukrainian-Canadian interests. The first recipient of the award was Michael Starr. He was honoured for his many years in parliament and also, for his previous services as mayor and alderman in Oshawa. The event was attended by numerous politicians from all political parties and included most of Michael Luchkovich's family.[49]

On June 1, 1987, Starr was appointed to the Refugee Status Advisory Committee in Ottawa. The committee heard claims from asylum seekers who had been interviewed by immigration officials. The thirty-member committee was an independent body appointed to distance the refugee process from the Department of Immigration. The committee was created in 1978 to give claimants a more impartial hearing of their cases than immigration officials allegedly provided. If the committee made a negative decision regarding asylum-seekers, the refugee claimants could ask for their case to be heard by the Immigration Appeal Board for a fuller hearing and, eventually, take the case to the Federal Court. The hearings kept Starr busy with weekly trips to Ottawa to review applications for refugee status in Canada. During these trips, Starr had the opportunity to renew acquaintances, visit old friends who were still active in politics and observe sessions of the House of Commons, where he spent many years.[50] Shortly after his appointment to the advisory committee, Starr visited the House of Commons on June 10, 1987, when several members were honoured for their thirty years of service in parliament. It was the thirtieth anniversary of Starr's election to parliament as part of the victorious Diefenbaker electoral sweep. Starr was also honoured when Alvin Hamilton announced Starr's presence in the public gallery. Hamilton said,

> I am doubly glad to see my friend, Mike Starr, in the Gallery because we set out to try to co-operate with the provinces. I well remember in 1958 when we were hard pressed to provide jobs for people. We had a high unemployment rate in those days of about 6 percent and were catching Hail Columbia from the Opposition. Bill Hamilton, the Postmaster General, and I were doing our level best to build post offices across the country and tear up the bush. We were spending a lot of money but not creating many jobs. Mike Starr suggested that we go to the municipal governments which had lots of jobs they wanted but no money.

---

49. *Ukrainian Voice* (Ukrainskyi Holos), September 15, 1986.
50. The Refugee Status Advisory Committee of Employment and Immigration Canada was dissolved on December 31, 1988.

Figure 20.3 Mike Starr received this honour on October 18, 1979. The ceremonial position as honorary Colonel of the Ontario Regiment, based in Oshawa, was previously held for many years by R. S. McLaughlin, the President of General Motors. Image courtesy of Walter Kish.

> As the House very well knows, municipalities are the creatures of the provinces. But how did Mike Starr get around that? He simply proposed to the municipalities that all of these programs were eligible for help if they could get the consent of the provincial government. One had to see the reactions of the provincial governments. How can one turn down a request from a municipality to have something done in its riding when nothing had to be spent?
>
> I can still remember Premier [Maurice] Duplessis of Quebec calling me and saying, "That Mike Starr, he is a devil. He puts a proposal before me that I cannot refuse." He thought the world of Mike, who was a very sensible person. He only dealt with Duplessis over the phone. Let me say that, to my recollection, Mike Starr was the first person to describe the type of program we are conducting with all the provinces and territories as a co-operative type of government. I changed that name somewhat, to co-operative federalism.[51]

Starr continued to maintain an active interest in local community affairs and served on the executives of a number of organizations. He had been Chairman of the Board of Trustees

---

51. *House of Commons Debates*, June 10, 1987, p. 6957.

Figure 20.4 Michael Starr Building, in Oshawa. Photo: Melissa Cole.

of the McLaughlin Arts Gallery of Oshawa, for which he had served as a trustee since December, 1957. In 1976, Starr was appointed Officer of the Order of St. John and, in 1978, he was appointed Commander of the Order.[52] In Oshawa he had also been Honorary President of the Oshawa Boy Scouts, the Honorary Colonel of the Ontario Regiment and the Honorary Chairman of the Folk Arts Council of Oshawa.[53] Working with the council, ethnocultural groups organized a Fiesta Week that publicizes their contributions to the cultural life of Oshawa. Fiesta Week began as Fanfare for Oshawa in 1961, organized by the council. In 1972, the festival grew into a week-long celebration of ethnocultural cuisine and culture, with pavilions representing over a dozen cultural groups in Oshawa. Fiesta Week takes place annually during the third week of June to this day. Starr was President of the Folk Arts Council of Ontario in 1970–71. Later, he was Honorary President of the council.[54]

During these years, Starr was also involved in various fund-raising projects and, in October 1987, Starr was General Campaign Chairman of the Oshawa-Whitby-Newcastle United Way Campaign. He accepted this position on condition that he would have an active role, being more than just a figurehead.[55] In 1988, he was Honorary Chairman of the Men's Hostel in Oshawa and helped to raise $300,000, and another $50,000 for the Arthritis

---

52. Press Release, Office of the Prime Minister of Canada, Ottawa, July 7, 1983.
53. *Oshawa This Weekend*, October 20, 1979.
54. Young, *Oshawa Folk Arts Council*, p. 14; Kieran Simpson (ed.), *Canadian Who's Who, 1989*, Volume XXIV, University of Toronto Press, p. 840.
55. *Oshawa/Whitby This Weekend*, October 28, 1987.

Society. He was a patron of the John Howard Society and served as a member of the board to study a proposal to establish a university in Oshawa.[56] The University of the Ontario Institute of Technology was founded in Oshawa in 2002 and the first students were accepted in 2003. This institution is among the newest universities in Canada. Starr accepted an active role in leading community organizations, especially with fund-raising, because he believed in the concept of "giving back" to the community in which he lived and that he felt was "good to him."[57]

---

56. *This Week*, March 19, 2000.
57. Ukrainian Canadian Research and Documentation Centre, "Memoirs of the Honourable Michael Starr" (1998).

Chapter 21
Final Years and Mike Starr's Legacy

At the local level, Starr continued to maintain his membership in various local voluntary organizations in 1987. He was Director of the Oshawa Arthritis Society's Residential Campaign and an honorary member of the Oshawa Rotary Club and Canadian Corps Association. He continued to head many fund-raising campaigns for Oshawa and the Durham Region.

Starr suffered a personal tragedy when his son, Robert, passed away on March 13, 1988, at age fifty-four in Thunder Bay. At that time, he was practicing dentistry for the Ontario Ministry of Health in northwestern Ontario. Robert Starr was a former member of the Ajax Rotary Club, president of the Oshawa Branch of the Ukrainian Professional and Businessmen's Association, and a member of the Royal College of Dental Surgeons and the Ontario Dental Association. The funeral service was held at the St. George Ukrainian Catholic Church in Oshawa.[1]

Following a long political career, Ed Broadbent stepped down as leader of the NDP on March 4, 1989, and he resigned as the Member of Parliament representing Oshawa on December 31, 1989. He had represented Oshawa successfully since he won the federal election in 1968 by fifteen votes over Starr. Broadbent was the federal leader of the NDP from 1975 until 1989.[2] He also held the position of Vice-President of the Socialist International from 1979 until 1989. Broadbent was appointed the Director of the International Centre for Human Rights and Democratic Development from 1990 to 1996. Broadbent's resignation in 1989 also marked the end of an era in NDP history in Oshawa.

Starr maintained a life-long interest in politics at all levels. At the international level, he felt fortunate to witness the collapse of the Soviet Union and the establishment of an independent Ukraine in 1991, and he was particularly happy that Canada was the first Western country to recognize the independence of Ukraine on December 2, 1991; the dream of his parent's generation, and as well those Ukrainians who immigrated to Canada after the Second World War, had been realized. Starr, who spoke on this issue many times throughout his political career dating back to the early 1950s, supported the movement for the independence of Ukraine. Locally, he became involved in a project to twin the Durham Region with the city of Dnipropetrovsk (now Dnipro), Ukraine.

It was during the tenure of Prime Minister Brian Mulroney that the concept of a value-added tax pioneered in the European Union was adapted in Canada as the goods and services tax (GST) by the federal government and as the provincial sales tax (PST) by many provincial governments. As per some federal-provincial agreements, a combined harmonized sales tax (HST) was also negotiated. Despite some early opposition and disagreements regarding this

---
1. Obituary, *Oshawa/Whitby This Week*, March 16, 1988; *The Globe and Mail,* March 15, 1988.
2. *The Globe and Mail*, September 29, December 1 and 14, 1989.

value-added tax and its administration, the HST became part of Canadian business and commercial life and its implementation was described by some scholars as a "tax revolution."[3] Starr had been heavily criticized during his leadership campaign for the Progressive Conservative Party in 1967 for proposing a similar approach to raising revenue for the federal government, criticism that, no doubt, negatively influence his leadership prospects.

At the national level, the emergence of the Reform Party in the 1990s began to erode the support for Progressive Conservatives, especially in Western Canada. Reviewing the history of the Progressive Conservative Party of Canada, Starr suggested that Reform and Progressive Conservatives should amalgamate, that a united party would revive the PCs and provide Reform with more exposure in Eastern Canada; one strong party could defeat the Liberals, a fractured one would not. He was disappointed and angry about current Progressive Conservative policies. He blamed the party's declining fortunes on the leadership of Mulroney and his tendency to formulate federal policies in reaction to the political situation in Quebec. In response, he threw his support behind Reform Party candidates. Preston Manning, the leader of the Reform Party and, after 1993, of the Official Opposition in Ottawa, was grateful for his support.[4]

Starr continued living at 25 Olive Avenue in the house he built himself with the assistance of friends and family. The walls of his den were covered with photographs of himself with public figures such as John Diefenbaker, Queen Elizabeth II, and John F. Kennedy. During drives around Oshawa he took pride in pointing out various municipal buildings that were built during his tenure as mayor. On occasion, retired public servants who had worked at the Department of Labour when Starr was minister would stop in for a visit with Starr to reminisce; he enjoyed their friendship and appreciated their expressions of loyalty.

By the 1990s, the ethnocultural neighbourhoods and enclaves of south Oshawa were pale shadows of their former existence. As the post–Second World War generation of immigrants that populated this area of Oshawa aged and integrated into the larger society, the local churches and community halls had to adapt to the new conditions.[5] A significant percentage of the Canadian-born generation attended colleges and universities and moved away for employment reasons. The introduction of robotics on General Motors assembly lines reduced the number of workers required to produce the same number of automobiles as during the previous decades. A number of local factories which had employed immigrant labour for several generations were closed and repurposed. Those remaining in Oshawa tended to live outside traditional ethnocultural enclaves. Plus there was a growing tendency towards intermarriage and language loss that eroded the unique character of the ethnocultural communities. Although there were a number of political refugees arriving in

---

3. Richard M. Bird, *The GST/HST: Creating an Integrated Sales Tax in a Federal Country*, International Center for Public Policy, Working Paper 12-21, April 2012. http://scholarworks.gsu.edu/cgi/viewcontent.cgi?article=1070&context=icepp.
4. Chris Bovie, "Unite the right says Mike Starr," *This Week*, November 1, 1998; Jane McDonald, "Mike Starr's legacy is unforgettable," *Oshawa This Week*, March 19, 2000.
5. Helen Bajorek MacDonald, "The Power of Polonia, Post WWII Polish Immigrants to Canada: Survivors of Deportation and Exile in Soviet Labour Camps," MA thesis, Trent University, 2001; in particular, see chapter "Oshawa Polonia – The Imagined Village: A Community of Memory," pp. 284–306.

Oshawa—Czechs and Slovaks in 1968, Vietnamese in 1979, Poles after 1981—the collapse of the Soviet Union in 1991 eliminated the threat of Communism as a significant political issue in community politics.

Shortly before the celebration of the hundredth anniversary of Ukrainian immigration to Canada in 1991, Starr received the exciting news that Ramon Hnatyshyn was appointed Governor-General of Canada on December 14, 1989. Hnatyshyn was sworn in during a ceremony in the Senate chamber on January 29, 1990. He was the son of Starr's good friend Senator John Hnatyshyn and had been raised on national politics from an early age. This appointment marked another significant political achievement among Ukrainians in Canada.

On May 13, 1990, the Oshawa branch of the Ukrainian Canadian Congress held an evening to honour Michael Starr. This event was held at the Ukrainian Heritage Centre on Jackson Avenue. On June 3, 1998, another "Appreciation Night" was organized to honour him and his accomplishments, this one at the Club Lviv Hall on Jackson Avenue; proceeds went to Scouts Canada and the Oshawa General Hospital.[6]

In October 1998 Starr was interviewed by Peter G. Budnick, a lawyer of Ukrainian descent, and filmed by Walter Wasik, a filmmaker responsible for a number of films about Ukrainians and Canadians. Budnick's questions provided Starr with an opportunity to reflect on his own political career and give his opinions about Canadian politics. Starr said that, in retirement, he received most of his news from reading newspapers and he was concerned about recent developments. He had supported Prime Minister Trudeau and the use in October 1970 of the War Measures Act to control radical political events in Quebec. Starr agreed Trudeau had a difficult decision to make. Although he had supported the Canadian Bill of Rights proposed by Prime Minister John Diefenbaker and passed in 1960, Starr was concerned about the influence of the Canadian Charter of Rights and Freedoms on the political direction of the country. According to Starr, the 1982 Charter empowered the Canadian Supreme Court to change legislation passed by Parliament and this tended to defend criminal rights more than those of victims. Starr felt this was interfering with democracy. He was particularly concerned about events in Quebec, where the provincial government had passed the Charter of the French Language, Bill 101, in 1977 that made Quebec unilingual. He also complained that the Quebec provincial government did not fly the Canadian flag on their buildings and felt that this was "not right." Also, he questioned the policy of official bilingualism in the federal government especially since, he believed, that some public servants were obliged to learn the other official language.[7] Starr mentioned he did not always follow the Progressive Conservative party line: for example, he supported the Pickering Airport project although his party was opposed. He also supported retaining capital punishment when the Conservative Party favoured its abolition; according to opinion polls, the majority of Canadians supported the death penalty. Regarding the controversial events surrounding Diefenbaker and questions about his leadership, Starr admitted he always disliked closed meetings and he felt he was, for all practical purposes, a lone wolf in politics. Throughout the interview, Starr stressed that the role of the politician was to serve the people.

---

6. *Courtice Bowmanville News*, May 27, 1998.
7. Ukrainian Canadian Research and Documentation Centre, "Memoirs of the Honourable Michael Starr," 1998.

In September 1999 the Oshawa Historical Society renamed its annual history award—presented to the top graduating students in Oshawa schools—The Honourable Michael Starr Award. During the presentation he was described as "Mr. Oshawa," an integral part of the history of Oshawa.[8]

By this time, Starr was beginning to suffer from a number of health problems. He began experiencing a slowly failing heart, a condition that continued for almost two years and was followed by a shortness of breath that, on January 20, caused him to enter the local hospital. Starr had been undergoing treatment for two months when he died on March 16, 2000.[9] The funeral was held on March 17 at the St. George Ukrainian Catholic Church in Oshawa. It was presided over by clergy from the Ukrainian Catholic and Ukrainian Orthodox churches, both of which Starr attended during his life in Oshawa. He was buried next to Anne in the St. Wolodymyr and St. Olha Cemetery near Oshawa. Starr was survived by his daughter, Joan Nicol, and her husband, Robert, and three grandchildren; also by his two sisters, Pearl Damoff of Toronto and Anne Hercia of Windsor.[10]

With the announcement of his death, tributes began flowing. He was described as the "very embodiment of the 20th century self-made man" and a "friendly, open person, easy to speak to and always ready with a fascinating anecdote." It was noted that Starr took tremendous pride in his relationships with his friends, neighbours and constituents. He maintained a remarkable level of activity and was the true definition of aging gracefully. Starr was a "people person" who made a career of serving others.[11] The various obituaries published in the English-language press mentioned his Ukrainian immigrant parents, his rise from an immigrant family to Alderman, Mayor, Member of Parliament, and Minister of Labour.[12] All mentioned he was the first Canadian of Ukrainian descent to be appointed to the federal cabinet. Among his many influential accomplishments was the winter works program that he expanded and promoted in 1958. He was described as being, after Col. R.S. McLaughlin, the most famous son of Oshawa.

Mike Starr's Legacy

Starr was awarded many honours throughout his career: the Most Venerable Order of the Hospital of Saint John of Jerusalem; the Queen Elizabeth II Coronation Medal; the Canadian Centennial Medal; the Taras Shevchenko Medal from the Ukrainian Canadian Congress and the Queen Elizabeth II Silver Jubilee Medal; Honorary Colonel of the Ontario Regiment; an Ontario government building in Oshawa named in his honour; even a

---

8. *Oshawa This Week*, September 24, 1999.
9. Jane McDonald, "Mike Starr's legacy is unforgettable," *Oshawa This Week*, March 19, 2000.
10. Shortly after the death of Michael Starr, his daughter, Joan Mary Nicol, passed away on May 30, 2000. She was the wife of Robert Nicol, who had served as a campaign manager for Starr in several elections. (Obituary: *The Globe and Mail*, May 31, 2000.)
11. Tim Kelly, "It was our honour to have Michael Starr with us," *Oshawa This Week*, March 19, 2000.
12. Donn Downey, "Labour minister had reputation for fairness," *The Globe and Mail*, March 21, 2000; Christy Chase, "Last respects for a favourite son," *Durham News*, March 21, 2000; Trevor Hache, "Politician Michael Starr never forgot his roots," *Toronto Star*, March 16, 2000; Myron Momryk, "Michael Starr, 89, Ukrainian Canadian Pioneer, dies," *The Ukrainian Weekly*, April 2, 2000.

walking path, the Mike Starr Trail, was officially opened a short distance from his home in 2001.

To commemorate the centenary of Starr's birth, an anniversary commemoration committee was organized in Oshawa in August 2010; its first meetings were held, appropriately, in the Michael Starr Building. Plans were discussed for the induction of Mike Starr in the Oshawa "Walk of Fame," a Mike Starr Exhibit with photos and materials, a Michael Starr Scholarship and an anniversary banquet. On the hundredth anniversary of Starr's birth, a banquet was held at the Dnipro Community Centre in Oshawa. In addition to family members, the event was attended by Ukrainian community leaders, local politicians and many friends and acquaintances who remembered Starr and his wife during his long political career.

Michael Starr was a political pioneer in Canadian history responsible for many firsts in the Ukrainian-Canadian community. When references are made to the political history of the Ukrainian community in Canada, inevitably Mike Starr is mentioned as the first federal cabinet minister of Ukrainian origin, although credit for this is usually given to the vision of John Diefenbaker for making the appointment. Other scholars give Starr credit for initiating the Do It Now campaign of the winter works program that changed the yearly cycle of work in Canada and stimulated work in the winter months—a program that marked the evolution of Canada from a primarily agricultural to an industrial society. Still others underline the federal aid to vocational schools that greatly assisted the various provincial governments to build and expand the secondary schools and college systems that absorbed the baby boom as the students born after the Second World War began to attend educational institutions in the late 1950s and early 1960s.

Starr was a modest person who did not seek opportunities to grandstand and he did not think of himself as a "big shot."[13] He was not known to make deliberate efforts to court the national media in Ottawa and this may have been a serious obstacle when he ran for the Progressive Conservative leadership. He was more concerned about his Oshawa constituency than in gamesmanship in Ottawa. Starr did not see himself as a historical figure, at least not until later in his political career. He did not keep a record of his activities, nor did he preserve correspondence from other politicians, community leaders and organizations. He did not maintain an archive or a library of information about his life and career: it was Anne who began keeping a scrapbook of newspaper clippings, correspondence, and related material, but not in an organized and systematic manner. Letters of congratulations on various birthdays and anniversaries from prominent individuals such as John Diefenbaker were rarely preserved despite their autograph and historical value. His awareness of his historical role in the Ukrainian Canadian community was stimulated during the Progressive Conservative leadership campaign and Starr became increasingly open to requests for interviews, where he reminisced about his early life and career.

Although Starr had been a cabinet minister he maintained the lifestyle and schedule of an ordinary Member of Parliament. He made every possible effort to visit his constituency in Oshawa to attend community, political and cultural events, and maintained his membership in local service organizations and enjoyed speaking when invited. It may be debated

---

13. Ukrainian Canadian Research and Documentation Centre, "Memoirs of the Honourable Michael Starr" 1998.

Figure 21.1 Headstone of Mike and Anne Starr.

that Starr shared his fame as the leading politician from Oshawa with his political rival, Ed Broadbent. However, Broadbent continued living in Ottawa after retiring from active politics while Starr never really left, and continued living in Oshawa until his death. He remained involved with the local community and assisted local voluntary organizations with fund raising projects and activities.

From very early in his political career, Starr was identified, and remained, a populist.[14] He rarely spoke about his conservative political philosophy. Within Progressive Conservative circles he was considered to represent the radical wing, and by others the progressive wing, of the party.[15] Some may be tempted to describe Starr as a Red Tory because he did not hesitate to use the financial and material resources of the federal government to fight unemployment in Canada. Starr supported this policy often in the face of opposition from his more traditionally conservative colleagues who believed in less state involvement in the lives of Canadian citizens. In reviewing his life and career, it is possible to identify principles that provided a foundation for his political actions: fiscal responsibility; a fair and reduced tax burden; sensitivity for the disadvantaged; a practical can-do approach to governmental problems; international relations based on democratic values and a strong national defence against the threat of international Communism.[16]

Starr's concern about the fate of Ukraine, his ancestral homeland, was a constant theme in his speeches throughout his career, especially during the Cold War years. He spoke on behalf of the waves of Ukrainian immigrants who arrived in Canada as political exiles, and although they integrated well into Canadian society, their hearts were always with Ukraine. This interest in Ukraine became an entrenched part of the Progressive Conservative Party, and later the Conservative Party agenda; as Prime Minister, Steven Harper on more than one occasion raised the fate of Ukraine during his tenure, both nationally and internationally. The cause of Ukraine continues to be an important issue in Canadian foreign affairs.

Through the example of his political career, Starr opened the political doors for many Canadians, especially for those from the ethnocultural groups, beginning with those from his very own Ukrainian Canadian community. Canada has benefited from his example, and there are now politicians and public servants at all levels of government, from all communities and ethnocultural groups, promoting Starr's life-long goal of contributing to the building of a better Canada through a widened and longstanding participation in the political process.

---

14. The Hon. Allister Grosart fonds, MG32 C65, Volume 8, File 9.
15. Thomas Van Dusen, *The Chief,* McGraw Hill Company of Canada Ltd., 1968, p. 18.
16. *Ottawa Citizen,* June 9, 2014 [Hugh Segal on Conservative principles].

Bibliography

Newspapers/Periodicals
Brantford Expositor
Canadian Farmer
Canadian Labour Defender
Canadian Tribune
Courtice Bowmanville News
The Daily Times Gazette
The Globe and Mail
Homin Ukrainy (Ukrainian Echo)
The Labour Gazette
The Melting Pot, Oshawa, (SWOC Lodge 1817)
Narodna Hazeta (People's Gazette)
The New Canadian
The New York Times
Novyi Shliakh (New Pathway)
The Oshawa Daily Reformer
Oshawa Daily Times
Oshawa News
Oshawa/Whitby This Week
Oshawaworker
Oshawa Workers Tribune
Ottawa Citizen
Peterborough Examiner
The Province
Sudbury Star
Time
Times Gazette
Toronto Daily Star
Toronto Telegram
Ukrainian Canadian Review
Ukrainske Zhyttia (Ukrainian Life)
Ukrainski Visti (Ukrainian News)
Ukrainskyi Holos (Ukrainian Voice)
Vancouver Sun
Vilne Slovo (Free Word)

Archives
Library and Archives Canada (LAC)
Sound Archives, Interview with Mike Starr by Leo LaClare, October 9, 1973.
LAC, The Hon. Allister Grosart fonds, MG32 C65.
LAC, Hon. G. Churchill Papers, MG 32, B 9.
LAC, The Hon. John G. Diefenbaker Papers, MG26.

V.J. Kaye fonds MG31 D69.
Michael J. Fenwick fonds, MG31 B17.
Michael Starr Papers, MG 32, B 15 (*The Mike Starr Story*).
Pedlar People Limited fonds, MG28 III 70, R3076-O-1-E.
LAC, Peter Stursberg Papers, MG31, D 78.
Thomas Van Dusen fonds (R11596-0-4-E).
LAC, Canadian Labour Congress Fonds, MG28 I103.
LAC, Progressive Conservative Party Collection, MG28 IV 2.
LAC, The Hon. Paul Yuzyk fonds, MG32 C67.
LAC, George Vickers Haythorne fonds, MG31 E23.
LAC, Communist Party of Canada Fonds, MG28 IV 4.
LAC, The Hon. J. Edward Broadbent Papers, MG32 C83.
LAC, Hon. Stanley Haidasz fonds. R1273-0-8-E.
LAC, Association of United Ukrainian Canadians fonds, MG28 V154.
LAC, RG2 Privy Council Offices fonds.
LAC, RG25 Department of External Affairs fonds.
LAC, RG26 Department of Citizenship and Immigration fonds.
LAC, RG146 Canadian Security Intelligence Service.

Ontario Archives
Oshawa, City of Oshawa Council Minutes, MS 671.
Ukrainian National Federation Collection, Oshawa Branch.
Ukrainian Sporting "Sitch" Association, Branch no. 3, Oshawa.
Ukrainian Professional and Businessmen's Club, Oshawa.

Ukrainian Canadian Research and Documentation Centre (Toronto)
"Memoirs of the Honourable Michael Starr," 1998.

Canadian Museum of History, Archives
Prokop (Prokopchak) Family fonds.

Publications
Abella, Irving, *On Strike, Six Key Labour Struggles in Canada, 1919–1949*, James Lewis and Samuel, Publishers, Toronto, 1974.
Almanakh Tovarystva Ukrainskyi Robitnycho-Farmerskyi Dim v Kanadi, 1918–1929 [Almanac of the Ukrainian Labour-Farmer Temple Association in Canada, 1918–1929], Winnipeg, 1930.
Beskyd, Julian (ed.), *Eparchy of Toronto, A Quarter of a Century on the Episcopal Throne 1948–1973*, Nasha Meta, Toronto, 1975.
Bird, Richard M., *The GST/HST: Creating an Integrated Sales Tax in a Federal Country*, International Center for Public Policy, Working Paper 12–21, April 2012.
Bliss, Michael, *Writing History, A Professor's Life,* Dundurn, Toronto, 2011.
Cadieux, H. L. and G. Griffiths, *Dogwood Fleet, The Story of the British Columbia Ferry Authority From 1958,* Cadieux and Griffiths (Publishers), Nanaimo, 1967.
Camp, Dalton, *Gentlemen, Players and Politicians*, McClelland and Stewart, Toronto, 1970.
Campbell, Lara, *Respectable Citizens, Gender, Family and Unemployment in Ontario "Great" Depression*, University of Toronto Press, 2009.
Campbell, Robert Malcolm, *Grand Illusions: The Politics of the Keynesian Experience in Canada, 1945–1975,* Broadview Press, Peterborough, 1987.

Chappell, Frank, *Oshawa Rotary in Retrospect, 1920–1952*, General Printers, Oshawa.
"Comment Réné Levesque est devenu independantiste," *Le Magazine Maclean*, Fevrier, 1969.
Conrad, Margaret, *George Nowlan, Maritime Conservative in National Politics*, University of Toronto Press, Toronto, 1986.
Darcovich, William and Paul Yuzyk (eds.), *A Statistical Compendium on the Ukrainians in Canada 1891–1976*, University of Ottawa Press, Ottawa, 1980.
Diefenbaker, John, *One Canada, Memories of the Right Honourable John G. Diefenbaker, The Years of Achievement 1952–62*, Macmillan of Canada, Toronto, 1976.
Diefenbaker, John, *One Canada*, Volume II, Toronto, Macmillan of Canada, 1975.
Donaghy, Greg, *Grit: The Life and Politics of Paul Martin Sr.*, UBC Press, Vancouver, 2015.
Drew, Dr. George, "On the Menace of Communism," *Revue de l'Université d'Ottawa*, Vol. 18, No. 1, January–March 1948.
Dupré, J. Stefan et al., *Federalism and Policy Development: The Case of Adult Occupation Training in Ontario*, University of Toronto Press, Toronto, 1973.
Edwards, Peter, *Waterfront Warlord, The Life and Violent Times of Hal C. Banks*, Key Porter Books, Toronto, 1987.
Fairbairn, Barbara J., *The Gentlemen's Strike: The Radio-Canada Television Producers' Dispute, December 29, 1958 - March 9, 1959*, MA thesis, Carleton University, 1982
Fedorowycz, W., "The Ukrainian National Federation of Canada: Its Presence in Ontario," *Polyphony, The Bulletin of the Multicultural History Society of Ontario*, Volume 10, 1988 (Ukrainians in Ontario).
Figol, Mykola (ed.), *25 Years of SUM Canada, 1948–1973*, Toronto, 1973.
First World Congress of Free Ukrainians – Proceedings, Winnipeg, 1969.
Fleming, Donald, *So Very Near: The Political Memoirs of the Hon. Donald M. Fleming*, Vol. 2., *The Summit Years*, McClelland and Stewart, Toronto, 1985.
Ford, Robert A.D., *Our Man in Moscow, A Diplomat's Reflections on the Soviet Union*, University of Toronto Press, Toronto, 1989.
Fortieth Anniversary, St. John's Ukrainian Greek-Orthodox Church in Oshawa, Ontario, 1935-1975, Harmony Printing, Toronto, Ontario.
The Fourth Ukrainian Canadian Congress, Winnipeg, Manitoba, July 8, 9, 10, 1953.
Fortieth Anniversary of the Proclamation of Independent Ukraine, 22, 1, 1918 – 22, 1, 1958, Ukrainian Canadian Committee Headquarters, Winnipeg.
Fraser, Alexander, *A History of Ontario*, The Canada History Company, Montreal/Toronto, 1907.
Friends in Need: The WBA Story, WBA, Winnipeg, 1972.
Hibbitts, Bernard *CBC International Service as a Psychological Instrument of Canadian Foreign Policy in the Cold War, 1948-1953*, MA thesis, Carleton University, 1981.
Hilliker, John F., "Diefenbaker and Canadian External Relations," in J. L. Granatstein (ed.), *Canadian Foreign Policy: Historical Readings*, Copp Clark Pitman Ltd., Toronto, 1986.
Hood, M. McIntyre, *Oshawa, The Crossing Between the Waters, A History of Canada's Motor City*, 1968.
Horner, Jack, *My Own Brand*, Hurtig Publishers Ltd., Edmonton, 1980,
Hryniuk, Stella, "A Peasant Society in Transition: Ukrainian Peasants in Five East Galician Counties 1880-1900," PhD thesis, 1985, University of Manitoba.
Iliustrovanyi Kaliendar Kanadyiskoho Ukraintsia na Rik 1926 (Illustrated Calendar of the Canadian Ukrainian for 1926), Winnipeg, 1926.
Johnston, James, *The Party's Over*, Longmans Canada Ltd., Don Mills, Ontario, 1971.
Kaplan, William, *Everything That Floats, Pat Sullivan, Hal Banks and the Seaman's Union of Canada*, University of Toronto Press, Toronto, 1987.
Kashtan, W., "Diagnosing Anti-Communism," *The Marxist Quarterly*, Autumn, 1962

Kaye, V.J., *Dictionary of Ukrainian Canadian Biography, Pioneer Settlers of Manitoba, 1891-1900*, Ukrainian Canadian Research Foundation, Toronto, 1975.

Kelley, Fraser, "Labour Minister Starr: Service at the Cleaner's Shop," *Saturday Night*, June 21, 1958.

Kieran, Jon W., "Unemployment Crisis: How Will the Tories Weather the Winter?" *Saturday Night*, Vol. 72, No. 25, December 7, 1957.

Kordan, Bohdan S. and Lubomyr Y. Luciuk, *A Delicate and Difficult Question, Documents in the History of Ukrainians in Canada 1899-1962*, The Limestone Press, Kingston, Ontario, 1986.

Kostash, Myrna, *Long Way From Home, The story of the Sixties generation in Canada,* James Lorimer and Company, Toronto, 1980.

Kwavnick, David, *Organized Labour and Pressure Politics; The Canadian Labour Congress, 1956-1968*, McGill-Queen's University Press, Montreal, 1972.

Kyba, Patrick, Alvin, *A Biography of the Honourable Alvin Hamilton, P.C.,* Canadian Plains Research Center, Regina, Saskatchewan, 1989.

Lazarus, Morden, *Up From the Ranks, Trade Union VIP's Past and Present,* Regent Press, 1977,

MacDonald, Helen Bajorek, "The Power of Polonia, Post WWII Polish Immigrants to Canada: Survivors of Deportation and Exile in Soviet Labour Camps," MA thesis, Trent University, 2001.

Manthorpe, Jonathan, "One of Our Agencies is Missing, The Crisis of Change at the Workmen's Compensation Board," in Donald C. MacDonald (ed.), *Government and Politics of Ontario,* MacMillan of Canada, 1975.

Martin, Paul, *A Very Public Life, So Many Worlds*, Volume II, Deneau, Toronto, 1985.

Martynowych, Orest T., "The Ukrainian Bloc Settlement in East Central Alberta, 1890-1930: A History," Occasional Paper No. 10, Historic Sites Service, *Alberta Culture,*.

———, *Ukrainians in Canada, The Interwar Years, Book I*, CIUS Press, 2016.

Marunchak, Michael H., *The Ukrainian Canadians: A History*, UVAN, Winnipeg, 1982.

McDougall, A.K., *John P. Robarts: His Life and Government*, University of Toronto Press, Toronto.

Momryk, Myron, "Mike Starr, From mayor to cabinet minister," *The Archivist*, July-August, 1987.

———, "The Royal Canadian Mounted Police and the Surveillance of the Ukrainian Community in Canada," *Journal of Ukrainian Studies,* Volume 28, No. 2, 2003.

———, "From the Streets of Oshawa to the Prisons of Moscow: The Story of Janos Farkas (1902–1938)," *Hungarian Studies Review*, Vol. XXXVIII, Nos. 1-2, 2011.

Morton, Desmond, *Social Democracy in Canada*, Toronto, 1977.

Nash, Knowlton, *The Microphone Wars, A History of Triumph and Betrayal at the CBC*, McClelland and Stewart Inc., Toronto, 1994.

Newman, Peter C., *Renegade in Power: The Diefenbaker Years*, McClelland and Stewart Ltd., Toronto, 1963.

———, *A Nation Divided, Canada and the Coming of Pierre Trudeau,* Alfred A. Knopf, New York, 1969.

———, *The Distemper of Our Times, Canadian Politics in Transition: 1963-1968*, McClelland and Stewart Limited, Toronto, 1968.

Nicholson, Patrick, *Vision and Indecision: Diefenbaker and Pearson*, Longmans Canada Limited, Don Mills, 1968.

Normandin, Pierre G., *The Canadian Parliamentary Guide.* (Various Years).

Old Home Week, Programme, Oshawa Silver Jubilee, June 30-July 4, 1949, Oshawa Old Home Week Committee.

Otvorennia Ukrainskoi Pravoslavnoi Tserkvy Rizdva Presviatoi Bohorodytsi v Oshavi, Ont, 1916-1953 [The official opening of the Ukrainian Orthodox Church Blessed Virgin in Oshawa, 1916-1953] November 1, 1953, Oshawa, Ontario.

Palmer, Bryan D., *Canada's 1960s, The Ironies of Identity in a Rebellious Era,* University of Toronto Press, Toronto, 2009.

Pascoe, Harold N., *Take My Hand*, Harold N. Pascoe Publisher, 1978.
Pelletier, Gerard, *Les Années d'Impatience, 1950-1960*, Editions Internationales, Alain Stanké, 1983.
Pendergest, James Alexander, "Labour and Politics in Oshawa and District, 1928-1943," MA thesis, Queen's University, 1973.
Pickersgill, J. S., *My Years with Louis St. Laurent: A Political Memoir*, University of Toronto Press, Toronto, 1975.
———, *The Road Back, By a Liberal in Opposition*, University of Toronto Press, Toronto, 1986.
Prymak, Thomas M., "The Ukrainian Flying School in Oshawa," *Polyphony, The Bulletin of the Multicultural History Society of Ontario*, Vol. 10, 1988, (Ukrainians in Ontario).
Richardson, B. T., *Canada and Mr. Diefenbaker*, McClelland and Stewart, Toronto, 1962.
Riddell, W. Craig, *Labour-Management Cooperation in Canada*, University of Toronto Press, Toronto, 1986.
Robertson, Heather, *Driving Force: The McLaughlin Family and the Age of the Car*, McClelland and Stewart, Toronto, 1995.
Robinson, H. Basil, *Diefenbaker's World: A Populist in Foreign Affairs*, University of Toronto Press, Toronto, 1989.
Rowe, Frederick W., *The Smallwood Era*, McGraw-Hill Ryerson Ltd., Toronto, 1985.
Salutin, Rick, *Kent Rowley, The Organizer: A Canadian Union Life*, Toronto, 1980.
Saywell, John T. (ed.). *Canadian Annual Review for 1960*, University of Toronto Press, 1961.
Scher, Len, *The Un-Canadians: True Stories of the Blacklist Era*, Lester Publishing Limited, 1992.
Sharp, Mitchell, *Which Reminds Me . . . : A Memoir*, University of Toronto Press, Toronto, 1994.
Simpson, Kieran (ed.), *Canadian Who's Who, 1989*, Volume XXIV, University of Toronto Press.
Smallwood, Joseph R., *I Chose Canada: The Memoirs of the Honourable Joseph R. Smallwood*, Macmillan of Canada, Toronto, 1973.
Smith, Denis Smith, *Rogue Tory: The Life and Legend of John G. Diefenbaker*, Macfarlane Walter and Ross, Toronto, 1995.
Sokolyk, K.W., *Their Sporting Legacy: The Participation of Canadians of Ukrainian Descent in Sport, 1891-1991*, The Basilian Press, Toronto, 2002.
Star, Myhailo, "Shcho Ia Zavdiachuiu Prosviti," in *Zolotyi Iuvilei Tovarystva 'Prosvita' im. Tarasa Shevchenka v Montreali-Point St. Charles 1913-1963*, pp. 35–36.
Steed, Judy, *Ed Broadbent: The Pursuit of Power*, Viking (Penguin Group), Markham, 1988.
Stevens, Geoffrey, *Stanfield*, McClelland and Stewart Ltd., Toronto, 1973.
———, *The Player: The Life and Times of Dalton Camp*, Key Porter Books, Toronto, 2003.
Suchan, Laura, *Ukrainians in Oshawa, 1900-1955*, Oshawa Historical Society, Historical Oshawa, Vol. VI.
Stursberg, Peter, *Diefenbaker: Leadership Lost 1962-67*, University of Toronto Press, 1976.
Thomson, Dale C., *Jean Lesage and The Quiet Revolution*, Macmillan of Canada, Toronto, 1984.
UNYF of Oshawa, 35th Jubilee, May 15-16, 1971, UNF Hall, 68 Bloor Street.
Van Dusen, Thomas, *The Chief*, McGraw-Hill Company of Canada Limited, 1968.
Whitaker, Reg and Gary Marcuse, *Cold War Canada: The Making of a National Insecurity State, 1945-1957*, University of Toronto Press, Toronto, 1994.
Yates, Charlotte, "From Plant to Politics: The Canadian UAW 1936-1984," PhD thesis, Carleton University, 1988.
Young, Sharon, *Oshawa Folk Arts Council, 1961-1981*, Oshawa Folk Arts Council, 1982

Official Documents
Annual Report of the Department of Labour, 1961-62, Ottawa, Queen's printer, 1963.
Barrand, L.R. (compiler), *City of Oshawa, Municipal Manual*, 1957.

Canada, Industrial Inquiry Commission Concerning Matters Relating to the Disruption of Shipping on the Great Lakes, the St. Lawrence River System and Connected Water, Report, Ottawa, Queen's Printer, 2 volumes, 1963.
Canada Year Book 1957-58, Dominion Bureau of Statistics, Ottawa, 1958.
Canadian Annual Review for 1961.
Canadian Annual Review for 1962.
Canadian Annual Review for 1963.
Denton, Frank T. and Sylvia Ostry, *An Analysis of Post-War Unemployment*, Economic Council of Canada, Queen's Printer, Ottawa, 1965.
Department of Labour, *Annual Report for the Fiscal Year Ended March 31, 1957*, Ottawa, 1957.
Department of Labour, *Annual Report for the Fiscal Year ended March 31, 1963*, Ottawa, 1963.
Drouin Collection, Quebec Vital and Church Records, 1621-1967, Wasyl Starchewski, Baptized 15 February, 1913.
Ethical Conduct in the Public Sector, DSS, Ottawa, 1984.
House of Commons Debates. (Various Years).
National Winter Employment Conference, Ottawa, July 14 and 15, 1958, Summary of Proceedings, Department of Labour.
Press Digest, Department of Citizenship and Immigration.
Province of Ontario, *The Vital Statistics Act,* Delayed Statement of Birth, 23 February, 1970 (502691).
Province of Ontario, Canada, *Marriages 1933-1934.*
Regional Studies Program, Research Publications, Number Three, Population C.O.J.P.B., Oshawa, 1967, Ontario.
Report of the Chief Electoral Officer, Twenty-Sixth General Election 1963, Queen's Printer, Ottawa.
Report of the commission of inquiry into matters relating to one Gerda Munsinger, Ottawa: Queen's Printer, 1966. Commissioner: The Hon. Wishart F. Spence.
Twenty-Fourth General Election 1958, Report of the Chief Electoral Officer, Queen's Printer, Ottawa, 1959.
Twenty-Fifth General Election 1962, Report of the Chief Electoral Officer, Queen's Printer, Ottawa, 1963.
Twenty-Seventh General Election 1965, Report of the Chief Electoral Officer, Queen's Printer, Ottawa, 1966.
Twenty-Eighth General Election 1968, Report of the Chief Electoral Officer, Queen's Printer, Ottawa, 1969.
Twenty-Ninth General Election 1972, Report of the Chief Electoral Officer, Information Canada, 1973.
Thirty-Third General Election 1984, Report of the Chief Electoral Officer, Supply and Services, Canada, 1984.

Directories
Lovell's Montreal Directory for 1914-1915, John Lovell and Son Ltd., Montreal, 1914.
Vernon's City of Oshawa Directory for the Year 1955, Vernon Directories Ltd., Publisher, Hamilton, Ontario, 1955.

Interviews
Conversation with Mrs. Anne Hercia at her home in Windsor, Ontario, on June 9, 1988.
LAC, Signature Series, Guy Bertiaume, Librarian and Archivist of Canada in conversation with the Hon. Ed Broadbent, [Public Discussion], February 7, 2017.

www.ingramcontent.com/pod-product-compliance
Lightning Source LLC
Chambersburg PA
CBHW061128010526
44116CB00023B/2998